Praise for
I Am a Woman

"In a world where it's controversial to state both biblical and objective truth, *I Am a Woman* is a beacon of direction for the return of common sense and morality. You can expect to be challenged in every sense of the word in the process of equipping you with the effective tools to be a better sister, daughter, mother, Christian, and woman."

—**Riley Gaines**, twelve-time NCAA all-American swimmer, five-time SEC champion, and ambassador for the Independent Women's Forum

"If the world says a man can be a woman, then according to the world, there's nothing distinct or special about being a woman. If a man can identify as a mother, then in the eyes of the world, there is no unique purpose of motherhood beyond the act of birthing. The world may be going along with the erasure of womanhood and motherhood, but we as warrior women know we are not a 'social construct.' *I Am a Woman* reminds us of who we are in God's eyes. Women don't exist to validate the feelings of man or the world. We exist to fulfill the mighty promise and purpose God gave us as daughters of the one and only King. *I Am a Woman* is an equipping to counteract the unprecedented attacks on women today. Jennifer beautifully illustrates the true essence of our womanhood, helping us embrace a deeper understanding of the biblical foundation to our femininity. This is the ultimate female empowerment."

—**Landon Starbuck**, founder of Freedom Forever

"Bravo . . . *I Am a Woman* is a must-read for anyone grappling with the question 'What is a Woman?'. *I Am a Woman* boldly stands up to answer this question with clarity, conviction, love, and biblical truth. This insightful book does more than just define what a woman is; it unlocks the ancient meaning of gender and sex in the context of biblical wisdom, challenging readers to rethink modern constructs on gender and identity."

—**Misty Phillip**, founder of Spark Media and host of *It Is Time to Stand Up*

"This book is a refreshing voice of truth in a cultural wilderness of deceit and confusion. If only the message that Jennifer has so brilliantly and fearlessly written in these pages could be infused into every heart and mind, the world would experience a jolt of common sense and clarity for a return to sanity!"

—**Grant and Robin Luton**, founders of Torah Today Ministries

"It's time to speak the truth, and Jennifer Strickland does just that. With grace, humility, honor, and common sense, she reminds us that God created woman on purpose and for a special purpose. No matter how culture tries to distort this, we have a sacred calling and a beautiful opportunity to lovingly advocate for femininity in the wake of gender confusion."

—**Heather Creekmore**, podcast host and bestselling author of four books, including *The 40-Day Body Image Workbook* and *Aging Gratefully*

"Jennifer Strickland bravely, yet lovingly, reminds the older generation and teaches the younger generation the true meaning and definition of a woman. And she does so right in the middle of today's cancel culture when so many are terrified to speak up for Truth and common sense. *I Am a Woman* takes a biblical, historical, and anatomical view of woman, returning the reader to the origin of our name that gives us worth, all while Strickland returns us to a healthy understanding of gendered bodies, roles, and relationships that inspire rather than confuse people. This is a must-read!"

—**Dr. Victorya Rogers**, life coach and author of *Finding a Man Worth Keeping*

"Women are life-givers. We are the guardians of the home, messengers of God's Word, and the answer to the world's cries for help. Women are change-agents in a culture that has forgotten who we are. In *I Am a Woman*, Jennifer not only empowers women, but honors the men at our side. This book will help you use your voice to shift the conversation about gender back to God's original design. It completely upends the cultural lies about womanhood and points us back to Genesis, where male and female are created to walk in unity to bring life to the world. Jennifer, I genuinely thank you for writing this book. The world needs it. It's a book in due season. It's a book for now."

—**Trina Titus Lozano**, co-author of *Home Experience*

"Finally, we hear a Christian woman answer the 'What is a Woman?' question with thunderous truth. Unapologetic, grace-laced, and deeply profound, this book is a tool in the hands of mothers, daughters, and leaders to define womanhood correctly. What others are afraid to say, Jennifer articulates with love that cannot be denied. She is a voice in the wilderness, breaking through the confusion. As she mines the word 'woman' for gold, you will find a richness to our name that cannot be erased, because it comes from God's first words about 'male and female' that awaken the best in us all."

—**Tracey Mitchell**, international speaker and
award-winning author

"In a world where we are forced to believe a man is a woman, this book offers a powerful rebuke of the modern-day gender ideology movement and how women are being forced to play along with the narrative. Through faith, biblical verses, and exploring the inner workings of God's creation of women, *I Am a Woman* delivers a powerful and uplifting message to women across the world. Women everywhere can use this book to raise their voices and be heard and reclaim the word 'woman' for themselves."

—**Oli London**, author of *Gender Madness*

"I am a part of a movement called the Whosoevers, and we travel to speak to youth all across the world. Jennifer's new book *I Am a Woman* is truly an answer to the lies that I see permeating the minds of our youth all around the world when it comes to gender. The world is undergoing an attack on the image of God and who the Lord designed us to be as women and men. This book addresses the truths found in God's Word to help bring clarity to the spirit of confusion that has lied to this generation about their sexual identity. It helps restore what the enemy has tried to steal, which is our femininity as women and masculinity for men. Please take the time to read this book and share it with the youth and women in your world. This truth is for today and this message is for this time."

—**Christina Boudreau**, global ambassador for the Whosoevers

"Jennifer's writing is so eloquent and passionate. Her book reminds us of how beautiful it is to be a woman. I appreciate that reminder, and I'll never let gender ideology sway me from the truth. This is the book young women need to be reminded of how beautiful their womanhood is and to never take it for granted."

—**Pamela Garfield-Jaeger**, LCSW

"Our words matter, and *I Am a Woman* dives deep into the language of womanhood to find hidden, surprising gems. You may not agree with everything Jennifer writes, but if you come with an open mind, you'll undoubtedly find jewels that spark wonder in the purpose and beauty of being a woman."

—**Jessie Minassian**, author, speaker, and founder of LifeLoveandGod.com

"Many years ago, my wife, Devi Titus, was literally rescued by Jennifer Strickland. Devi had slipped out of a closing conference session to use the women's restroom before returning home. When she reached up to open the stall door handle, she discovered it had jammed, and she couldn't get out. She began yelling, 'Help, I'm stuck!' Fortunately, Jennifer, who was the last woman in the building, ran out of the elevator to use the restroom, and rescued her. What an inauspicious way to meet one of her dearest friends and future disciple.

"Devi returned home to tell me of this incredible woman she had met, Jennifer, a former professional model and now a profound, powerfully anointed author, speaker, and voice for godly women. That began years of a fruitful relationship. Whenever Jennifer called, all else was dropped so she could sow into this anointed woman of God and future world-changer.

"Devi went home to be with Jesus on December 28, 2022. I could only wish she would have lived long enough to read this book and to see the impact Jennifer is making in the lives of countless women, children and families.

"I read the manuscript for *I Am Woman* by Jennifer Strickland at thirty-nine thousand feet on a mission trip to Dubai, United Arab Emirates. I have never been more impacted by one book. My mind is racing. Thoughts are going in all directions. How can we get this information out? I need to be memorizing these statistics. I never knew that. I need to be taking notes. My mind is exploding with new revelation. I'm crying. I'm rejoicing at the potential this new information provides. How can I get this book into the hands of every man I mentor and every leader I influence?

"If I were you, I would set aside every other book you're now reading and dive into the life-changing truths revealed in *I Am Woman*. Make this book a priority. You will never be the same. Your world will be challenged and changed. You will have tools with which to destroy the lies of the enemy. You will rescue the lost and dying youth. The timeliness of this book cannot be overestimated."

—**Larry Titus**, founder and president emeritus of Kingdom Global Ministries in Dallas, Texas

I
Am
a
Woman

I Am a Woman

Taking Back Our Name

JENNIFER STRICKLAND

REGNERY
FAITH

Unless otherwise noted, all Scripture quotations are taken from the Holman Christian Standard Bible®, Copyright © 1999, 2000, 2002, 2003, 2009 by Holman Bible Publishers. Used by permission. Holman Christian Standard Bible®, HSB®, and HCSB® are federally registered trademarks of Holman Bible Publishers.

Scriptures marked ESV are taken from ESV® Bible (The Holy Bible, English Standard Version®), copyright © 2001 by Crossway, a publishing ministry of Good News Publishers. Used by permission. All rights reserved.

Scriptures marked KJ21 are taken from the 21st Century King James Version®, copyright © 1994. Used by permission of Deuel Enterprises, Inc., Gary, SD 57237. All rights reserved.

Scripture quotations marked NASB are taken from the (NASB®) New American Standard Bible®, Copyright © 1960, 1971, 1977, 1995, and 2020 by the Lockman Foundation. Used by permission. All rights reserved. www.lockman.org.

Scriptures marked NIV are taken from the Holy Bible, New International Version®, NIV®. Copyright © 1973, 1978, 1984, 2011 by Biblica, Inc.® Used by permission of Zondervan. All rights reserved worldwide. www.zondervan.com. The "NIV" and "New International Version" are trademarks registered in the United States Patent and Trademark Office by Biblica, Inc.®

Scriptures marked NLT are taken from the Holy Bible, New Living Translation. Copyright © 1996, 2004, 2015 by Tyndale House Foundation. Used by permission of Tyndale House Ministries, Carol Stream, Illinois 60188. All rights reserved.

Regnery Faith books may be purchased in bulk at special discounts for sales promotion, corporate gifts, fund-raising, or educational purposes. Special editions can also be created to specifications. For details, contact the Special Sales Department, Regnery Faith, 307 West 36th Street, 11th Floor, New York, NY 10018 or info@skyhorsepublishing.com.

Regnery Faith™ is an imprint of Skyhorse Publishing, Inc.®, a Delaware corporation. Please follow our publisher Tony Lyons on Instagram @tonylyonsisuncertain.

Visit our website at www.regnery.com.

10 9 8 7 6 5 4 3 2 1

Library of Congress Cataloging-in-Publication Data is available on file.

Cover design by Daniel Bruffey
Cover photo by Meshali Mitchell

Print ISBN: 978-1-68451-588-2
Ebook ISBN: 978-1-5107-8160-3

Printed in the United States of America

for Olivia:
אוליביה

The fruit of the olive tree, bright, illuminating oil.

for Zachary:
זכרי

The one who remembers the commands of God and lives them out.

for Samuel:
שְׁמוּאֵל

He who hears God and is heard by Him.

Thank you for believing in me. You are our legacy.

Wisdom calls out in the street; she raises her voice in the public squares. . . . at the crossroads, she takes her stand.
—Proverbs 1:20, 8:2

Contents

Introduction

The other day I watched a video where Turning Point USA co-founder Charlie Kirk interviewed students on a college campus and asked them a simple question: "What is a Woman?" One of the girls tossed her trash on the table and said, "That's a stupid question! That's a dumb question!" More girls chanted, "Someone who identifies as a woman!" Charlie challenged them not to use the word "woman" in the definition. "That's a trick question!" they cried. "How about you talk to someone in media training?"

"I don't need media training!" Charlie said, laughing. "The college kids of America, going hundreds of thousands of dollars into debt, think it's a trick question."[1] The rest of us knew what a woman was the moment we were born.

We have indoctrinated a generation with "gender-inclusive" language that annihilates the beauty of gender. These students grew up with mantras about "owning a body" they cannot even define. The culture is lambasting them with a firehose of muddy water that laces womanhood with toxicity. Whether it is the billions of pornographic images, the transgender stars dancing on TikTok, the new language of nonsensical terms for sex and gender, or the legislation that allows men in female spaces, young people are overrun with lies about what it means to be a woman.

When a culture dismantles womanhood, it tears apart the fabric that holds us together. It is high time that we take back our name.

When Dictionaries Change

I am a dictionary nerd. A word girl. I still have my tattered red Webster's dictionary that I studied as a *hobby* in high school and college. Yep, it's true. I am *that nerdy*. But this is one thing I understand: Language that has concrete meaning is the basis for human society, and dictionaries reflect the culture in which they were written.

Check out the definition for man and woman in the *1828 American Dictionary of the English Language*:

MAN,[2] *noun plural* men. [Hebrew. species, kind, image, similitude.]
1. Mankind; the human race; the whole species of human beings.[3]
   - And God said, Let us make *man* in our image, after our likeness, and let them have dominion—Genesis 1:26.
   - It is written, *man* shall not live by bread alone—Matthew 4:4.
2. A male individual of the human race, of adult growth or years.

The full definition has seven Bible verses in it. Let's look at woman:

WOMAN,[4] *noun plural* women. [a compound of womb and man.]
1. The female of the human race, grown to adult years.
   - And the rib, which the Lord God had taken from the man, made he a *woman*—Genesis 2:22.

Over time, the word "womb" and all the biblical references disappeared, but the definitions remained the same. In the foggy years of the COVID-19 pandemic, however, the Cambridge dictionary slyly altered the definitions of man and woman to cave to woke ideologues. We now read:

MAN,[5] *noun.*
1. an adult male human being
2. an adult who lives and identifies as male though they may have been said to have a different sex at birth:

- *Mark is a trans man (= a man who was said to be female when they were born).*
- *Their doctor encouraged them to live as a man for a while before undergoing surgical transition.*

WOMAN,[6] *noun*
1. an adult female human being
2. an adult who lives and identifies as female though they may have been said to have a different sex at birth:
   - *She was the first trans woman elected to a national office.*
   - *Mary is a woman who was assigned male at birth.*

Mary is now referred to as *a woman who was assigned male at birth.* "She" is really a he, and the doctors must have made a grave error when looking at her genitalia, chromosomes, and DNA. If we dig up "Mary's" bones centuries after "their" death, they will still read *male.* Binary sex has been an immutable fact forever. Yet it is now "inclusive and tolerant" to say male and female are interchangeable—something that does not exist among mammals. Today, rational-thinking adults, psychologists, liberals, and even feminists are labeled "homophobic, transphobic, hateful right-wing bigots" if they stand squarely on the definitions of man and woman that have been in place since the dawn of time.

In my 1990 tattered red dictionary, the definitions of male and female are crystal clear:

MALE[7], *adj.*
1. Designating or of the sex that fertilizes the ovum
2. Of like, or suitable for men or boys, masculine

FEMALE[8], *adj.*
1. Designating or of the sex that bears offspring
2. Of, like, or suitable for women or girls

In 2020, Merriam-Webster slipped in these alterations:

MALE[9], *adj.*
1. a (1): of, relating to, or being the sex that typically has the capacity to produce relatively small, usually motile gametes which fertilize the eggs of a female
   b: having a gender identity that is the opposite of female

FEMALE[10], *adj.*
1. a (1): Of, relating to, or being the sex that typically has the capacity to bear young or produce eggs
   b: having a gender identity that is opposite of male

Prior to the 1950s, "gender" meant male or female but applied only to grammar, not people. This changed during the 1960s when sexologists realized their sex reassignment agenda could not be defended using the word "sex." Since changing the sex of human beings is impossible, their solution was to hijack the word "gender" and infuse it with a new meaning that applied to people. Due to feminist mantras intent on abolishing sex stereotypes, "gender" now refers to one's social sex and *internal feeling* of being male or female—or neither. According to the American College of Pediatricians, this manipulation of our language has led to teaching children that gender is fluid, and they can have an "innate gender identity" that presents along a continuum.[11]

Being male or female is now being touted as a feeling, not a reality. According to this theory, since feelings are fluid, gender is too.

In 1990, Webster's definition of gender was crystal clear:[12]

1. the classification by which words are grouped as masculine, feminine, or neuter
2. a person's sex

Simple as that. Fifteen words.

At the time of this writing, Merriam-Webster devotes precisely 666 words to define gender, the biblical number of the rising Antichrist—yet that will continue to change.[13] Merriam-Webster provides these examples for "gender identity":

Facebook provides more than 50 options beyond "male" and "female" for users to describe their *gender identity*, from "gender questioning" and "neither" to "androgynous."[14]

In 2021, [the governor] . . . said schools should allow transgender students to use restrooms and locker rooms that match their *gender identity*.[15]

The prioritization of race and *gender identities* means that no one is happy.[16]

That last sentence says it all. Today, our youth are unhappier than ever. Instead of looking at the underpinnings of a society that has turned away from truth and biological reality, most kids are being taught about gender identity in school, ranging from kindergarten to college. Forty-two percent of Generation Z—born between 1997 and 2012—have been diagnosed with a mental health condition, and 90 percent believe they are not set up for success.[17] When college girls suggest "media training" to answer the question "What is a Woman?" we have a problem.

What's at Stake

From the top of our government to the corners of our classrooms, a lie has woven into the culture. The lie is:

Gender is only a social construct.
Therefore, womanhood is only a social construct.

The notion that gender is socially constructed is now steeply baked into our laws and customs. In many places, males who feel like females can change their birth certificates and freely enter female bathrooms, sports, beauty pageants, and prisons. Never mind that gender identity does not exist in all of creation. Never mind that the plant and animal kingdoms are not defined this way. Never mind if women and girls feel scared, exposed, and vulnerable due to prior experience with male violence. Never mind that 90 percent of sexual assaults, voyeurism, and harassment in changing rooms occur in unisex facilities.[18] Never mind that in every part of the world, 98–99 percent of sex offenders are male.[19] If a man feels like he is a woman, he can identify as one. Never mind, never mind, never mind!

When feelings dictate laws, we are in big trouble as a society. If a male can be female—then there is no longer a defense for female sororities, sports, changing rooms, boarding schools, summer camp cabins, Girl Scout tents, youth detention centers, jails, prisons, gynecologists, domestic violence support groups, rape crisis centers, lesbian associations, teenage locker rooms, elementary school bathrooms, or even girls-only sleepovers. Will your daughter be charged with discrimination for not including boys who believe they are girls in her safest places imaginable? The disregard for biology is irresponsible, but the disregard for the female experience is *inexcusable*.

Don't think too hard about it; it doesn't affect you, you might say. But it does. Due to this teaching that has permeated society at every possible level, an entire generation of children is becoming increasingly confused and mentally unstable. Teens are turning on their bodies in droves, from eating disorders to self-harm to denying biological sex altogether. Many are even attempting to "change their sex" before puberty—a biological impossibility that slews of doctors, therapists, teachers, and parents are supporting and even celebrating. This can lead children down a very painful road that causes sexual dysfunction and sterility.

We need to pay attention to what is happening to the kids. If we do nothing to protect future generations from being brainwashed by dictionaries that change, we will be responsible for the loss of the meaning of the words *man* and *woman*.

Understanding the purpose of sex and gender is essential to a thriving society; without it, we will fall—and we are *falling*. We can either clap our hands over our ears and pretend it's not happening, or we can take a stand. We can fearlessly answer the question: "What is a Woman?" without stuttering. This is *not* a time to be silent; this is a time to *speak*. And it takes courage to do it. Because if you do, you will be accused of hating trans people—when the reality is, you love them so much, you want to tell them the truth: Womanhood is a gift and a calling; it is in our bones, and it is *the answer* to humanity's cry for help.

Our Goal

Looking at the dictionary in 1828, we find there was a time when people derived their definitions from the Bible, an ancient text that is endlessly deep and unchanging. In preparation for this book, I have read volumes of works written by feminists, journalists, and activists, all of which I will share. Yet I cannot deny who I am—a word nerd and a girl who drinks daily from the Bible. In my studies of sex and gender, there has been no clearer spring to draw from.

Though the world and its languages may change, God's Word does not change.[20] As Jesus said, "Heaven and earth will pass away, but my words will never pass away."[21] Whether you believe the Scriptures are true, false, or you wrestle with their precepts like most of us, I respect you—but I also want to challenge you. Do you know where we can find an eternal definition of *woman* that will not conform to the whims of man's ideologies? Though the history of biblical interpretation is wrought with wrongdoing and misapplication—especially about women—the original languages of the Bible still tell us who we are.

In this book, we are going to weigh sex and gender as God defines them on a scale next to the gender ideology movement that is sweeping across our nation and world. My goal is to look closely at the definitions of male, female, man, and woman that throw open doorways which enlarge, rather than diminish, who we are. And where womanhood has been improperly translated, I plan to severely challenge the culture's religious assumptions as well.

Why do most Christians remain silent on this? They are afraid to speak the truth about sex and gender for fear of backlash. Yet Thomas Campbell challenges us:

> Where the Scriptures speak, we speak;
> And where the Scriptures are silent, we are silent.[22]

The Scriptures are not silent on this; they are a megaphone of truth laced with love, power, and authority about the purpose of gender. George Orwell said he never sat down to write a bestseller, but instead to expose a lie and give it a good hearing:

> My starting point is always a feeling of partisanship, a sense of injustice. When I sit down to write a book, I do not say to myself, "I am going to produce a work of art." I write it because there is some lie that I want to expose, some fact to which I want to draw attention, and my initial concern is to get a hearing.[23]

This book is that hearing. In his book *What Is a Woman?*, commentator Matt Walsh exposed the dark foundations of gender ideology. I'd like to take it on from a different angle. In *I Am a Woman*, I want to remember womanhood. I want to go back so we can go forward. I want to remind the world what it means to be a woman.

Remember

This book is dedicated to our children. Our middle son, Zach, has a name I will refer to often because it means male. It also means *to remember*. Variations of this word occur over 1,200 times in Scripture. Genesis 9:16 is a classic example:

> Whenever the rainbow appears in the clouds, I will see it and **remember** the everlasting covenant between God and all living creatures of every kind on the earth.[24]

We are commanded over and over to *remember* who God is as He remembers us. When we see a rainbow, we see a sign of remembrance, a promise after a storm, a symbol of hope. The rainbow is not a symbol of pride; it is a sign of God's promises kept.

Embedded in the word male is a calling to remember who God is and act upon that truth. This is not a backward motion of remembering but a backward-and-forward motion. Like the Spirit hovering over the waters, like the waves of the sea, it drifts back and sails forward. We remember so we can write new letters in the sand. We go back so we can sail forward with new understanding.

By recalling the original meaning of our name, we light a flame to lead the way. My thesis is this: If we return to a biblical understanding of gender, we will attract people to it. Not only is it incredibly free-ing, but God-given gender helps us rise to the calling of the day. If we uphold positive femininity and the power we carry, girls will naturally be drawn to womanhood. The same is true for manhood. But for us to do that, we must return to the original names for sex and gender that expand and multiply their meaning. Jesus used the name *woman* often, knowing the beautiful mystery that word opens for us.

The Language of Sex and Gender

Because of the life-changing impact studying the word *woman* has had on me, I am excited to share it with you. But I want to make something clear: The purpose of this book is not to debate those who embrace gender ideology. Nor is it to negate their experiences. Instead, it is to return us to the origin of our name that gives us worth.

When writing about sex and gender, each author must choose their language and definition of terms that best suits their discussion of the subject. That is the right of the author, and it should be respected. I have chosen a simplistic understanding of sex and gender; whenever possible, I use them synonymously. Specifically, I use gender to refer to masculinity or femininity in language and in people, and sex as biology. My goal is to align people with their biological reality, not divorce them from it. A divided house cannot stand, and my goal is not to create division, but unity.

For the purpose of this book, the notion that gender is guessed at by a doctor and is fluid—changing as quickly as feelings do—is not helpful. Whatever you believe about these things, I plan to look at the *meaning and function* inside our names *male* and *female, man* and *woman, son* and *daughter, mother* and *father*. I am more interested in returning us to a healthy understanding of gendered bodies, roles, and relationships that inspires rather than confuses people.

In no way is this meant to diminish the struggles of trans-identified people or youth with gender dysphoria, which is a psychological condition in which a person experiences a marked incongruence between their experienced gender and the gender associated with their biological sex.[25] I only have empathy and love for those who feel like they are "trapped in the wrong body." It is incredibly painful to feel misaligned with one's biological sex. This calls for love for the long road. At the same time, love that abandons the truth is no longer love. I am deeply devoted to people who struggle with their bodies. All my work is directed toward helping young people be the best they can be in the skin they are in. It has been my life's mission to help them align their minds with the truth that God formed them with great love and intention.[26]

The entire objective of this book is to appreciate who we are as sexed image-bearers and help us bring out the best in the word *woman*. The way we will do this is by unpacking the gendered words penned in Genesis that introduce us to woman with purposeful design that is not only physical, but as active as the breath we carry.

Opening the Door to Woman

Sam Kneller writes, "A biblical Hebrew word is like a door, waiting to be pried open, eager to ramble across the threshold and explore the dazzle of a thrilling discovery."[27]

This book is an invitation to go back to the beginning—to return to the ancient scrolls of the Old Testament, where every tittle and scratch is weighted with meaning, and gender is woven into the language like a beautiful tapestry. *Every letter* of the Hebrew words *male, female, man,* and *woman* is a gold mine waiting to be discovered. When we excavate a Hebrew word, we open a giant glass door to a brand-new world. On the other side of that door, we find secrets for marriages, families, communities, children, neighborhoods, churches, and nations. Liberating and true, ancient and timeless, beautiful and profound—fascinating realizations await us.

For seven years, I dreamt of writing this book, but it wasn't until I cracked open the door to peer inside the name woman that I found revelations for all of us. The ancient Hebrew definitions of sex and gender are so rich in meaning that everyone—regardless of their political or religious beliefs—would greatly benefit by understanding them.

By embracing the purpose of gender as Scripture unveils, we unearth our calling as men and women which is not interchangeable with the opposite sex. There is meaning in our sex that is endlessly fulfilling. Embracing the *action* of manhood and womanhood is so empowering, so freeing, and so essential to our families that we *must* pass it on as a legacy from one generation to the next.

Mining for Gold

I Am a Woman started with a personal challenge to rise to the meaning of my name, *woman.* The fires of adversity drove it out of me. In a deeply personal journey, I lost who I was. As the trials of life ravaged my identity as a wife, mother, sister, and friend, I mined the Scriptures for jewels of understanding. When I felt like I was disintegrating and could barely stand, I found myself sinking to the depths of who I was. At the bottom of a well of pain and thrashing, I found gold. I found my truest calling in this world.

I refer to this time in my life as "the crucible," the place of pain where everything we believe is tested. It is the trial by fire, the gauntlet of adversity, *the initiation into the person we are meant to be.* When we are in a crucible, we want out of it, but the best thing we can do is stay in it and let it change us for the better. Tales tell the story of a silversmith who won't take the spoon out of the fire until he sees his reflection in it. So it is with us. We remain in the fire until He's burned off the impurities which do not reflect the best of who we are. If we trust God has His careful eye upon us, we come out of the fire reflecting His image in the spoon. We become the person we are meant to be. In my crucible, I learned the meaning of *female* ♀, *woman*, *daughter*, *wife*, *mother*, and *sister*. I learned what it means to be *male* ♂, *man*, *son*, *husband*, *father*, and *brother*.

These discoveries changed everything for me—how I spoke to my husband, how I mothered my children, how I lived in every possible essence. I saw my daughter differently, my sons in a brand-new light. As the torrents of relational challenges swirled around me and threatened to take me down, I began responding to the engulfing waves of grief and sorrow differently; I learned to stand on solid ground and speak with love on my lips and grace in my heart. And when I made mistakes, I felt their weight differently. The Hebrew word for *woman* has challenged me, humbled me, and liberated me to love like no other and live my best life.

The more we reach for the treasure inside this word, woman, the more we become her—an advocate, a builder, a guardian, a helper, and a voice that is both a purifying fire *and* a breath of fresh air. This is a definition worth fighting for. It is worth the hard work of remembering so we become the people we are meant to be.

Most believers don't realize that according to John 20:15, the first word Jesus spoke after He rose from the dead was "Woman." If we taught the true definition of this priceless name, the girls of this generation would rise to it. Not only does this book answer the "What is a Woman?" question, but it also calls out the best in men and women, husbands and wives, fathers and sons, mothers and daughters, sisters and brothers in a way that creates a legacy worth leaving. In the pages before us, we will find that God's design is that men uphold women and women uphold men. We will find that sons are like vines and daughters are pillars. We will find that the ribcage from which the first woman was formed contains secrets to her relationship to mankind.

These secrets will lead us to revelations about ourselves that we may already know but can strengthen. As we take back our name, we will rise to the call of the hour to preserve the meaning of God-given gender and hold it up as a jewel to be valued.

Can an entire book be written about the golden manna inside the word *woman*? Yes. You are holding that book in your hands.

We are going to go back to the beginning and remember. Then—and only then—will we carry a torch to light the way forward.

Let's open the door.

—Jen

Chapter One

I Am Not a #NastyWoman

Woman under Fire

She seduced him with her pretty speech and
enticed him with her flattery.
He followed her at once . . . awaiting the arrow
that would pierce its heart.
—*Proverbs 7:21–23 (NLT)*

"I am a Naaaaaaaasty Woman!" actress Ashley Judd snarled as she stalked across the stage like an animal hunting its prey. It was the Women's March of 2017, and half a million people swarmed our nation's capital while many more echoed their mantras in sister marches around the world. With my passion for women's causes, I was very curious about this movement. Plastered across the TV screen, women of all ages walked through the streets in throngs, wearing bright pink knit caps they called "pussyhats." Women held signs representing their various causes, including "My Body My Choice!" "Free Melania!" and other insults against former President Donald Trump, who had just been inaugurated. It was the largest single-day protest in U.S. history, totaling an estimated 4.5 million people worldwide, from Antarctica to Zimbabwe.[1]

I stood in my living room in wonder and amazement at the sheer number of women and girls—and even men—marching for a cause

I couldn't grasp. Did they want women's rights? Abortion rights? The right to gay marriage? The right to speak up against sexual harassment? Since American women already have those rights, I couldn't fathom what they were so passionate about. Yes, it had been a contentious election. Trump's inauguration ignited a maelstrom of anger in some circles. But why on earth were women wearing something representing vaginas on their heads? This seemed like a departure to me, *a step down* rather than a *step up* for women's dignity. "Women's rights are human rights!" they claimed, marching to guarantee our "reproductive freedom." They called themselves "the resistance" and took to the streets *en masse*, with a sea of cotton candy pink on their heads. These women were *on fire*, and that is an understatement.

Their signs read: "I am not a Human Incubator!"; "We are the Granddaughters of the Witches You Could Not Burn"; "The Future is Female"; "Nasty Women Will Change the World!"; "Keep Your Filthy Laws off My Silky Drawers"; "Make America Gay Again"; "I'm Not Going to Be Ignored, Don" (with a picture of the woman from *Fatal Attraction* on it); "We Are the Resistance"; "God hates Trump"; and "This Pussy Bites Back." The most striking photo for me was of a six-year-old girl standing next to her mother, holding a sign that read, "The Future is Nasty."[2]

That word took hold. Women mimicked it like a chorus, and things were about to get nastier.

First, Madonna took the stage and said she'd like to blow up the White House.[3] Then Ashley Judd strutted to the microphone.

"I am a feminist . . . and I am a Naaaaasty Woman," she drawled.[4]

In a bellowing voice, she recited a poem written by a nineteen-year-old girl that declared their fight against white supremacy, homophobia, transphobia, and misogyny—words we never heard when we were nineteen. In some of the most shocking language about women the world has ever heard, she compared us to "blood-stained bedsheets" and declared a commitment to embody this nastiness. "I am a Crusty, Bitchy, Loud, Nasty woman," she declared while the crowd hollered and stirred. "And our pussies ain't for grabbing. . . . They're for birthing new generations of Filthy, Vulgar, Bossy, Brave, Proud, Nasty women. . . . So if you a nasty woman, say hell yeah!"[5]

"Hell ya!" The crowd thundered.

I studied their signs and examined their motives. When I saw grandmothers and mothers and daughters linking arms in unison, I wondered if this was the message we really wanted to pass on to our daughters. As a speaker, I am used to telling girls they are loved, valuable, resilient—so this was *the opposite of* what I try to call out in women.

Maybe they were echoing the sarcasm of the president.[6] Maybe they hated men. Maybe—and more likely—their anger stemmed from the longstanding sexual abuse, exploitation, and silencing of women in Hollywood. Maybe a lot of women in that crowd had been grabbed, harassed, abused, or forsaken by male figures who should have protected them. This, I could empathize with. This, I understood.

But I wondered if these American women were marching for a worthy cause? What if we marched for women still under Sharia law, which grants permission for men to rape their wives, beat women to death for showing their ankles, sell little girls as child brides—a religion that hangs homosexuals as capital punishment? What if we marched for the millions of children in our own country sold into sex trafficking? What if we marched to abolish Pornhub, where women are beaten and demoralized for entertainment? What if we marched to open pregnancy centers next to every Planned Parenthood in the nation, making adoption accessible and inexpensive for parents? What about banishing TikTok videos that incite the sexuality of children? The possibilities are endless for what women can do when they join forces.

Had women been so victimized that their default mantra was nastiness? Or had they been so indoctrinated that they believed Trump and his supporters were really "racist, misogynistic, transphobic, homophobic white supremacists"? I was seriously confused. Hadn't we already achieved equal rights? What were we marching for? Is this the message we wanted to send? What in the world was going on?!

I struggled to understand their mission until much later, when I took a deep dive into the roots of the feminist movement. But one thing

I knew: This is not the voice of womanhood we want our daughters to emulate.

Pro-life women were "uninvited" to the so-called Women's March—which says a lot, considering we account for over half of the women in the United States.[7] If women uphold the meaning of life in the womb, does that mean we are no longer "women"? If this was a "women's march," couldn't they have invited volunteers from pregnancy centers, where women volunteer every day *to do something sacrificial to help women in crisis, regardless of their political persuasion?* That seemed like a strange message to send to all the brave mothers who chose life despite the inconvenience of an unplanned pregnancy—Mary included.

I wondered what the response of the uninvited would be. I figured the younger generation would be very curious about this movement, and maybe they'd be drawn to it. Little did I know that the voice of this crowd would get nastier over the next seven years—until people across America would be scratching their heads, asking, "How did this happen? Why are men demanding to be called women? Why are girls suddenly rejecting femininity?"

A New Language for Women

The next day I had a conversation with Devi Titus[8], my late great mentor, a worldwide leader for women. "We need a new language," Devi told me. "That holds the plumb line of who we are."

We discussed how this new wave of feminist leaders coalesced their language and had the massive backing of George Soros, who funded the event.[9] We wanted to respond in unison as women who believe in God, honor men, value home and family, and set an example for girls. We ended our phone call with the agreement that we needed a new language for how to talk about womanhood, not knowing where it would come from.

Within a couple of days, I was stretching in exercise class when in a moment quite indescribable, I experienced an outpouring of language that splattered like raindrops through my soul. It was as if my head was open to a heavenly portal, and words showered through my mind and landed in the soil of my heart. Speedily they came in a downpour, easily remembered words coursing through my veins like rain hammering a windowpane, and I feared I would not be able to remember them all.

When I told a friend about this experience, she insisted I write them down—quickly. So I did.

Those words would become my lifeline over the next several years.

They would bring out the best in me. They would challenge me. Expect more of me. Finish me.

In childhood, I filled stacks of journals with rhymes. Now as an adult, I recorded this endless stream of words and found that they needed shaping. As I pondered over the formlessness of the prose, I remembered the language of sonnets—fourteen-to-sixteen-line poems that Shakespeare wrote to be memorized and recited from the stage.

After quite a bit of chiseling, there came seven poems.

I AM A DAUGHTER
I AM A WOMAN
I AM A MOTHER
I AM A WIFE
I AM A FRIEND
I AM A SISTER
WHO I AM

The last one is an acrostic which calls out our best and worst character traits from A to Z. *Angry or Able; Bitter or Beautiful; Cantankerous or Courageous.* None of the poetry represented who I was at the time of writing. Instead, the words represented who I *wanted* to be, or rather who God created us to be. [10]

For me, the identity poetry provided that "plumb line" Devi talked about. They raised the bar on womanhood, on me, and my little life that felt so big at times. The adjectives that describe us elevate the potential of humanity and the role we play in the world, redefining woman with rhythm and prose. They challenge American women to be brave and bold and grateful and humble, standing not in opposition to men or in competition with one another, but in unison as we raise our voices for the truly oppressed women of the world. They call out the excellence in who we are and remind us to rise to the meaning of our name.

Time and again, those words resonated in my spirit and called me higher. Bent me lower. In a way, I became accountable to them. In the heat of my crucible, I cried while memorizing them in the shower. When I recited the poetry over audiences from coast to coast, these words had the amazing power to heal and set free. It felt like the language we had been looking for.

The Crucible in America

In a weird and awesome way, those words counseled me for three straight years, from 2017 to 2020, when I returned from a ski trip with my boys to a world reeling with the coronavirus. The world seemed to have come to a halt, a pause, a gap in time. It was a time to reconcile who we are with this life we live. It was a time of refreshment and reprieve but also a time of grief and chaos.

Then, in the summer of 2021, the Taliban took over Afghanistan and abortion became illegal in Texas. Living in Texas and knowing how hard the women at our pregnancy centers work, I watched to see how American women would respond. While an image of an Islamic woman throwing her baby over the barbed wire to marines to spare its life went viral, just a few days later, liberal women in Texas were marching, yelling, and demanding their "constitutional right" to end the lives of their own children in what should be the safest place on earth, the womb. I wondered if anyone saw the hypocrisy of it all.

I kept wondering what on earth these women were yelling about. Here they were in the blessed land of America, carrying signs that screamed "My Body My Choice!" while women in Afghanistan were being ripped from their families, denied an education, raped, belittled, stoned, and slaughtered in the streets. Girls were being sold to the

Taliban as child brides, a terror we do not understand. I wanted more for American women. I wanted us to stand for *them*. But we can only control ourselves, and this was something I still needed to learn.

The coronavirus did so much to us. It separated families and loved ones. It stole time, energy, and focus. Many of us, including myself, lost our compass. Through the hysteria and disfunction, people became fearful of one another, afraid to touch.

The fear blasted its way into our home for about a month. Then I covered our doorframes with oil, spoke life over our home, and we moved on with our lives as much as possible. But I kept trying to wrap my brain around it all. The Christian community saw it as a sign of the times. Many people in the black community, struck by the death of George Floyd in May 2020, raged. Athletes stopped pledging allegiance to our flag, a silent way to say they didn't honor the America we so loved. Doctors were silenced for sharing their medical expertise, and big tech acted not unlike China, limiting the information we received. Our government rushed forth a vaccine for the coronavirus, pitting us against each other. Some eagerly took it, and others cautiously held back. We became pro-life versus pro-choice; pro-Trump versus anti-Trump; black versus white; mask-wearers versus non-mask-wearers; the vaccinated versus the unvaccinated. We ended up farther apart instead of #bettertogether.

Then, the oddest moment in women's history occurred right before our eyes.

The Senator and the Judge

During the 2022 confirmation hearings for the first female black Supreme Court nominee, we overheard this conversation:

Senator Marsha Blackburn, a Republican from Tennessee, asked, "Can you provide a definition for the word *woman*?"

Judge Ketanji Brown Jackson replied, "I can't. I'm not a biologist."

The judge could have quoted Merriam-Webster's dictionary:

woman noun

1. a: an adult female person

Or Dictionary.com:

woman noun

1. a: an adult female person

Or the Cambridge dictionary:

woman noun

1. a: an adult female human being

Or, she could have drawn on the detailed description of a woman from Wikipedia, which says we have two X chromosomes; are capable of pregnancy and childbirth; and have a female reproductive system, larger breasts, less facial and body hair, higher body fat, and are usually shorter and less muscular than men.

> A woman is an adult female human. Prior to adulthood, a female human is referred to as a girl. Typically, women have two X chromosomes and are capable of pregnancy and giving birth from puberty until menopause. Female anatomy is distinguished from male anatomy by the female reproductive system, which includes the ovaries, fallopian tubes, uterus, vagina, and vulva. The adult female pelvis is wider, the hips broader, and the breasts larger than that of adult males. Women have significantly less facial and other body hair, have a higher body fat composition, and are on average shorter and less muscular than men.[11]

Or I can imagine the conversation going like this:

Senator: "Can you provide a definition for the word *woman*?"

Judge: "You're looking at one, Senator, and we've come a long way, baby!

          Or. . . .

Senator: "Can you provide a definition for the word *woman*?"

Judge: "Women protect and uplift their families. At one time, women were considered second-class citizens; today they serve in every arena in the public sphere. Women can be wives and mothers; businesswomen and bosses; up front and behind the scenes; and we come in all colors, shapes, and sizes. Women are an answer to a problem; an aide to humanity; a breath of fresh air. We have a long history of abuse and over-sexualization, which we are working to change. We have made significant strides, but we can do better. There are still women around the world and in our own nation who are not free from oppression. And as the first potential Supreme Court nominee who also happens to be a black female, I promise to protect the dignity and value of women as long as I hold this office."

Instead, her answer was that she "didn't know" what a woman is.

A respectable, brilliant woman, raised by a woman, with sisters at her side, cannot—or *will not*—tell us what a woman is? Why couldn't she tell the story of her mother or grandmother or Corrie Ten Boom? Rosa Parks? Maya Angelou? She could have at least given us a history lesson on how a black woman ascended to the Supreme Court.

Nothing. Silence.

I guess Victoria's Secret's recent campaign—with the word UNDEFINABLE written across a woman's naked body—had become gospel truth.[12]

There we were, on the heels of #internationalwomensday and #womenshistorymonth and #feminism—and we couldn't define what a woman is anymore.

In my view, this was a high point for black women and liberals, but this was a low point for feminists, Catholics, Mormons, Christians—Muslims and Arabs too—who have long been fighting for women to be treated as equals. It felt odd to say, "This is a great day for women!" when a woman in the highest court of the land could not—or would not—define who we are.

I wanted to call her bluff. I wanted to say, "We have ovaries, lady. We are female. We nurse babies. We battle infertility and miscarriages and periods and cancers unique to women. We do breast cancer marches with pink ribbons pinned to our hearts. We have lost friends and marriages and sisters and husbands and babies. We feed children, dress them in dignity, and rise in the night when they need our help. We are managers of households and husbands and hope. We carry sons and daughters on our hips. We run schools. We run communities. We run rape crisis centers. We rescue girls. We light a flame when the night is darkest. We are mothers, wives, sisters, daughters, friends. We are black, brown, yellow, white, and we bleed red every single month. We are fighters. We are more than the dictionary definition. We are teachers, nurses, doctors, ministers, lawyers, artists, judges! We lead *nations*. Must I go on?"

When we lose the meaning of woman, we lose our fight for mankind. But we will not lose this fight. I will not, and you will not if you dare to take the name "the land of the free and home of the brave."

What on earth is a judge to do when atrocities like rape, incest, and abuse come before her seat? Will she defend girls from sexual slavery, which is based upon the fact that they are *female*? Will she admit girls are not as physically strong? Will she recognize our bodies are weaker and more vulnerable because we carry life into this world? Will she admit our curves make us softer and more in need of legal protection? Will she defend our name, *woman*?

I knew womanhood was under attack, but I had no idea it could get to this level. So I went to the well. I looked deep inside of it, all the way to the bottom. As fast as I could, I wrote a quick definition and posted it on Facebook:

A woman is the valuable, equal counterpart to man. She is a companion and comfort to those in need. The name "woman" means guardian, helper, spiritual protector and opposing voice to sin. Made in the image of God, she is an aide to humanity— designed to breathe life into her home, community, and nation. She is the breath of life and brings revelation through the power of her voice. She is also a wife, mother, daughter, sister, and friend. (Source: Bible.)

I tried to boost it, but Facebook denied my request, saying I didn't have the right to comment on current events, even though I've been writing about the impact of media on teen girls since 2006. It didn't matter though; people shared it thousands of times. This told me something.

The world is groaning for this message.

The Senator asked the question. This book is my answer.

Chapter Two

I Am Woman Wisdom

The Choice before Us

Do not forsake wisdom, and she will protect you; love her, and she will watch over you. . . . She will give you a garland to grace your head and present you with a glorious crown.
—*Proverbs 4:6, 9 (NIV)*

Like fathers teaching their children, womanhood is learned through legacy. The unforced rhythms of femininity are passed from one generation to the next. Ideally, we learn beauty, service, and gratitude from our mothers, sisters, grandmothers, and friends. The hard-fought truths of identity are passed down from our elders. This can be positive or negative; legacy is *learned*.

The answer to the "What is a Woman?" question is found in our grandmother's eyes, deep as a cool blue lake from all the times she's gazed at the mirror that never changes. Dictionaries may change, cultural norms may change, but those pages don't change. With the Word as her lens, she finds a depth of meaning in our name that enlarges who we are. She is the satisfied woman, the Woman Wisdom.

Womanhood Is Learned

There are two women in the Book of Proverbs who tell us who we can be: the Woman Wisdom and the Woman Folly. One is constructive; the other is destructive. The choice is as ancient as the one presented in the Garden: Fear God, keep His commands, and eat from the tree of life; or reject His instruction and choose to go our own way, eating the bitter fruit of deception. Lady Wisdom and Lady Folly: We can choose one, or the other.

A wise woman builds her house; the foolish one tears it down with her own hands (or mouth). A noble woman protects her home, marriage, and family; a toxic woman rejects God, destroys men, and annihilates the family. She doesn't realize this is what she's doing—which is the key to the foolishness of the fool. She acts out of her flesh—doing what she wants to do, regardless of what God thinks about it. The fool literally *does not know what she is doing*—but the Woman Wisdom knows exactly what she is doing. Prepared for the day of battle, she intentionally builds her home and legacy.

In the Book of Proverbs, the culmination of toxic womanhood warps femininity into a lifestyle of reckless sexuality. The "forbidden" woman, the adulteress, leads men down crooked alleys that descend into the pit of darkness. She lures them through her slick-sounding words and ultimately becomes their noose. Not only does she lead others to Hell, but she also destroys herself.

In contrast, life-giving women model the way of life. They breathe life into mankind, uphold the men at their side, and express faithfulness through wise stewardship of resources. The Woman Wisdom is fastidious, bringing good and not harm to her man all the days of his life. She fears God and ushers abundance and favor upon her family. One is rash; the other is deliberate. One steals and kills; the other is a channel of the abundant life. Both have a voice at the city gates.

Both call out for others to follow them; both beckon the clueless to follow their lead.

The Wise Woman

When we witness our grandmothers, friends, and sisters standing on behalf of valiant womanhood, we learn. As they stoop low in prayer closets, heads bowed, the word of life on their lips and in their pens, we learn how to war for our marriages, sons, daughters, homes, and nations. Their hands are a record of diligence and dedication. Their eyes are like purified water, and they speak to us with tangible strength. They have a legacy to leave, and nothing can steal it from them. By watching them, we want what they have; we see what we need.

Wise women rise in the early morning light and pray for their families. Their churches. Their schools. Their nations. They manage their homes as the center of family life and create sanctuaries to shelter their husbands—or any worn traveler—after a hard day. They cook, they clean, they pay bills, and they stir the sauce while holding babies on their hips. They know there is a time to be silent and a time to speak—and this is the most important lesson we learn.

When we speak with wisdom, we nourish souls. But when the bitter fruit of condemnation drips off our lips, we poison people with our words. Wisdom builds her house; the foolish woman tears it down. In the marketplace of ideas, wisdom raises her voice in the public square. Above the noisy crowd, she calls out:

> Speak up for those who cannot speak for themselves; ensure justice for those being crushed. Yes, speak up for the poor and helpless, and see that they get justice. (Proverbs 31:8–9 NLT)

The Wise Woman confronts injustice without nastiness. She seeks to live righteously and refuses religiosity, pride, contention, belittling, insult, derision, threats, and strife—because she knows it leads to her own demise, man's destruction, and the family's falling apart.

The Wise Woman's faith is real. Her faith is lived. It is experienced. It is active. She lifts her voice in the public square to speak on behalf of the vulnerable and voiceless. She is not a victim; she is victorious, and she knows the power in her tongue to bring life or death.

Women of Valor stand in front of microphones when it's easier to stay home. Or stay home to do noble, unseen work while others slay dragons with mighty swords. The Wise Woman utilizes her time to bring good and not harm. She humbles herself at the Word's reproof, works hard, prays long, grasps the spindle, and does not look back. She leads by example.

Woman's name has meaning, and it is *lived*. It is the Holy Spirit— the Helper—on the move, hovering over nothingness like the furious flapping of a hummingbird's wings. Women hover. Women move. Women create from nothingness. Women link arms with other women and provide good, solid counsel to instill values that uphold—and not destroy—the family unit. Like the beautiful wind of the Spirit, we advocate for one another. When the heat of the crucible feels too hot to bear, we get into the fire together. We hold up one another's hands and wipe one another's tears. We know how to war on our sisters' behalf.

Wise women carry strength, identity, and valorous living. They drink deep from the living spring and meditate on God's Word day and night. They know they are imperfect, unholy, sinful human beings who are in desperate need of a Savior. His strength empowers them to rise while it is yet night and carry His light into shadowed rooms, illuminating the unseen. They know it is the light of Christ that beckons hurting souls; they know that Jesus came to heal the sick, the lame, the blind, the poor, the brokenhearted, the fool—because that was them once.

As tempting as it may be, wise women won't blame, shame, or condemn because they know there is no condemnation that bears good fruit. They may be abused; they may be belittled; they may not be believed—but like the women chosen first to announce Christ's resurrection, they speak into the night. They may be called crazy or lunatics or shameful or sinful or freaks—but those that find their value in His eyes carry gold that no one can steal.

The Wise Woman knows she is not perfect but returns again and again to the living spring of water that quenches her thirst. She leans into the God who never forsakes her. She prays in faith to the One who resurrects dead things. She builds something new from piles of rubble.

Woman Wisdom knows who she is and knows a God who empa-
thizes with our pain. She knows He fills these weak bodies of ours
with power and places us at a table of triumph over the enemy that
tries to destroy us. Women of Valor are the Esthers of this generation,
called for such a time as *this*. We are the Deborahs, the mothers, the
survivors, the advocates. Together, we are a formidable force—and if
anyone threatens to steal, kill, and destroy the daughters' legacy, they
have another thing coming—because our girls were also born for such
a time as this, and they have everything they need to overcome.

Woman Wisdom conquers not by force but with a heart of understanding. You will see her strength in her ferociously solid, faith-filled
eyes; in the blue veins of her hands worn from dishes and cooking and
wrapping and gardening the soil of the family. You will catch a glimpse
of the spirit of life in her eyes when she dances, cooks, laughs, serves,
and models valorous living to a generation of girls who don't know yet
what it takes to be free. You will admire the way she leans in to hear
your story and speaks of her own wounds with fearless tears. You will
be captivated by her love because she loves you for the long road. She
does not walk out or threaten to; she knows the status of her position
as a beloved Daughter of God and won't settle for less.

The Woman Wisdom's voice is a gentle whisper, a declaration of
victory. She is unbendable, immovable, unstoppable. She stands for
God, family, nation—and she will not bend to man's ideologies. She is
the wind of the Spirit. The movement of Woman is as breathtaking as
the Spirit over the deep. Women are life-givers, light-bearers, and wise
women walk in the way of life to the full.

Women see what others cannot. In the unseen, they speak life; they
bring life; they *are life—for the first woman's name means Life.*

The Woman Folly
But the Foolish Woman believes she can go her own way. She is proud
and wise in her own eyes. She exalts her own wisdom, and any of us
can be her. She rejects God as Creator and mocks the divine order of

male and female unity as power against the enemy. The Foolish Woman is brash, above correction, a loud-mouthed wren who spurns the One who created her. She questions God's instructions and puts herself in the place of a god. She is the one who calls the shots. She refuses to repent from her selfish acts of temptation that lead others away from Him. She is such a fool that she doesn't even realize the words dripping from her mouth are a bitter poison.

Any one of us can break a Proverb and act a fool: We can mismanage our money, show no self-control over our mouths, tear one another down with our words, refuse correction, lead men to sin, become an adulteress—and these are just a few ways of the fool. Yet the key difference between the way of wisdom and the way of the fool is the fear of the Lord. The hallmark of the fool is rejecting the essence of who God is. "Fools despise wisdom and discipline." But "wisdom will multiply your days and add years to your life. If you become wise, you will be the one to benefit. If you scorn wisdom, you will be the one to suffer" (Proverbs 1:7, 9:10–12, NLT).

The Woman Wisdom values good counsel, responds to correction, listens to a rebuke, binds God's Word around her heart, and fears Him—which leads to blessings in this life and the next.

The Woman Folly, on the other hand, rejects God, believes her ways are better, and continues down that road. She won't receive correction and scorns a rebuke. She cannot be questioned or reasoned with, and when essential correction is offered, she runs from it. She also calls out in the streets, beckoning others to follow her ways. How does she lure them? With her smooth talk.

> The woman named Folly is brash. She is ignorant and doesn't know it. She sits in her doorway on the heights overlooking the city. She calls out to men going by who are minding their own business. "Come in with me," she urges. . . . But little do they know that the dead are there. Her guests are in the depths of the grave. (Proverbs 9:13–18, NLT)

Woman Folly uses her mouth as a tool for the enemy. She separates from her husband, mocks God, chooses death (albeit warned) and doesn't turn back via humility. She lacks self-control and uses her tongue as a ravaging sword. She blames, resents, and puts down rather than protects. She dishonors instead of honors. When she should keep her mouth shut, she speaks. When she is angry, she lets people have it, then blames others for the taste of bitter fruit on her lips. She is contentious, critical, and divisive.

Just as the Woman Wisdom reaches her full expression in the Woman of Valor, so the Woman Folly maximizes her impact through flesh-driven ways that destroy families. When a foolish woman becomes toxic, she uses her slick words to lure men away from their wives and into the den of death. She does not regard her voice as sacred, her money as sacred, her husband as sacred. With her mouth dripping with allure, she is the epitome of the flesh-driven woman, the personification of the adulteress. Through her hyper-sexuality, she gains power and control. She is foolish, nasty, and clueless. She is the woman we warn our sons about. The Foolish Woman drives men to one place—destruction. Then she demolishes her own life:

> For she has been the ruin of many; many men have been her victims. Her house is the road to the grave. . . . A wise woman builds her home but a foolish one tears it down with her own hands. (Proverbs 7:26–27, 14:1, NLT)

Not only does she destroy men, but she ultimately destroys herself and her household, which comes crashing down around her.

Her legacy is pain.

Any one of us can become her. The choice is ours.

We Get to Choose

The choices presented in the Garden are the same choices you have now. You can use your womanliness to seduce men or sanctify them. You can use your power and influence to build the house or tear it down. You can use your voice to deny God's existence or trust His Word and obey. You can burn down your house with anger and contention or flow with life-giving water for the thirsty travelers who come to your door.

Valiant womanhood woos us to be wiser, stronger, and more self-controlled while defeated womanhood entices us toward blame, shame, and judgment. As we experience one another's suffering, we discover what kind of women we want to be; there is always a choice.

We learn by failing. We choose to reject an angry way of life when we finally come to the realization that we can rise above whatever circumstances life dishes us. We choose to reject bitterness when we witness it mercilessly aging our faces. We choose to reject the demeaning sound of women's voices when we hear our own words jolt through the air, piercing those who need life from us. Instead of being cranky, critical, and cantankerous, we learn that true courage bites its tongue and the words of the wise bring healing.

We reject the name "I am a nasty woman," when nasty words drive us below the depths of who we are. We learn to build up when we realize the folly of tearing down. We learn through practice, trial, and error. Valiant women win when we dispel fear, love deeply, and live a life worth modeling for our daughters. This modeling happens as we rest in the nobility of our name: *woman*.

We are women. We are mothers. We are daughters. We are grandmothers, granddaughters, sisters, and friends. We are not "cis-gender" or any other label people try to slap on us. We are not categorized by race nor by feelings of "gender identity"; we are women, period.

We are Deborahs who war on behalf of Israel, Magdalenes who feed the disciples, Sarahs pregnant with a promise. We are the women Jesus called "Dear." And when He used this word to address us, He knew the power we carry.

I am a WOMAN, and there is deep meaning in my name.

A Circle of Women

The movement to annihilate gender is personal to me, because I have been both the Wise Woman and the Foolish one. Stubborn and opinionated, I once believed I knew the way to live life "to the full." Driven, smart, and filled with wanderlust, I traveled around the world by myself in my late teens and early twenties, working as a runway, commercial, and print model. With a modeling contract I called my "ticket to freedom," I pursued money and fame as if it would fill my heart's desires. While working as a model in Milan, Italy, I descended into anorexia and refused to listen to those who told me how sick I had become. The more I starved myself to attain what I believe to be perfection, the darker my thoughts became.

I soon found myself at the tip of the Italian boot, in a Wise Woman's home in the South of Italy.

"I'm going to teach you to eat," she declared as she stirred the burgundy sauce with a worn wooden spoon and formed orecchiette pasta with the thumb of her aged hand. Cold and shivering, I suddenly remembered my mother and grandmother. The Señora, the name for the Italian grandmother, changed my lenses. As her calloused hands broke fresh bread on the table before me, I remembered who I was—a daughter who had lost her way. In my search for success and glamour, I had believed the lies of the devil and paid a high price for it. Depressed, lonely, and confused, I had to make a new way. The early twenties are tough for young women. When we bite into the media's promises of attaining a full life on our own terms, we end up on the brink.

It was in the belly of this experience that I read the Word for the very first time. It fed my soul like water dripping into a hollow well. Given the choice to worship God or money, I chose the way of freedom and walked away from modeling for good. As recorded in my first book, *Girl Perfect*, I entered into an unknown field of possibility in search of an authentic life.

I took the money I made modeling and returned to school to get a master's degree in writing and literature with an emphasis in biblical studies. But then I got sucked into *another movement* that confused me even more. Back in the States, I met a woman who invited me to a Bible study and soon found myself in a church that enveloped me with attention and community. I moved in with three of the women, and we spent all our time together. They even baptized me in the cool waters of the Pacific. During this time, my aunt tried to warn me that this church was a cult, but I wouldn't listen.

After being a part of the group for three and a half years, I went on a family vacation, only to find out on the first morning that my family had planned a cult intervention. Bewildered and betrayed, I walked out of my aunt's house to figure out what on earth to do. Infuriated, I threw my thick burgundy Bible on the grass and demanded that God give me direction. The tattered pages flipped open to Proverbs 18–19, which basically said stupid people run from correction and that to be wise, you must seek knowledge and not be afraid of it. The verses said wise counsel can save your life and that a rebuke to a wise man is oil on his head. So I turned around, walked back into the house, and listened carefully to what my family and their counselors had to say.

The movement I was a part of was made up of mostly well-meaning people who believed only *they* had a corner on truth. Vulnerable people like me were love-bombed and consumed with their community, then disregarded if we raised legitimate questions about their teaching. As I dug into the tenets of the movement, I discovered they believed everybody outside the group was *lost and missing it*. According to them, it was their way or the highway.

So I ended up on the highway again. I had walked away from the only life I ever knew once before, and I could do it again. Truth mattered more to me. And the truth is, this movement was damaging people. People were getting deeply hurt, and I was one of them.

With Jesus holding my hand, I walked away from the only church I'd ever been a part of. Less than a month later, I met my husband, Shane, "the Cowboy," as I call him—and we started a brand-new life together. He drove me to a healthy, evangelical free church every Sunday. It took all the strength I had to resist the urge to throw my Bible at the pastor and run screaming from the church. Most of the time, I looked down at my lap and quickly wiped the tears off my face while Shane wrapped his strong arm around my shoulder and gave me a squeeze.

Although the women of my first church led me astray, faithful women from our new church surrounded me as I ventured into marriage and motherhood. As I stepped into ministry, they supported me and helped me. When I messed up, they were there to pick me up. They challenged me, celebrated with me, and modeled for me the way of life. This circle of women taught me what it looks like to walk with God in freedom and courage. Collectively, God has worked through women to transform me into the wife, mother, sister, and friend I am today. I would never have made it without these women and the Word.

In the Bible, Wisdom is a she.

> She is more precious than jewels; nothing you desire can equal her. Long life is in her right hand; in her left, riches and honor. Her ways are pleasant, and all her paths, peaceful. She is a tree of life to those who embrace her, and those who hold on to her are happy. (Proverbs 3:15–17)

But the Fool is stubborn and contentious. Folly is easy the beginning but very hard in the end.

> Because they hated knowledge, didn't choose to fear the lord, were not interested in my counsel, and rejected all my correction, they will eat the fruit of their way and be glutted with their own schemes. . . . the complacency of fools will destroy them. But whoever listens to me will live securely and be undisturbed by the dread of danger. (Proverbs 1:29–33)

There are two women we can be. We can reject God's ways and be the Fool. Or we can apply His Word and be the Wise. Whatever roads we have walked down, we can take a turn. We can try again. We can wake up the morning after the storm and see the rainbow arching over the dimly lit sky. We can believe that better days are coming. We can go back to the well and remember. When we get up off the floor and walk forward—head held high—we will be wiser for the journey we have taken. Because we have taken the wrong way, we can have grace for those who are on that road right now.

Chapter Three

I Am Made in God's Image

In the Beginning, Elohim

God's name is a verb.
We do not pronounce it with our lips,
but with our lives.
—L. Grant Luton[1]

After getting my master's in writing and literature, I taught junior high and high school English, so I had to teach grammar. *Yawn,* I know! But I made it fun! Like every grammar teacher, I did something with my students that helped them understand how humanity works. When I taught the parts of speech, we underlined the subject and circled the verb. Why? Because the subject and the verb are the power of the sentence. *Olivia runs across the street to rescue her brother.* Olivia is the subject; runs is the verb. Her brother is the object, and the action of the sentence is *Olivia runs to rescue.* The articles and pronouns in the sentence have little meaning, so we skip right over them. *Olivia running* to save her brother is all that counts—which is why it is so irresponsible that social media, schools, and institutions have focused an entire generation on pronouns—the most meaningless parts of speech in language. Tell me your verbs, and that will tell me *a lot* about you.

A Language of Action and Gender

In 2022, the United States House of Representatives replaced the words "father, mother, son, daughter, brother, sister, husband, wife, father-in-law, or mother-in-law" and inserted "parent, child, sibling, spouse, or parent-in-law" in their written language.[2] Like today's universities which encourage students to write in non-gendered terms, our government claims this is "gender-inclusive language." But for those of us who believe we are to honor our fathers and mothers, this new language is meaningless and offensive. When we weigh these changes in light of a biblical understanding of gender, what do we discover? Can gender be erased, and should it be?

While I don't believe most Americans want to see the erasure of women or the destruction of the family, the meaning of male and female has quickly unraveled before our eyes. When the gender-bending movement began taking hold, I wondered if there was such a thing as "gender identity" in the Bible, and if it can be incongruent with biological sex? In a language of action, can one be separate from the other? At first, I thought the words "gender" and "identity" should *not* go together. They seemed out of whack. But as I searched the Scriptures for the meaning of *woman*, I learned more about gender than I could have imagined. Now I believe there is a "biblical gender identity" that brings out the best in who we are.

In my search for the definition of woman, I looked at biblical Hebrew, what the sages call the language of transcendence. Hebrew words carry meaning for the body, soul, and spirit—and they have *action* in them. The language of Genesis is a verb-based language—a language of *movement*. God is a *verb*. Jesus is a *verb*. Man is a *verb*. Woman is a *verb*. They may be classified as nouns, but they have *action* in them. When God tells Moses His proper name, יהוה, an abbreviated form of "I Am Who I Am," it is made up of three "be" verbs: *I was, I am, and I always will be.*[3] His name has *action* in it: *He has existed; He does exist; and He will always exist.*

As L. Grant Luton writes in his landmark book *In His Own Words: Messianic Insights into the Hebrew Alphabet*, "God is the ultimate

'Be-er' and we are His 'be-ings.' Hence, we are not to be parrots who merely mouth sounds, but we are to proclaim God's name with deeds."[4] Since no one knows how to pronounce God's name, the sages say, "We don't pronounce God's name with our lips. We proclaim it with our lives."[5]

It is the activity of God and of the believer that holds meaning. To be human is to be one who is made in the likeness of God and *represents* Him in the earth. In Hebrew thought, to not represent Him is to *not be human*. We see this definition in the 1828 dictionary: Man is likened to an image or similitude, a vessel of God.

To be a man or a woman is to reflect the God who made us. There is *life, purpose, and function* in the words *mother, father, son, and daughter*. Humanity is not an object; it is an *action*.

The English word for female comes from the Latin *femina*, which means "woman"—but dictionaries no longer make note of this. In Latin, or Romance languages, nouns are either *feminine* or *masculine*. In Italian, the beautiful woman is *la bella donna*. The article, adjective, and noun are feminine—everything works together. English, however, is a non-gendered language, which is why people can try to make it gender neutral. This is not the case with Romance or Semitic languages. Italian, French, and Spanish are Romance languages; Hebrew is Semitic.

The Hebrew of the Old Testament is gendered through-and-through, and *it cannot be neutralized*. You *cannot* take gender out of it; that is impossible for good reason. The feminine and masculine complement one another; they do not compete. Not only are pronouns, adjectives, and nouns gendered—but verbs are as well. In Genesis 1:1, we read *God created*, but in English we cannot see the gender of this action. In Hebrew, *God* is masculine and *created* is masculine as well. In the New Testament, Greek has three genders—masculine, feminine, and neuter. Gender is woven into these languages like a dynamic tapestry that cannot be unraveled.

Masculinity and femininity are some of the most beautiful features of the Bible, not only in language, but in identity. Gender *enlarges*—

it doesn't diminish—who we are. It has nothing to do with cultural stereotypes—Jesus was single, Paul was single, Mary Magdalene was single—and no one knows if they liked pink or blue. That is not the point. Masculinity and femininity are *actions*; they have dignity that is far above styles, fads, and pronouns.

The Bible as Literature

When I was in graduate school for my master's in writing and literature, I wrote the first draft of my book *Girl Perfect*. Written as fiction, it told the ups and downs of my character's life as a fashion model and the reasons she walked away. But my cut-and-dry thesis advisor told me to change the end. He thought someone other than Jesus should "save" the girl in the story. But that wouldn't work because the girl in the story was *me*.

He told me to go back to the drawing board. Stunned, I sat in his office and tearfully admitted the story was my own. Still, he insisted I change it and threatened to not approve my thesis if I didn't. But there was *no other ending*. So three hundred pages later, I had to write a new thesis. Called "Eve, Mary, and Me," it paralleled my story with women of Scripture. At the time, I was taking a "Bible as Literature" class taught by a fierce feminist, so I invited her to be on my thesis committee. We hit a roadblock: The thesis committee claimed I couldn't use the Bible as my source literature. That was odd, since they were teaching a class by that name.

I stood before the committee and argued my case: Even Shakespeare considered the Bible as the foundation for all literature. He alluded to the Bible hundreds if not thousands of times in his work. Ernest Hemingway, William Faulkner, Herman Melville, Nathaniel Hawthorne, John Milton, Mark Twain, and Leo Tolstoy all referenced the Bible or based entire works on it.[6] A literature course without it would do its students a terrible disservice; they wouldn't even be able to understand Shakespeare. It is the fundamental backbone of western culture.

I won my case.

I wonder what would happen if the gender-benders had an open mind about the creation of woman. Since their gender vocabulary is ever-fluid and expanding, I wonder if we could present a voluminous definition of woman that crystalizes rather than confuses who we are. You can read the Bible through the lens of faith, the lens of literature, or both. They are stories, yes, but they are also dramatic films of living history. If we forget them, we forget who we are and where we came from. We fail to remember, to *zakar*.

To be male in biblical Hebrew, *zakar*, is to remember who God is and pass it on to the next generation. To be female, we will discover, is *neqevah*, to bring life by sharing our unique perceptions to the world. We do this best through the lens of the *imago dei*, the made-in-God's-image aspect of gender the world is forgetting. Emily Brontë, the author of *Wuthering Heights*, alludes to every type of biblical genre in her work. The Brontë sisters reveal over 450 allusions to and quotations from the Bible, referencing nearly every book in both the Old and New Testaments in their writing, including the Pentateuch, historical poetic and wisdom literature, major and minor prophets, the synoptic Gospels, and Paul and Peter's epistles.[7] Toni Morrison, Maya Angelou, and a slew of other writers have done so throughout history. Let's be real: Corrie Ten Boom led a freedom march upon a solid foundation, and our sons and daughters are longing to be free.

Without the lens of Scripture, we will never be able to define gender clearly. So I am taking the road of the Brontë sisters, of Milton, Hemingway, Twain, and Shakespeare—I am going as far back as we can remember to light the way. If you dare take this road with me, you will learn more about gender than a million magazines could tell you.

Gold in the Letters

When I say we are going to go back, I mean we are going to go *all the way back* to the first recorded language of Genesis, the ancient pictographic alphabet reaching as far back as 2000 B.C.[8] The first recordings of Hebrew are pictographic. While modern Hebrew is hard to decipher, the pictographs are super easy; they look like caveman letters. A child could easily read and memorize them, which is why I use them in this book to illustrate the actions of gender in the words *man, woman, male, female, mother, father, son, daughter, sister,* and *brother.*

The words, the roots of the words, and *every single letter* illuminate the divine meaning of words and deepen our understanding of the actions of familial roles and relationships. The best way to understand Hebrew words is to first look at the definition, then examine their roots, then peer inside the letters, which further illuminate their meaning.[9] The real treasure is when we look at the letters; each one is a glass doorway that deepens our understanding of who we are.

In the Beginning, the Son

Since we are going back to the beginning, let's look at the first two *letters* of the Bible. I promise this is going to be easy and fun. In Genesis 1:1, we read "In the Beginning, God," which is one Hebrew word, *Bereshith* בְּרֵאשִׁית. In English we cannot see the *letters that begin this word.* In ancient Hebrew, they are the *bet* ◻ and the *nun* ﬧ. The *bet* ◻ represents a house, family, or dwelling. It can represent the house of God, the home of the family, or the house of the Word, the Bible. The *nun* ﬧ looks like a tadpole. It represents a sprouting seed, offspring, or descendants. It also represents humility.

Together, these letters spell son. In ancient Hebrew, son looks like this: ﬧ◻. I point this out to show God's heart. At the very beginning, He lifts up His Son Jesus. This mirrors John's Gospel, which says: "In the beginning was the Word, and the Word was with God, and the Word was God. He was in the beginning with God. And the Word became flesh, and dwelt among us . . ."[10]

As the "house of humility" that embodies the family of God, Jesus was there with God in the beginning.

What is the meaning of this word, Son?

- Son: bên בֵּן [11]
  - Noun Masculine
    - Son, grandson, young men
    - Male child
  - A Builder of the family name
  - People (of a nation)
    - Sparks, Stars, Arrows
  - Afflicted one, Anointed one, Appointed to
    - Arrow; Warrior
    - Servant, Soldier, Steward
    - Tumultuous, Worthy, Mighty
    - Very Fruitful
  - Root: bânâh
    - To build, rebuild, establish, repair, cause to continue
    - To build a house (establish a family)
  - Pictograph (read right to left): בנ Seed | House

On the surface, son means *servant, soldier, steward, worthy, mighty,* and *very fruitful.* He is the builder of the family name, tumultuous and mighty. The son is symbolized by arrows, sparks, or stars. He represents the Arrow Warrior that defends homes and nations. This is where we get our symbol for masculinity: ♂.

In the Beginning, Elohim

The second word of the Bible is *Elohim,* or God: "In the beginning God [Elohim] created the heavens and the earth."[12]

God is called by many names, but this is our first introduction of who He is. In Jewish thought, a name is not a random series of letters or sounds. It means *your reputation.* It is the mark of your *individuality, authority,* and *character.* The word for name is *shêm.* It is the *signifying factor of identity.*[13] So as we look at God's *shem,* we see the nature of who He is and what He does. Who is Elohim?

- God: ĕlôhîym אֱלֹהִים [14]
  - Noun Masculine (Plural)
    - Rulers, judges
    - Divine ones
    - Angels, gods
  - The (true) God
  - Pictograph (read right to left):
    - ᴍᵧ⚥ᴜᴸ Water | Hand | Breath | Shepherd | Strength

Elohim is a plural term meaning gods, rulers, or judges. It can also mean *supreme*, *great*, and *mighty*. While God is neither male nor female, *Elohim* is the masculine plural of a word that looks feminine in the singular (*Eloha*).[15] It makes sense that our first introduction to God is in the plural: He is God the Father, Jesus, and the Holy Spirit, three-in-one. He reveals His function in the very next word: God *created*. His name has *action* in it. His action is to create.

But the gold is in the letters. This is where the pictographic letters are helpful in understanding who He is. In Hebrew, we read right to left.

- The first letter of *Elohim* is the *aleph* � which means "**Strength.**"
- The second letter is the *lamed* J which represents the "**Authority of the Shepherd.**"

God is often called "*El*," a shortened name for *Elohim*. These two letters depict him as a strong shepherd in authority—exactly the name of God in Psalm 23: The Lord is my **shepherd**; I shall not want.

- The third letter is the *hey* ⚥, the letter of femininity, the **Breath of God.**
- The next letter is the *yud* ⊣, the letter of masculinity, the **Hand of God.**
- The last letter is the *mem* ᴍ, which means *Chaos*, or the *Deep*. It can also mean **Water or Blood.**

A related word, ⲯⲩⳑⳑ, spells power: The power or might of one who rules or teaches; the one who yokes two things together. Putting the letters of his name together, we see *Elohim* in greater depth: A strong Authority and Shepherd who spoke the world into being with His breath and created the heavens and earth with His mighty hand. He is a powerful Ruler and Teacher who yokes us to Him through His blood. When you look at the letters, you may see something new or different.[16] This is just what I see, and the more I study the letters in God's names, the more I respect Him.

Is the Spirit Feminine?

So far we have the Son, *Ben*, and the Creator, *Elohim*. Then the Spirit comes on the scene in Genesis 1:2: "Now the earth was formless and empty, darkness covered the surface of the watery depths, and the Spirit of God was hovering over the surface of the waters" (NASB).

Spirit—*ruach* in Hebrew—is a feminine word meaning wind, breath, mind, or spirit. It can also mean temper, disposition, and the energy of life. There is action in *ruach*—like the mighty wind that blows a ship's sails over the waters, to be filled with the Spirit is "to be given a fresh wind; to be wide with space or understanding; to be enlarged."[17] It is the *breath of God*. L. Grant Luton explains:

> In Hebrew, the word for "spirit" (*ruach*) is always feminine. In Greek, the word for "spirit'" (*pneuma*) is always neuter. But, never is it a "he". Due to the suppression of these grammatical facts, translators have bowed to tradition and capitalized "Holy Spirit" as if it were a proper name.[18]

While the Spirit is neither "male" nor "female," the Spirit or *ruach* is feminine. We find the character of the Spirit in Proverbs, where a woman personifies Wisdom:

> She is like merchant ships . . .
> She rises also while it is still night
> She girds herself with strength
> She senses that her gain is good;
> She stretches out her hands to the needy.
> Strength and dignity are her clothing,
> And she smiles at the future.
> She opens her mouth with wisdom,
> And the teaching of kindness is on her tongue.[19]

Do you see all the *actions* in these phrases? She *rises* in dark times; she *girds* herself with strength; she *perceives* that her work is profitable; she *dresses* herself with dignity; she *smiles* at the future and *opens her mouth* with kindness. Valiant womanhood is an *action,* not a fantasy. It is not a feeling and not an outfit. It is the *action* of womanhood that is engrained in our DNA.

This passage is translated in English as "The Wife of the Noble Character," and while noble is a nice word to describe women, the translation is incomplete in English. In Hebrew, wife and woman are the same word. A woman does not have to be a wife to be a life-giver. The Hebraic understanding of her is a *Woman of Valor, Strength, and Might,* a metaphor for the Holy Spirit.

There is a warrior mentality inside of her.

The Holy Spirit is the movement of God, the breath of believers, and the voice of Heaven. Jesus called the Holy Spirit "the Helper," the same exact word God uses for woman in Genesis. Just as the *ruach,* or Spirit, brings life to man, so a woman's voice can bring life or death. Silencing her is not in our best interest. Yes, women can have seriously *bad breath* (remember "I am #Nasty!"). Or women can speak truth that brings *life to her name.* The power of life and death are in the words we say. As James 3:6 says, the tongue is a raging fire. Fire either destroys life or brings it. Woman has *this much power.*

God creates. The Spirit hovers. Like the furious flapping of a hummingbird's wings, *ruach* brings *life, movement,* and *expansion.* It stirs the earth, creating wind that ripples in the deep. The movement of the Spirit is *fluid* and its *function* is to bring *life*, like woman.

When our oldest son, Zach, left for college, he said, "Mom, I will always remember you on your feet." That's what women do; we move; we stir; we breathe life (or death) into our homes, families, children, and men. "If mama ain't happy, nobody's happy." Women set the tone and multiply our influence. Like the hovering of a mother bird over the affairs of the household, women are moving, speaking, helping, influencing.

We have a ranch in our family called Legacy 8. Nana envisioned it; Papa built it; Nana designed it; Papa established it; Papa maintains it; Nana fills it with life. The truth is, they do all of this *together*, and because they do, future generations will benefit. In order for the next generation to take hold of it, we will need male and female, man and woman, mother and father, brother and sister to partner in unity—appreciating one another's gifts and honoring our unique roles in the family. Honoring the feminine touches the women imprint on the ranch—the gardens, the walkways, the linens, the smell of cornbread, cakes, and stew; the lit candles and throw blankets folded *just so* on Papa's favorite chair—these are touches of the feminine that honor who we are. As the breath of the Spirit breathes life into the man, so the woman breathes life into the home. The name of the Spirit, like the name woman, means *life*.

Honoring the men who carved the family ranch out of the hard and stubborn earth—the men who fix the tractors and lawnmowers and trucks and water wells with sweat, blood, and dirt caked on their faces in the blazing Texas sun—the men who maintain the deer blinds, the fields, the cattle, the fences, and protect the property with strength and ammunition—this is not patriarchy. This is a deep, abiding respect for the masculine. To me, this is attractive. To God, this is unity.

We help one another. We protect one another. We complement one another.

This is *faith, family, and wholeness: Each one brings their gifts to create the whole.*

I—2—I

If we look at the pattern of creation in Genesis 1, we see that God takes what is one, separates it into two, then calls it one again. The pattern is 1—2—1, and only in *oneness* does He call it "good."

He separates and then unites:

- Light from darkness—calling them "day" and "night"
- Waters of the heavens from waters of the earth—calling it "sky"
- Waters of the earth from dry ground—calling the whole earth "good."
- Plants from trees—calling the garden "good."
- Sun, moon, and stars—calling the solar system "good."
- Creatures of the water, sky, and land—calling them "good."
- Wildlife, livestock, and creatures that crawl upon the ground—calling them "good."

In His final act of creation, He creates mankind.

"Let Us make man in Our own image, according to Our likeness. They will rule the fish of the sea, the birds of the sky, the livestock, all the earth, and the creatures that crawl on the earth."

So God created man in his own image;
he created him in the image of God;
he created them male and female.[20]

When girls struggle with their identity, we begin right here. We help them see that the mirror does not define them and the opinions of people do not define them; God defines them. As the saying goes, "What He creates, He names." Just as the sun and moon are beautiful representations of His being, so is our biological sex. As human beings, we are God's only creations that represent *Elohim* in both His masculinity and femininity. You cannot tear the masculinity out of

Him: the *yod* ⊐⌐, the hand that works on our behalf. You cannot rip the femininity out of Him: the *hey* ⚇, the breath that brings life.

Once the first man and woman are created in His likeness, He ordains them with *purpose and biological sex*. He immediately gives them the purpose of taking dominion over the earth and everything in it. They are equally given the command to be fruitful and multiply, which can only come from male and female together. As one force—1—2—1— they will rule and reign over all He has provided—and this he names "very good."[21] The Hebrew word for "good" is another glass doorway. It means *pleasant, agreeable, rich, excellent, valuable, beneficial, noble, pure, right, beautiful, favorable, loving, joyful, sweet, abundance*. The masculine form of "good" means *welfare and happiness*. The feminine form means all that, plus *bounty*.[22]

All of His creation is "good," but what does He mean when He says "*very good*"? *Very* means *abundantly, exceedingly, vehemently good*.

So, when the world tells children *it is not good* to be masculine or feminine, man or woman, male or female, we stop in our tracks. We say, "No, that is not right." It is *not good* to reject your gender, because that reflects the God who made you in His likeness and His image. Again, in English, we do not see the gendered words in this phrase: "Let Us make man in Our own image, according to Our likeness." The word for *image* is *tselem*—which is masculine. The word for *likeness* is *dᵉmûwth*, which is feminine. So when people say that God made a mistake in creating them male and female, they substitute light for darkness, good for evil. As Isaiah warns us:

> Woe to those who call evil good
> and good evil,
> who substitute darkness for light
> and light for darkness,
> who substitute bitter for sweet
> and sweet for bitter.
> woe to those who consider themselves wise

and judge themselves clever . . . to those who . . .
deprive the innocent of justice.[23]

There Is a Lie in the Garden

Some say that if you want to sum up the character of God in one word, it would be *unity*. Others say *justice*. Some say *truth*. Even more say *love*. God is serious about unity, justice, truth, and love. He creates us as His representatives in His "image," *tselem* (masculine) and "likeness," *dᵉmûwth* (feminine). To be silent when the world calls evil good is to be a coward—and His name means *Strength*. To be silent is to be negligent—and His name means *Shepherd*. He tells us 365 times in the Bible not to be afraid. If we are weak in times like this, we are not image bearers who reflect His nature through *action*.

A lie has crept into the garden. The lie is this: You can have all this abundance apart from *Elohim* and apart from one another. You can have it through separateness. You can go about it your own way. You should build a family without male and female in oneness; women should rule and men should take a back seat; or men should rule and women should sit down. This is all wrong. This is not God. This is not who He is. This is not the picture of the Trinity. This is not our Creator's character or nature.

The lie goes like this: You are your own maker. Your own ruler. *You are Elohim.*

You can unify with whomever you please and call it good—you can redefine words and call them good—you can alter the genitalia of human beings through drugs and surgery and call it good—you can have sex with whoever you want as long as it feels good. Because men call it good. Media calls it good. The government calls it good. But it is not good in God's eyes, because it does not fulfill the command to be fruitful and multiply.

Closer to home, sometimes we think we can be divided from our husbands or brothers and make them the enemy—while we call ourselves good. We think we can turn our backs on our beloved brothers and dig in our heels. We can insist on having our own way—insist on being right. We can divide mother from father, brother from sister, husband from wife, man from woman—and call it good. But when we do this, we demolish what God calls vehemently good. We suffer because we worship ourselves; *we* define what is good and ignore what He says about it.

We must realize that not everything that looks good is good. Not everything that sounds good is good. Not everything that feels good is good. Not everything we think is good is good. Certainly, Adam and Eve learned this in the garden. Yet sometimes we have to learn it again and again, as I have.

When I decide what is good—when I trump God with my opinions or my jabbering mouth—I lose my way as a woman. I forget who I am created to be. In the forgetting, I suffer. The whole family suffers—and it is in the suffering that He calls us to humble ourselves and turn back. Turn over. Face one another; pick unity. Stop fighting. Confess. Say sorry. Forgive. Reach. Hold on. Believe in one other, because only in oneness do we find what is truly good.

In the beginning, God created. The Spirit hovered. The Word spoke: Let there be light, and the light was good.

1—2—1: one image, two sexes, called to be one. That is *fruitfully, abundantly, vehemently good.*

The Secret Letters in God's Name

Devout Jews believe God's name (יהוה) is so holy that we should not write it, lest it be destroyed. So to be sensitive to our Jewish brothers and sisters, I call Him God or Lord. But the spelling of His name is very important to our discussion of gender. In English, it looks like this: YHVH. While no one knows its proper pronunciation, His name probably sounds like roaring waters, or a deep breath and exhalation, and if that's true, we are saying it *with every breath we take.*

When Moses asked God what He should be called, He told him:

"Say this to the Israelites: YHVH [יהוה], the God of your fathers, the God of Abraham, the God of Isaac, and the God of Jacob, has sent me to you. This is My name forever; this is how I am to be remembered in every generation." (Exodus 3:15)

Perhaps His name means "The Existing One," the one whose *action* is *to abide with us*:

- **The LORD: YHVH**[24] **יהוה**
  - ○ **Proper Name**
  - ○ **The Existing One**
  - ○ **Root: Made up of the letters that spell "was", "is", and "will be."**
    - • **To be, become, come to pass, exist**
    - • **To arise, to appear, to stand, to execute, to finish**
    - • **To abide, to remain, to continue**
    - • **To accompany, to be with**
  - ○ **Pictograph of YHVH (read right to left):**
    - • ⽊ Υ ⽊ ⹁ **Breath | Nail | Breath | Hand**

Is there gender inside His name? In order to answer that question, we have to open up the letters, and this is easiest by taking a look at the pictograph of YHVH: ⽊ Υ ⽊ ⹁

In Hebrew, we read right to left, so the *yud* ⹁ is the first letter of God's name. Each letter symbolizes something much deeper. His name is masculine-feminine-masculine-feminine.

- • *yud* ⹁   is the letter of masculinity: the Hand of God.
- • *hey* ⽊   is the letter of femininity: the Breath of God.
- • *vav* Υ   is the masculine letter of the cross. It joins two together. It unites.
- • *hey* ⽊   is the letter of femininity: the Breath of God.

Not only is gender alive in His name, but it also reveals the beauty and power of the reconciliation of the sexes. The first letter is the letter of masculinity, the *yud*, ⊐ which represents the **"Hand of God."** It looks like an arm with a closed fist. It means to work, make, throw, or worship—the function of the hand. The *yud* represents a finished work or deed done. It is a symbol of productive labor, protection, and security. It is the strong image of the masculine hand that protects, provides, creates, and cultivates.

The next letter of His holy name is the *hey* ⚥, the letter of femininity which means **"Behold."** The pictograph looks like a person standing in front of a window with her arms raised. As a posture of praise, it signifies one who reveals, announces, and brings perception, life, and breath. We see it on the end of Isaiah, Jeremiah, and Sarah: it means *to be infused with the life of the Spirit.* When this letter is placed at the beginning of a word, it gives that word dignity and worth. When it is placed on the end of a word, that word becomes feminine; it means *she.* This is the letter of femininity, meaning **"the Breath of God."** Even the sound of this letter is a mere exhalation of breath. At the root of God's name we find *hâvâ'*, ⚥⚥, meaning "Breathe, Breathe."[25]

The third letter is the *vav* Y, which represents a tent peg, nail, or hook that joins two things together as one, securely fastening them. This letter can also mean **"and."** The *vav* binds two into one. It is the letter of unity and is symbolized by the nail, which unites man to God in oneness though the cross. The final letter is again the *hey*, ⚥, the letter of insight and revelation which means, **"Behold!"**

In God's name, we find *man* and *woman* joined together in unity. The mnemonic meaning, the interpretation of the letters, has many possibilities. It can mean *Behold, the Hand,* and *Behold the Nail* or *Behold the Hand that Drove the Nail.* His name represents the hand of masculinity and the breath of femininity bound into one. You will find this represented throughout Scripture, where we see Him arising like a warrior in His zeal to take out our enemies and gathering us under His wings to protect us as a mother hen.

The Secret Letters in Jesus's Name

Finally, we are going to close this "biblical gender identity lesson" with Jesus's name, Yeshua. In His name you will see the *action* of the Son of YHVH:

Jesus: Yêshûwa'[26] יְשׁוּעַ

- **Proper Name Masculine**
  - ○ **Salvation**
  - ○ **Root Verb**
    - • **To be liberated, saved, rescued**
    - • **To help, avenge, defend, deliver from trouble**
    - • **To be open, wide or free**
    - • **To be safe; to preserve**
  - ○ **Pictograph (read right to left):**
    - • **ᵔYᴗᴗᴗ See | Nail | Devour | Hand**
    - • **When one of the flock is in trouble, the sheep cry out and the shepherd will deliver them.**

Jesus's name is not just a random series of letters. His name is the *action* of *saving*. As Matthew 1:21 says, "She will bear a Son and you shall call his name Jesus [Yeshua], for He will save [yesheia] His people from their sins." The root of Jesus's name is *yâsha'*, which means *to be liberated or rescued*. It is closely related to *yeshuwah*, the feminine word meaning salvation and deliverance.[27]

When we open the doors to look at the letters of Yeshua, we find it means: "When the sheep are in trouble, they cry out and the shepherd rescues them." The shepherd takes delight in his sheep and watches over the flock with compassion and protection. This goes along with Jesus's description of Himself as the Good Shepherd who lays down His life for His sheep. What is the character of Jesus? He rescues people when they are fighting for their lives.

This is why I couldn't change the ending of my first book. He was the one who rescued me. He was not just a character in the story; He was the beginning and the end of the story. So it is with the name

Son. When our nation's leaders attempt to eliminate His name from government documents, they are trying to erase the foundational history of our nation. From the beginning, He saves people when they are in trouble. You will not find this meaning in the words *spouse* (which doesn't exist in the Bible), or *parent*. You will only find these truths in the gendered words that make up the human family. The actions of *sons* are to save, rescue, and liberate people when they are in trouble.

In the first letter of Jesus's name is the *yud* ⅃, the masculine hand of protection. The second letter is the *vav* Y, the tent peg or nail that joins two as one. The last two letters of His name mean "watch, shepherd, and delight."

The letter *shin* ɯ is a picture of the teeth used for devouring or destruction, and the letter *ayin* ◎ is a picture of the eye and represents sight. Combined, these two letters mean "the destroyer watches." His name literally means a shepherd who keeps a careful watch over the state of His flock. When a predator comes to attack, the shepherd destroys the enemy on behalf of the sheep.[28]

When we say, "His name is higher than any name, and at the name of Jesus, every knee shall bow," we must understand who we are talking about.[29] He is both the Good Shepherd and the Destroyer of our enemies. He came to save us as a mighty Deliverer and guide as a humble Shepherd at the same time.

As the Shepherd carefully tending to His flock, He is watching over His beloved sons and daughters with a loving eye—and He will leave the ninety-nine to rescue the one. He is our first example of what it means to be *male*.

A Binding Force for Unity

When we look at the battle of the sexes, we have to recognize that men often don't see Jesus as their model for masculinity—the hand that protects, rescues, and saves those who are in trouble. Instead, abuses against women have caused so much pain between the sexes that women have revolted against masculine energy that does not protect them. But healthy masculinity is modeled by Jesus, our Defender and Advocate.

As we will see in the coming chapters, religious men have often silenced women and called it good—but this is something Jesus never modeled. Quite the opposite—He gave them a voice and brought forth their influence. The ultimate picture of the unity of the genders is in God's name. Biblically, this is represented by Christ and His Bride. Jesus died to lift up His Bride, not to devalue her. In the Bible, the people He loves are called His Beloved Daughter and Chosen Bride. To Him, we are collectively a "she / her." There are more revelations to unveil as we look at male and female that bring out the best in both of us, and men and women would do well to understand them.

From Genesis to Revelation, we will find God does not change. He never loses His character, His *shem*: He is the binding force for unity between the sexes. He is a 1—2—1 God who takes what is one, makes it two, then calls them one again. This is a mystery, and we are going to unravel it.

Chapter Four

I Am a Daughter

The Apple of His Eye

Anyone who touches you touches
the pupil of His eye.
—Zechariah 2:8 (NASB)

As much as we are tempted to blame feminists for losing sight of the definition of a woman, we must remember that God calls men to account first. Even in the Garden of Eden, when Eve bit the apple, God called on Adam. Why? Because Adam was the first human representation of Christ. Biblically, the male is held accountable to God for the state of the family.

As Carrie Gress reveals in her book *The End of Woman*, the founders of feminism suffered from neglect, violence, and abuse by the hands of men who were supposed to nurture and protect them.[1] This is why feminists came out angry and broken and firing spit. The founders of the feminist movement battled mental illness; divorced and cheated on their husbands; turned to sexual relations with women; and abused sex, drugs, and rock and roll to "liberate themselves" from carnal men.[2] The truth is, the men they loved brutalized them rather than shepherded them. So feminists came out raging like tongues of fire.

"Smash the patriarchy!" They hollered, believing if they could raise themselves as superior to men—and be nothing like their weak, subservient mothers—they would win. "These boots are made for stomping, and they'll stomp all over you!" They cried, but it backfired.

The sexual liberation movement has a lot of fallout for women. As we stand, the state of women is worse than ever:

- Ninety-two percent of victims of trafficking for sexual exploitation are female.[3]
- Ninety-nine percent of sex buyers are male.[4]
- The average rape victim is a fifteen-year-old girl.[5]
- One in four adolescent girls aged fifteen through nineteen have experienced physical and/or sexual violence from an intimate partner or husband.[6]
- Eighty-five percent of sex trafficking victims in the United States are *American women and children*.[7]
- Globally eighty-one thousand women and girls were killed in 2020. Fifty-eight percent of them died at the hands of an intimate partner or a family member, which equals **a woman or girl being killed every eleven minutes in her own home.**[8]
- In January 2020, Pornhub was the tenth most visited website on the planet, with more hits than Netflix or Amazon.[9]

With a billion hits on Pornhub in December 2021 alone,[10] we know there are far too many men and boys visiting this site. Even girls are turning to pornography for sexual entertainment in rising numbers every year. With every single hit, the feminist mantra "Sex work is work!" is destroying the relationship between the sexes. It is destroying marriages. Furthermore, it denies the command to be fruitful and multiply. Instead, it multiplies nothing but pain for both men and women. Instead of forging us in oneness, it creates division. Male and female are eating the apple of carnality, and the juice is dripping down their chins. The most bitter juice of all is the stolen worth of *woman*.

In December 2020, journalist Nicholas Kristof published an investigation in the *New York Times* proving that Pornhub was infested with rape videos. He writes, "[Pornhub] monetizes child rapes, revenge pornography, spy cam videos of women showering, racist and misogynist content, and footage of women being asphyxiated in plastic bags." Once his investigation went public, Pornhub immediately deleted 80 percent of its content—a staggering ten million videos—for degrading children on its site, mostly young girls, but boys too.[11] Nevertheless, the site is still raking in billions of dollars showing women being raped, choked, nearly suffocated, and humiliated every day, while the women pretend to like it, denying their constant pain, exhaustion, and trauma.

When women leave the porn industry, they say things like, "It was torture for seven years. I was miserable, I was lonely, I eventually turned to drugs and alcohol and attempted suicide."[12] "Most of the girls start crying because they're hurting so bad . . . I couldn't breathe. I was being hit and choked. I was really upset and they didn't stop."[13] "I have never been so frightened and disgraced and humiliated in my life. I felt like garbage. I engaged in sex acts in pornography against my will to avoid being killed. . . . Everyone who watches [that show] watches me being raped."[14]

No Wonder

For the last six years, the most popular search on Pornhub is *teens*. According to Fight the New Drug, "teens" got 33.8 billion hits in 2018.[15] With 98 percent of Pornhub videos featuring a white female, how can we wonder why white teen girls from middle-income families are the number one demographic of girls with gender dysphoria, rejecting their femaleness altogether?[16]

People scratch their heads and wonder, "Why don't girls want to become developed women? Why are they rejecting their feminine figures and dressing like men? Why can't they define *woman*?" The answer is obvious. According to Covenant Eyes, 39 percent of boys and

23 percent of girls have witnessed sexual bondage online—and sexual images stamp themselves in their brains; once they have seen them, they cannot forget. Eighty-three percent of boys and 57 percent of girls are exposed to *group sex* online. Two-thirds of teens have accidentally seen it on their phones, two-thirds have seen it in the last week, and two-thirds seek it out monthly. According to Covenant Eyes, nine out of ten boys and six out of ten girls are exposed to pornography before the age of eighteen, and the average boy sees it at age twelve.[17] The onslaught of images comes directly through their iPhones, which have *the apple bitten on it in plain sight!*

Studies prove this is harming their brains and causing sexual dysfunction while desensitizing them to sexual violence. Porn literally *trains* their minds in misogyny—the hatred of women. Meanwhile, radical feminists claim that "Sex work is work," as if men should make money off women's degradation. In the U.S., the porn industry pulls in more than the combined revenues of the NFL, NBA, and MLB, generating between $15–97 billion a year.[18] This is a true "pandemic," and I'd give anything to see women around the world rise up to put a stop to it.

Porn lies, and it's destroying the kids. It's destroying women too, turning themselves against their own nature as nurturers and as mothers. Every woman wants to be respected, and to deny that is to deny the meaning of our name. As mothers and fathers, we have to refuse to allow it into our homes and pray it is abolished as a nation. Yet the relentless focus on sexual "identity" in our culture only promotes it.

The Language of Sexual "Identity"

When people get sick, where do they go for answers? A common site to turn to is Healthline.com. Yet this site offers forty-seven terms describing sexual attraction, behavior, and orientation. Are you ready for this list? Hold your breath and see if you can read them all without taking a breath:

Allosexual, allosexim, androsexual, asexual, aromatic, auto-
sexual, autoromantic, bicurious, bisexual, biromantic, closed,
coming out, cupiosexual, demisexual, demiromantic, fluid, gay,
gray sexual, gray romantic, gynsexual, heterosexual, homosexual, lesbian, LGBTQIA+, libidoist asexual, monosexual,
non-libidoist asexual, omnisexual, pansexual, panromantic,
polysexual, pomosexual, passing, queer, questioning, romantic
attraction, romantic orientation, sapiosexual, sexual attraction, sex-averse, sex-favorable, sex-indifferent, sexual orientation or sexuality, sex-repulsed, skoliosexual, spectrasexual, and
straight.[19]

I decided to go through the list and see who the average woman in
America is according to Healthline.com. After taking the quizzes, I discovered that according to these "doctors," the average woman's "sexual
identity" is allosexual, androsexual (attracted to men), cisgender, cishet,
demisexual, and demiromantic (meaning she is romantically attracted
to someone due to an emotional relationship—which is *normal*.) On
top of that, she is heterosexual, monosexual, panromantic, pomosexual, straight, and sometimes sapiosexual and sex-indifferent when she's
not in the mood for sex. She could even be graysexual or grayromantic
at times (if I can figure out what that means), although I think that's
just when she's tired from taking care of the kids, house, and bills all
day and just wants to cuddle with her husband before bed rather than
have sex.

Should we focus now on pronouns? Or instead, should we recognize the infiltration of the most confusing doctrine known to man that
has permeated our public school system and universities and invaded
every form of psychiatry, medical care, and therapeutic environments?
This language is aimed at the mantra that "gender is fluid" and "sexuality" is too—for *everyone*. At this point, we have *elementary school
children* being brainwashed by pride videos, claiming they are *bisexual and gender fluid*, a statement that causes confusion and belittling
among their peers.

The Problem with Sexual and Gender Identity

I am the daughter of a former home economics and sex education teacher. My mother implemented and taught a values-based sex education program that promoted abstinence as the best choice for students their age. Most of my friends in the 1980s—including me—took sex education from my mom in the seventh grade. Totally embarrassing, I know—but back then it was more like a co-ed health class, and my mother was a great teacher.

I vividly remember sitting in her class, looking at videos and posters that documented the progression of a woman's body from conception to childbirth. These images showed the picture of the womb through a mother's transparent body. We could see her entire reproductive system at work, including the growth of the child from a fertilized egg into a fully formed human being. These images inspired me to see the miracle of birth as beautiful and profound.

My mother defined terms for her students, taught us the male and female reproductive systems, and the impact of risky behaviors like sex, drugs, and alcohol. Mom equipped us with an appreciation of the human body and an understanding of the consequences of sex outside of marriage, emphasizing abstinence as our best choice. When we were done with that unit, we learned how to bake, cook, and sew—both boys and girls, together—and it was great.

I wish we could go back to those days. Today, many school districts are promoting gender ideology as scientific fact, blurring gender lines, and presenting deviant sexuality as a healthy option. As Abigail Shrier writes in her revealing book *Irreversible Damage: The Transgender Craze Seducing our Daughters*, "The high school version of three of the most highly respected health curricula[20] that include gender identity and sexual orientation instruction are so raunchy, explicit, and radical that I couldn't decide whether they were trying to excite adolescents . . . or turn them off to sex entirely." In programs where gender theory is the new gospel, both children and teachers are told they must address boys as girls and girls as boys if the child feels like that's "who they are." This is a theory anyone can debunk by watching pregnancy videos from the 1980s. Today's new gender charts look something like the periodic table, but every one of them is different. A quick search for "gender symbols for kids" comes up with images like this one:[21]

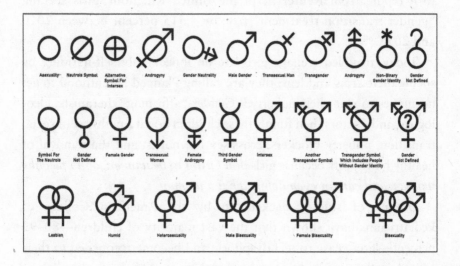

A 2022 report showed that three-quarters of Americans who call themselves nonbinary (a person who identifies as neither male nor female) are in Generation Z, under thirty years old. That is double the number from their 2017 report, only five years earlier.[22] The word *nonbinary* is relatively new; it didn't appear in the *New York Times* until 2014. But everyone is expected to accept the above chart as the new gospel. If we pose reasonable questions or disagree with its tenets, we are shunned and demoralized. Canceled.

Gender Dysphoria

The massive rise in gender dysphoria among young people is a *direct result* of this teaching. Gender dysphoria is a psychological condition in which children experience a painful incongruence between their biological sex and experienced gender; they feel like boys stuck inside of girls' bodies or vice versa. This condition used to show up primarily in toddler boys; today we've seen a massive spike in what's being called late-onset gender dysphoria in prepubescent girls. In the United States, the number of children and teens diagnosed with gender dysphoria nearly tripled between 2017 and 2021, according to a report from Reuters.[23] In the United Kingdom, girls seeking "gender transition treatment" rose by 4,515 percent between 2010 and 2018.[24]

Today, troubled teenage girls are no longer only self-harming by slicing their arms and legs; they are calling Planned Parenthood to get hormones to *stop* their puberty.[25] Gender-"affirming" therapists, ideologues, and doctors then funnel these children down a pathway of social transition, puberty blockers, cross-sex hormones, and the removal of healthy body parts because girls *don't want to be women, don't feel like women, and cannot even define what a woman is.*

Dozens of studies backed up by the American College of Pediatricians have shown that the vast majority of children—80–95 percent—later cease to feel dysphoric and become reconciled to their sex when they are *not* encouraged to believe that they are members of the opposite sex.[26] Nevertheless, America's pathway is this: Teach kids they can choose their gender from kindergarten to college, affirm them if they do, change their name and pronouns (sometimes over and over again), and applaud them as they walk down the road of medicalization. While not all doctors encourage this pathway, gender-"affirming" doctors do, and that is a major problem for teens' developing brains.

With teen girls who are extremely prone to social contagions, this is a fire burning out of control if we do not put a stop to it. As Abigail Shrier methodically lays out in *Irreversible Damage*, gender dysphoria has caught on in a similar way to the social contagions of self-harm and eating disorders; adolescents egg each other in adopting trans, bisexual, and nonbinary identities. But the difference is, we never affirmed girls in self-harm before, while the gender-"affirming" road is quite the opposite. If girls believe they are really boys, they are *encouraged* to bind their breasts, which smashes healthy breast tissue and lymph nodes. They can even purchase underwear from Target, Walmart, and Amazon that creates the illusion of a boy's bulge. For boys who believe they are trans, the process may begin with dressing like a girl and "tucking" their male organs to hide them as if they are a source of shame. (Online trans-activist communities will help them with this.)

The next step is puberty blockers, which may interfere with normal bone density development and put them at risk of osteoporosis. This also carries risks for brain development and may suppress their IQ peaking to its highest level.[27] If the adults around them affirm their delusion that they are "born in the wrong body," gender-"affirming" doctors will put them on puberty blockers like Lupron, which is used to castrate sex offenders but is not FDA-approved for children—without knowledge of the long-term impact on their bodies.

Studies show that nearly 100 percent of children who use puberty blockers go straight to cross-sex hormones, probably because their natural bodies have not been allowed to develop.[28] Remember—if they had been allowed to proceed with puberty, 80–95 percent of kids would find that their dysphoric feelings naturally went away. But after puberty has been suppressed, girls go on to take testosterone, a class III substance, which can induce menopause and cause vaginal atrophy. Intercourse becomes painful because their vagina is dry, cracked, and receding; their clitoris grows, and they experience painful cramping due to endometriosis. If they move straight from blockers to cross-sex hormones, "infertility is almost guaranteed—and sexual development and potential for orgasm may be foreclosed for good," Shrier writes.[29] Other side effects are muscle aches, increased moodiness, aggression, and uncontrollable appetite—among girls who often already have eating disorders. Their voice deepens; they grow facial and body hair like boys. Long term, they have a high risk of diabetes, stroke, blood clots, cancer, heart disease, and increasing mortality rates.[30] This process halts healthy biological functioning—all before or right around puberty; most often, these kids *have not even had sex yet*. This is all based on the *idea* that male and female can be swapped like apples for oranges.

After five years on testosterone, gender-"affirming" doctors may suggest the girls have their uterus and ovaries removed "to reduce their risk" of endometrial cancer.[31] The last step to the "happiness and peace" promised by this movement is the removal of healthy body parts; for boys, testicles and sometimes the penis; for girls, breasts, uteruses, and ovaries. They end up sterile. Sex is painful if not impossible. Breastfeeding is impossible, and so is childbearing—all while showing no proof to the improvement of their mental health.[32] The number of young detransitioners—those who regret their attempted transition to the opposite sex—has exploded on Reddit and YouTube. They record their heinous journeys of believing they were the opposite sex in which they took the road of medicalization. They are now clawing their way out of the indoctrination of gender theory and raising their voices to be heard. This entire pathway is based on the concept that gender is fluid and decided upon by the child and not their Creator.

Women's "Health"?!!

Meanwhile, magazines like *Teen Vogue* and *Women's Health* actually encourage this—which seems unbelievable, but it is true. Let's read an excerpt from *Women's Health* magazine that provides an overview on some commonly "confused ideas" surrounding gender identity.[33] Jackie Golob, a certified sex therapist in Minnesota, starts with the lie we are analyzing, "Gender is only a social construct," then proceeds to set us straight about gender identity.[34]

- **Genitalia does not equal gender.** "The sex characteristics a person is born with do not signify a person's gender identity. When people have 'gender reveal parties,' it really should be called a 'genital reveal party.'" Someone's genitals have no bearing on whether they identify as a man, a woman, non-binary, or anything else.
- **Once more: Gender isn't physical.** The best way to describe someone's gender identity is as a person's "internal, deeply held knowledge of their own gender," according to GLAAD's

Media Reference Guide.[35] You can't "tell" someone's gender by looking at them; that said, some people might choose to *express* their gender identity through their appearance, which might include "makeup, dresses, high heels, athletic shorts, sneakers, and more," Golob explains.

- **The gender binary isn't real.** There's a common misconception that there are just two genders: "male" and "female." But there are tons of other gender identities beyond those two. "[Most people] live in between [the binary], with personality traits that relate to gender identity, expression, and biological sex. Gender identity can change over time, and it is not fixed," says Golob. Just because you identify one way at one point in time, does not mean you will always choose that identity, or that your identity won't shift and evolve.

- **Sexuality and gender identity are not the same thing.** "Gender identity is how you feel about yourself and the ways you express your gender and biological sex," says Golob.[36] Meanwhile, sexuality refers to who you are emotionally, physically, romantically, or sexually attracted to, she says. In summary, "gender is how you feel about yourself, while sexuality is how you feel about others," says Golob.[37]

The article lists sixteen "gender identity terms we should know" but points out there are limitless options: "anatomical sex (sex 'assigned at birth'), cisgender, transgender, cishet, non-binary, intersex, gender queer, gender-fluid, gender non-conforming, gender-expansive, agender, gendervoid, bigender, omnigender, pangender, and two-spirit."[38]

According to this teaching, not only is gender different from sex—but these ideas go for *all of us*—even those who have never questioned our gender. That means that not only *gender dysphoric* children may believe they are meant to be the opposite sex—but *all children* must choose from a plethora of genders which will fluctuate throughout their lives. Nothing is concrete, nothing is true, and what is true now may not be true in the future.

There is no foundation to this teaching except the imaginary ideas of mankind. Not only is it not grounded in reality—but it also directly opposes God's intention in creation. Because gender "fluidity" is the hypothesized answer to gender confusion, impressionable children who trust their parents, teachers, and therapists are taught that their ever-changing feelings indicate who they are. *They decide who they are—and that can change from day to day.* Not only is gender fluid, but truth is fluid as well.

The critical thinkers ask, "Since when do we tell children that *feelings* determine identity? Since when do we advertise that sexual urges tell people who they are? Since when do we advise young people to explore bisexuality and transgenderism? And since when do we teach that sex is simply for pleasure?" We don't tell children this. We tell them to protect their sexuality for marriage and childbearing. But the culture is telling them the exact opposite. As long as they "consent" to it, their desires and the desires of others are "good."

Forming a Healthy Identity

Because this teaching combines the words "gender" with "identity," and "sexual" with "identity," the equation looks like this: Gay = your identity. Trans = your identity. Pansexual = your identity. But is this healthy? When I see you, I don't see "gay or straight, trans or cis." I see a person who is valuable, priceless, gifted, worthy, and has a purpose. I see your body as beautiful and sacred and worth protecting.

Identity in God's eyes is not based on sexuality; it's based on personhood. It is both fixed and constant. It is not found in feelings, mental health diagnoses, sexual persuasion, gender identity, or pronouns—and the very worst place to get our identity is from other people, good or bad. What people say about us or don't say about us is not our source of security. I know this because I lived it; it's in my bones, in my blood. When I was a teenage girl in the modeling business, for example, my identity was completely wrapped up in how I looked and what others thought of me—and that was a rollercoaster ride. It wasn't until I saw how I looked in God's unchanging mirror that my perception of myself changed for the better.

Identity in Christ does not arrive *outside in*. It arrives *inside out*, and it is not fluid. Healthy identity begins with knowing we are created by God with intentional design. Once we understand this, we have to look away from people and gaze long and hard into the Father's eyes. When we see ourselves in His eyes, we discover we are enough as we are. We see how valuable we are. We do not have to change to be loved. When we realize how loved we are, we change. We live as loved children of God from the inside out. The crystallization of our identity begins with turning towards the Father first.

The Father

One of the saddest things about gender theory is the attempt to remove the names of the family from our language. Although God is *Elohim* and YHVH, the name Jesus uses most often to refer to God is Father. If you suddenly stopped calling your earthly father by that title, that would certainly hurt him. Likewise, in a nation that claims to make God its foundation, the dismissal of the Father's name must grieve Him. We must not let the name of the Father go; it is by looking into His eyes that we see our true reflection.

- Father: av[39] אָב
  - Noun Masculine
  - Father; Family Determiner
  - God as father of his people
  - Head or founder of a household, group, family, or clan
    - Ancestor, grandfather, forefathers
  - Producer, generator
    - Of benevolence and protection
  - Term of respect and honor
    - Ruler or chief

- ○ **Root: avah** אבה
  - • **Submit to existing demand**
    - ▫ Conforming with and agreeing to wishes of others
    - ▫ Counselor
    - ▫ Related Roots: ripen, submit; fill; desire
  - ○ **Pictograph (read right to left):** ﬡﬥ House | Strength
    - • **Stand, Fruit**

The father is the *family determiner*. He is *the producer and generator of benevolence and protection.* He is the head or founder of a household, the ruler or chief, and his name is an indicator of honor and respect. In the root of his name, we discover the word counselor, the word Jesus uses for the Holy Spirit. In Hebraic thought, the father is the commander of the family army, provider of offspring, priest, and teacher. His name also means fresh fruit, the father of the next generation of trees in the family line.[40]

The pictograph further illuminates his name. By standing tall through righteousness and humility, he is the *strength of the house.* Where does his strength come from? In the word *father* we open a glass doorway into a little-known secret: The root of his name means to *submit to existing demand, to conform and agree with the wishes of others.*

To *submit* is the *action* from which the word father is derived. It can also mean *to fill, desire, and ripen.* Hence, the word "fruit" for father. In God's economy, the one who comes underneath others to lift them up is the strongest one. It has been devastating to our society that so many men don't understand where their strength comes from. They think it is in dominating women that they become strong, when the truth is the opposite. The strength of the father comes in laying down his life to save us. When men absorb this identity, everyone flourishes—especially their wives, sons, and daughters.

Cloudy Lenses

Ever since my starve-myself-till-I-was-sick days as a model, I've had trouble with my vision. If I wear a single contact in my right eye, I can see long distance. But when I need to look at my phone, it looks like a water-color painting. It is *so annoying*. So I stick my finger in my eye, toss the contact out, and it shrivels like plastic baked in the sun.

When we look at ourselves through the lens of gender and sexual fluidity, we do not get a clear picture of who we are. We are under a delusion when we combine the words "sexual" with "identity." The terms do not match. Sexual urges change over time, so labeling ourselves by sexuality does not create a fixed identity. Labels can stick to us, then fall off and shrivel in the sun. And they should, because when sexuality is identity, we have blurry vision.

As one of the main spokespeople against this movement, ex-trans influencer Oli London realized, when he identified as a Korean woman, his inner white boy eventually came out. He tried the surgeries and costumes, but they failed him. He came to Christ, wrote a book called *Gender Madness*, and is shouting from the rooftops how this ideology steals identity in young people.[41] Once he found Jesus, his lenses changed. This is what happens for all of us. What once was foggy suddenly becomes clear.

I Call You Daughter

A biblical story which illustrates this point is the bleeding woman.[42] Forever recorded in the annals of history because she bled for twelve aching years, her identity was reduced to her biology. Worse, her identity was *a feeling*: She was rejected and ostracized by her community. Anything she touched was considered contaminated. Her labels were Dirty and Rejected. No matter what she did, her body would not conform to the confines of her culture.

Today, the bleeding woman might be called "asexual, born in the wrong body, not really a woman, gender neutral" (for who knew why she bled for twelve long years—and no one would touch her). Separated from others due to biblical purity laws, she likely believed something was *wrong* with her. Unworthy of love and acceptance, she was a bloody mess when she pressed through the crowd to reach for Jesus's robe. Yet when she did, she found healing in the fringe of His garment. Immediately she shrunk back, afraid. But Jesus searched to see her face in the crowd.

Finally, she approached Him, trembling with fear. What would she see in the reflection of His eyes? Would she see how she *felt* inside: Dirty, Stained, Rejected? Would He *affirm* the lies she believed about herself—that she was *asexual* because her body didn't work right? That she was *born in the wrong body*? That she was *not really a woman* because she couldn't bear children? Would His eyes affirm that she was unlovable and untouchable, disposable even?

No. He called her the highest name a woman can be called on this earth: *daughter*.

> "Daughter," He said to her, "your faith has made you well.
> Go in peace and be free from your affliction."[43]

The word "affliction" means whipping, scourging, plaguing. It is the exact description Isaiah wrote seven hundred years prior to describe the whipping of Christ's body prior to laying down His life on the cross. Jesus was scourged. He was humiliated, browbeaten, and rejected by the very people He came to serve. He was a Man of Sorrows who knew bodily sickness and grief. His scourging was her scourging. His rejection was her rejection. His grief was her grief. His bleeding was her bleeding. And His rising was her rising.

Her reach for Him is the reach of every woman who feels soiled, dirty, rejected, alone, and uncomfortable in her body. From this single interaction with Jesus, she walked away with an identity that would last: He called her daughter. In Hebrew, daughter means "the Apple of My Eye." Jesus wanted to go face-to-face with the bleeding woman so she could see her reflection in His eyes. In Jesus's language, daughters are called branches. Like sons, they are builders, establishers, and repairers. They create new branches of the family, repair the broken places, and carry on the legacy of their father under a new name.[44]

- **DAUGHTER: bat** בַּת [45]
  - ○ **Noun Feminine**
  - ○ **Daughter, girl, adopted daughter, daughter-in-law, granddaughter, female child, cousin**
  - ○ **A polite address**
  - ○ **Description of character**
  - ○ **As personification**
    - • **Town, village**
    - • **Company**
  - ○ **Apple of the Eye**
    - • **Eye**
    - • **First, Branch**
  - ○ **Pictograph (read right to left):** תם **Cross | House**

As the Apple of Jesus's Eye, the bleeding woman who no man would touch would forever share in His inheritance, whether or not she would ever marry or bear children or be loved by a man. The lies she believed were annihilated by looking in His eyes.

The expression "Apple of the Eye" is used by Shakespeare and in the Old Testament to indicate a person who is valued *above all else*. This is how God sees His daughters and His sons. Even David asked God to be the "Apple of His Eye": "Keep me as the apple of your eye; hide me in the shadow of your wings" he prayed.[46] Literally this means, "keep me as the daughter of thine eye." To be the apple of someone's eye means that you are gazed upon with tender love and watched carefully by that person. Someone is keeping watch over your life. He sees your tears and hears your prayers; He knows your dreams and your fears. You are central in His gaze, and your image is reflected like a pool of water in His eyes.[47]

Likewise, Jerusalem is called the Apple of God's Eye. As Zechariah 2:8 says, anyone who touches Israel touches "the pupil of His eye." When Hamas—which means *violence* in Hebrew—slaughtered 1,500 Israeli civilians on October 7, 2023, this was like thrusting a pointed finger in the pupil of God's eye. In the brutality of the massacre, babies were decapitated, and grandmothers, mothers, and daughters were raped so badly their pelvises were crushed. The horror sent shock waves through the world.

When violent people hurt God's daughters—whether through pornography, violence, murder, or abuse—they thrust God in the eye. Not only have they deeply offended Him, but they have also received His full attention. It is a very serious offense to stab God in His eye. This is how the Father—who is our Generator of Benevolence and Protection—feels when His chosen ones are raped, mutilated, dragged through the streets, and beaten beyond repair.

When His daughters are hurt, He cries. As Jeremiah wrote: "My grief is beyond healing; my heart is broken. Listen to the weeping of my people; it can be heard all across the land. 'Has the LORD abandoned Jerusalem?' the people ask. 'Is her King no longer there?'. . . . I hurt with the hurt of my people. I mourn and am overcome with grief.'"[48]

So when Jesus called the bleeding woman "daughter," He represented the Father's heart for us all. In the same way, He cries for His people, Jerusalem, and mourns over the way women are devalued in our pornographic society. His desire is to see His daughters protected and healed. On purpose, He chose a hemorrhaging woman to be called the Apple of His Eye. This was His way of saying, *I see you. I see your suffering and the places where your heart bleeds. I hear the names they call you and how they treat you as if you are disposable!*

What about the brazen prostitute who cried uncontrollably at Jesus's feet? Did He call her pansexual, pomosexual, or sexually fluid? No. Even though she lived a sexually deviant lifestyle that brought pain, shame, and confusion, He still called her loved. In fact, He rebuked the religious people who assigned her a sexual identity by asking them a single question: "Do you see this woman?"[49] I imagine it like this: Do you SEE this WOMAN? Do you SEE how HURT she is? Jesus knew the meaning of the word *woman*. She was *not* their whipping post.

She had likely been raped multiple times, and yet it was the stigma of *her* reputation that followed her like a stench. When we see her in our mind's eye—really SEE her crying at His feet—should we pick a category she should fit in? Should we hold up a sign that says, "Sex Work is Work!"?

No. The questions we should ask are: How did prostitution *break* her? How did being sold *steal* her worth? How did sex with greedy man after greedy man ravage her soul? How many times did she wince in pain as they used her and discarded her like a filthy rag? How many men committed adultery with her and called *her* the sinner? What could mend her?

When we tell the truth about identity, we do not reduce people to biology, appearance, or sexual activity. We are more than that. We are loved daughters—and to tear that name from us is to dismantle our souls. When Jesus calls us loved, it is an indicator of deep respect. In our narratives of categorizing people according to their sexuality, we assign names to people that God does not call us. By doing this, we completely dismiss the truth of femininity. We conveniently ignore the truth: This lifestyle *hurts women*.

We know how the religious hypocrites labeled the sinful woman. They called her a whore. But Jesus called her legendary. He said that wherever the Gospel is preached in the entire world, her story would be told.

The Cross Is in Her Name

The daughter and the sister are the *only* ones in the family whose names carry the sign of the cross. The daughter's pictograph is a beautiful representation of her name: †ヽ⊔. The letters mean *the house that protects the seed of the cross*. The family of God ⊔ will continue through her descendants ヽ. The daughter is marked by covenant of ownership † by the Father Himself.

The daughter is the circle upheld by the cross, the universal symbol for female ♀.

Given the opportunity, Jesus upholds women, every single time. As author Kristi McLelland says, He takes them from a place of shame and lifts them to a place of honor.[50]

So is the Father casually standing by and watching the world steal our name, or does He have something to say about it? When He asks the question, "Do you SEE this WOMAN?" He wants to know, "Do you see what I see? Do you know that when you offend her, you offend Me? Do you know that when you tear the femininity out of her, you break my heart? Do you know how much I love her? For I am the LORD, and she is the Apple of My Eye."

Chapter Five

I Am Worth Remembering

What Does It Mean to Be Male?

Remember your Creator in the days
of your youth.
—Ecclesiastes 12:1

In my search for the biblical roots of the word *woman*, I found that we are intrinsically linked to men. In three-quarters of the Bible's references to female, we are listed "male and female." Everything about the female complements the male. This is the key feminists missed. By rejecting "the patriarchy" rather than calling men to account, feminists did themselves a great disservice. If they had reminded men who they were *supposed to be* as protectors of women, they would have protected themselves. But instead, they shot themselves in the eye.

The Eye of the Patriarchy

The rabbis have a way of measuring a person: He either has a "good eye" or a "bad eye." Having a "good eye" means a man looks out for the needs of others and is kind and generous to the vulnerable. One who has a "bad eye" is greedy and self-centered, blind to the needs of those around him.[1] The man who tramples the weak has a bad eye. The man who uses brute strength to overpower a woman into submitting to him has a bad eye. We must remember that the ancient language of Genesis reveals the word *submit* is in the *father's name*. The one with the good eye lays himself down for his bride; he doesn't squash her. He lifts her, and in turn, she lifts him.

As the Hebrew letter of femininity *hey* 𐤄 is pictured as "one looking through the window," womanhood is about perception. This is the feminine side of YHVH who beholds, shows, and reveals. Jesus says, "The eye is the lamp of the body. If your eye is good, your whole body will be full of light. But if your eye is bad, your whole body will be full of darkness."[2] If the eye is a symbol for woman, and the quality of a man's eye is determined by how he relates to those who are weaker, then I'm afraid unhealthy patriarchs have given the body of Christ bloodshot eyes. With pornography, abuses against women, and the silencing of women still rampant in the Western church, the daughters of God are still not valued the way God intends. Their pain is being mirrored in the daughters' rejection of traditional roles of marriage and motherhood and the lack of protection of female spaces, which most of the Church is silent about. If we want to restore the meaning of our name, these wrongs must be made right. The quality of a man's eye is shown in how he defends the vulnerable—and the truth is, women are more vulnerable, and we need men to stand up for our protections. Restoring our value is key to our healing.

Author Voddie Baucham says:

When you try to look at manhood in isolation, you've already got a problem. The God who created us. . . . He created us male and female. So you cannot understand maleness apart from femaleness. You have to understand what it means to be a man, first of all, by what it means to be made in the image of God, and second of all, by what it means to be made as this counterpart to a woman, and this idea that God created us to be priest, prophet, provider, and protector—God designed us that way.

And when you take us away from that, we are bigger than women, we are stronger than women . . . we have all of these things that allow us to take advantage of women. They get pregnant, we don't. We can just walk away from it and leave them with that. There are so many things that if left unchecked, they do allow for this toxic version of masculinity.

So what we have to call men back to, is this understanding of manhood that is outside of themselves. And you being a man is not just about who you think you are or even who you want to be. It is about you pointing back to the One who made you, it's about you pointing back to the purpose for which He made you, and it's about you pointing back to the relationship that He intends for you to have with the opposite sex. . . .

[Marriage is] an incredibly important part of the picture of what it means to be a man. This idea that we would be in a relationship, that we would be the head of a household, that we would be, like I said, priest, prophet, provider, protecter within that context—all of that gives us not only purpose, but it gives us greater understanding of what masculinity is all about, and it also keeps it in check, and it protects women. That's the irony of all this.

People are fighting against the patriarchy, people are fighting against marriage, people are fighting against traditional roles, and the result is, you leave women unprotected and you leave men unchecked to do whatever they will with those women.[3]

When men complain about having to take on all these responsibilities, Baucham says:

First of all, that's what you were created to do. Secondly, if a man is honest, it's what you yearn to do.[4]

When God created man, He embedded a function within his name: to remember who God is and what He requires and to act on this knowledge.

The greater a man understands the purpose of his maleness, the more likely he is to rise to it.

Here is the true definition that will never change—the one in Genesis:

- Male: zâkâr[5] זָכָר
  - ○ Noun Masculine or Adjective
    - Him, mankind, male, men
    - Son; boy; male animal, ram
    - Pointed or fixed in mind (indicating physique and mental toughness)
  - ○ Root: zâkar (verb)
    - To remember; call to mind; to be remembered by God; memorial; remembrance; mark or consider; mention, mindful, think, record, confess, draw attention to, proclaim, confess, memorialize
    - Remembering to redeem
    - Male; bearer of tradition
    - Historian
    - A recalling of events of the past or to act upon a past event
  - ○ Pictograph (read right to left): ꓵШ⌐ Head of Man | Open Palm | Weapon

There is a principle in Bible study called the "rule of first mention." This means that the first (and second) time a word is mentioned, that is its meaning *for the rest of Scripture*. Hebrew words contain physical truth, divine meaning, and implications for *action*. This is why it is called the language of transcendence; there are layers of meaning in the words.

Even the physical qualities of maleness are present in *zakar*—he is the *pointed one, the "arrow."* This is obvious in his physique. Even his sperm are like arrows. In physical as well as soul-like union, the male is the arrow, the giver ♂, and the female is the circle, the receiver ♀. Yet this pointedness is not just physical; it is also mental. The *action* of maleness implies a fixation of his mind on his purpose.

Here are three things to understand about the word "male":[6]

- A male passes his knowledge of the Creator to his children, and they receive the name of their father. A man is to act on behalf of his wife and children, demonstrating the commands of God through *action*. The male passes down the family history through story and name.

- *Zakar* means more than "to remember." It means "to act on what is remembered." *Zakar* means to recollect the past, apply it in the present, and consider the future outcome of conduct. It is more accurately defined as to "continually think": *past, present, and future.*

- It is also used as an action of God, in which God calls to mind His promise and commitment to you.

This fixation of thought and discipline of the mind is important for our understanding of maleness. It takes mental toughness to shoulder the responsibility of the family, community, and nation—and that is exactly what men do. In this fascinating verse, the wise teacher Solomon charges young men to *zakar*, to remember their Creator in the days of their youth:

> *Remember* him before your legs—the guards of your house—start to tremble; and before your **shoulders—the strong men—**stoop. Remember him before your teeth—your few remaining servants—stop grinding; and before **your eyes—the women looking through the windows**—see dimly.[7] (Ecclesiastes 12:3 NLT, emphasis added)

A father tells his son to remember—and draws a symbolic picture of the human body, calling his shoulders "strong men" and his eyes "women looking through the windows." These are the ancient Hebrew symbols for masculinity and femininity: the *yud* ⊐, the strong arm of work and protection; and the *hey* ⚔, the person looking out a window with her arms raised. Are men given the strength to shoulder the responsibility for the family? Are women windows to the soul through which God is seen and expressed? In Hebrew, the words male and female fit this description exactly—men shoulder responsibility and women perceive what men do not.

Zayin: A Sword, a Seed, and a Scepter

Volumes of books have been written about the hidden manna in the Hebrew alphabet. It is called the holy language because every letter contains infinite meaning. Each *letter* of the word male has a physical manifestation, an application for the soul (mind-will-emotions), and a connection to the divine.[8] It is *endlessly* deep, tapping into the body, soul, and spirit. Each letter is a doorway of its own, telling us who men are and how they are to relate to women.

Let's open the door to the word *male*. When we do this, we will see the secret power of his gender.

The first letter of the Hebrew word for male, *zakar*, is the *zayin* (z) ֡ which means *weapon*. In ancient Hebrew, this letter looks like a plow. In an agricultural society, a man puts his hand to the plow to extract a living from the earth. With the plow, he protects and provides for his family at the same time. L. Grant Luton writes:

> The name of the letter *zayin* (ז) can be spelled two ways. When it is spelled זין it means "weapon." But, when it is spelled זן it means "to nourish" or "sustain." These two concepts—"weapon" and "nourishment"—seem worlds apart until one learns that *bread* and *war* are closely related in both the Hebrew language and Jewish thought. The Hebrew word for "bread" is לחם and the word for "war" is מלחמה (*milchamah*). Note that the word for *bread* is in the center of the word for *war*. In Hebraic thought, success in battle is measured by how much land is won since land is the source of sustenance. Therefore, to win land is to win bread.[9]

The sages say the *zayin* has two faces, one representing a *weapon* and the other representing a *seed*. They are essential in understanding the role of the male. The *zayin* represents spiritual nourishment (a seed) and spiritual protection (a sword.) *Vav*, the letter that comes before *zayin*, symbolizes the figure of a *man*, and the *zayin* is depicted as *a man with a sword*. The modern letter is even shaped like a sword.

The *zayin* signifies the Sword of the Spirit, the Word of God, or Christ—which has two edges: warfare and nourishment. As a double-edged sword, the Word is like a seed that nurtures our souls and offers correction when we are going the wrong way. Just as the plow is a man's food and weapon, so "the Word of God must double as our spiritual food and weapon."[10]

Zayin's two faces—the seed and the sword—also signify the kindness and severity of God. Nowhere do we see this more powerfully displayed than in Jesus, who sternly "reproves and disciplines us," and in the next sentence, gently knocks on the doors of our hearts, offering to come inside and dine with us.[11] He will rebuke us *and* feed us—all for our good.

As the Sword of the Spirit represents the Word of God, Christ is called the Word. Jewish rabbis describe the modern pictogram of the *zayin* as a scepter—a small staff held in the hand, symbolizing the authority of the king. It is the emblem of royalty and sovereign power.[12] As Psalm 45:6 says, "The scepter of uprightness is the scepter of your kingdom."[13] Hold on to your hats, because we are going to go deeper. Like I said, *zayin* is constructed from the previous letter, *vav* (representing a man of the word) with the addition of a crown on its head. It is not just a sword; it is a scepter. And it is not just a scepter; it is a King. The *zayin* is the "Crowned Man (Jesus) equipped with the sword of the Holy Spirit."[14] Here is the modern form of the *zayin*, appearing as a man with a crown on his head upheld by a sword:[15]

Jesus was male. Hidden within the first letter of word *male* is a calling to use the tool of Scripture and the tools of the earth to sustain his family. The entire goal of a male is to pass his *shem* [name] to his descendants, just as the lineage of Christ is threaded through the male. The whole point of being male is to carry his name forward—and by name, I mean his *character and way of life*. Why was Christ male? Was He just a patriarchal figure? Or was Christ a kingly example to men everywhere to lay down their lives to lift up their brides?

The feminist mantra is that we are the SAME. Gender is fluid; it's how you feel, rather than how you are made. This is false for body, soul, and spirit. Not only is it biologically false, but it is untrue at the soul level—and most of all, at the spiritual level. Maleness, like femaleness, is a gift and a calling; an assignment and an existence; a way of being. It is not a choice; however, men get to choose how they will use their weaponry.

Every male has the warrior spirit inside of him, a spirit of kingship and authority. If this is channeled correctly, everyone flourishes. Maleness has *nothing to do* with whether a boy digs in the dirt or picks up a paint brush. It is the shouldering of responsibility. The male is the seed, the sword, and the scepter.

Sons

Remember that the word for son means *arrows, sparks, or stars*. The son, or *ben* in Hebrew, means *servants, soldiers, and stewards who are tumultuous, worthy and mighty*. If more fathers passed this understanding to their sons, boys would rise to this calling. They might even choose to be protectors instead of oppressors; nurturers instead of thieves; warriors instead of weaklings; prophets instead of problems. All men have a unique genetic code—but *all are made in His likeness*. Through the male, God wars on behalf of women and children, not against them—and He uses males to display this part of Himself.

If boys understood their purpose, they would fight for women instead of trying to dominate them or erase them, as gender theory does. If Christ-followers replaced lies about feminine guys, toxic masculinity, and gender stereotypes with true manhood, boys would learn to follow the example of Christ, who esteemed His mother by calling her "Woman." With His last breath on the cross, He ensured she would be provided for and protected by John.[16]

We must wake people up to the fact that gender "fluidity" warps masculinity—and it does not protect women. Instead of these confusing lies, we could teach boys that the greatest living example of manhood was Jesus Christ, who laid down His life for all. Maybe we could replace TikTok images of men faking womanhood and presidents who call this "good" with a *truly* good message: that to be male is *to understand your greatest weapon is laying down your life to protect women and children.*

If more pastors taught this, boys would rise to the divine calling of their gender. If gender theorists understood that the first letter in the word *male* signifies a Crowned Man equipped with the Sword of the Spirit—a weapon that nourishes, provides, and protects—they wouldn't *dare* stop the process by which boys become men. Next to female genital mutilation in China and Africa, cutting off their gonads is the greatest atrocity the world has ever seen against young boys who are effeminate in childhood. It not only steals their adolescence, but it also robs them of their purpose—to use their fully developed muscular bodies and fixed minds to protect and provide for others with a singular focus. If a fully-grown man wants to do this to his body, it is between him and his Maker. But to do this to children is *evil.*

The male is the one who sacrifices his life for the family; not only is this modeled by Christ, but by great men who have laid down their lives to defend our country. We respect women who serve in the armed forces, yet throughout history it is strong, self-sacrificing men who have fought for our liberties while women guarded the household and served a community in need, as the Wise Woman of Proverbs did.

In Judges 6, we see the story of Gideon who was hiding, cowering and afraid of the masses of enemies out to destroy him. When Gideon was acting like a weakling, hiding in the bushes—what did God call him? A "fem gay boy?" "Really a girl?" NO. Did He affirm his "gender identity?" NO. He spoke identity *into* him.

Then the Angel of the Lord appeared to him and said:
"The Lord is with you, mighty warrior."[17]

God "calls into being things that do not exist" (Romans 4:17 NASB). When he was anything but, God called Gideon a hero, a man of valor—and the valiant warrior inside of him rose up and defeated his enemies. When God went face-to-face with him, He spoke to him as if he was a fearless leader, and what happened? Gideon become one of the heroes listed in the Hebrews 11 hall of fame. He lived up to his name. As a male, he remembered who God was and struck down the altars of Baal, the god who makes people *forget* God and what He requires. He led an army of warriors to annihilate the enemy. Speaking the truth of Gideon's identity is all it took to empower him to become who he was meant to be. So it is with sons. Not all of them will seem masculine on the surface, but *all* are created to be heroes. God doesn't lie to people and affirm their feelings, equating them with identity; He speaks what is not as if it were so.

In her phenomenal book *Who Do You Say I Am?: Overcoming the Spirit of Identity Theft*, Kristen Smeltzer tells the story of her son Zachary suddenly being overtaken by what doctors would have diagnosed as psychosis, mania, or schizophrenia.[18] In her desperation, she cried out to God who showed her one simple strategy: *Tell him who I am and tell him who he is.* At times, her son was so troubled he saw tormenting visions and could barely speak. Repeatedly, she told him who he was. His name was Zachary David. Zachary means "God remembers," and David means "beloved." Her strategy was *calling him to remembrance.* The spiritual warfare eventually subsided, and her son came into his right mind. Today, her son is uniquely gifted in this very power. He literally became a "weapon," the first letter in his name, *zakar.*

Depositing the truth of his identity as a loved and remembered son of God called him back to his true name. This is what God does with us: He tells us who we are in His eyes—and that has the power to restore a person's true identity.

Kaf: Hands That Receive

The second letter in the word for male, *zakar*, is the *kaf* or K ש representing an open palm. It is the picture of a hand opening to the sky like one who receives from God. This letter represents productive labor and hard work.

When you take the image of the plow or weapon ⌐ and add the image of the open palm ש we see that a male's work is his offering. As Psalms 128:2 (NASB) says:

> When you shall eat the fruit of your hands [*kaf*],
> You will be happy and it will be well with you.

This letter also represents *potential* or *power*. When a man works with his hands as a gift from God, his labor will produce fruit and multiply. Interestingly, it can also mean "suppress." This sounds counterintuitive, but to bring out his potential, he will have to suppress the drives which are obstacles to his flourishing. On a physical level, men must suppress the forces that take them away from their identity to work for their families. A man whose hands do not work is not fulfilling his calling. He will use his hands for other purposes than to glorify God, and when he follows his fleshly desires, the family, community, and nation will suffer for it.

Resh: The Head That Bows Low

The third and last letter in the word male is the *resh* or R ר which signifies headship. Though it is near the end of the alphabet, *resh* means *beginning*—which is Jesus's leadership style: *The first shall be last*. The *resh* represents one who is first, chief, head, prince, commander, or leader.

The pictograph looks like a picture of a head covered by a hand ℛ. It symbolizes human reasoning versus obedience. When a man's head is covered by God's hand—and he bows in submission to it—he does not use human reasoning to decide how to live his life. He yields to God. Because "fear of the Lord is the beginning of wisdom," he doesn't think himself wise in his own eyes. Instead, he relies on the Lord's wisdom and direction for his life.

This is why men in Judaism wear the kippah, or skullcap—symbolizing they are "under God's hand." Their human reasoning is not above the Lord's. Under His authority, they are the head of their families. In the modern rendition of the *resh*, the figure represents a man with his head bent over—representing poverty. Again, this seems counterintuitive, but Jesus, as the Head of God's household, bent low to serve us. Our King became poor to lift us up. Jesus is the Servant King who came not to be served, but to serve. Only in stooping low do men mirror the life of Christ.

When we look at the names *woman* and *man*, we will see that both begin with *aleph* ℵ, the symbol of strong leadership. Both men and women are strong leaders, but only the male has the *resh* ℛ. As one who represents the family name, he is held accountable by God first. When Eve ate the forbidden fruit first, God called Adam first: "Where are you?"[19] Why? Because he is the head; he is the chief. As Paul wrote, death came through one man, *Adam*, and life came through one man—*Jesus*.[20] As the male, Adam is responsible to speak and act on behalf of the family, and God holds him accountable first.

In our family, we tell the men to "carry the boats." With the strong leadership of women by their side, men shoulder responsibility. They do whatever it takes to lead well, knowing they are accountable to God for their leadership. This aspect of headship is getting lost in our culture, and we must not let it be so. When we teach young men to "carry the boats," they understand the security of the family rests in their able hands, and they rise to the true meaning of their name, *male*. The "man" inside the boy rises up, because as Baucham says, "It's what he's made to do, and if he is honest, it's what he yearns to do."[21]

Restoring the Male

If a man submits to Christ, he makes it easy for the woman to honor his role as chief. Remember, the root of the Father has the word *submit* in it; he submits to God for the wellbeing of everyone in the home. When he takes this position, he naturally becomes a priest, provider, and protector. As the head of the family, he will cover his bride as God covers him. A male who understands his calling will wash and protect his bride physically, emotionally, and spiritually. He will also plant his seed inside of his wife to carry on his name—*his character and way of life*—to their descendants.

In our culture, we behave as if the woman has the final say regarding the destiny of her womb, and therefore she rules over the life and death of the male's descendants. This does not reflect the heart of God. There are two wombs the Bible speaks of. One is masculine and the other is feminine. The masculine word for womb, *rechem*,[22] is called "the seat of compassion." This is the word used to describe Jeremiah and David as prophets appointed *before the womb* [*rechem*].[23] This word is derived from a verb meaning *to love deeply, have mercy and pity, and behold with the tenderest affection.* The masculine word for womb literally means *love.*

Like an eagle, the male hovers over his children with fierce pride. The hidden manna inside the Father's name tells us he will submit to the wishes of others to maintain harmony. This is a good thing, a God thing. But this strength can also be a weakness, and it has been used against men in our society. The feminist demand for "rights" is so deafening that men have been taught to sit down and shut up. This movement has clearly directed men to release their role as protectors and providers and hand it over to the contentious women who want to take their place. In order to keep harmony with women, men are demanded to agree with "My Body, My Choice!" regardless of how they feel about it.

In a very domineering way, they are told to stand down when it comes to the male's rights to his own children. Yet males are meant to be chiefs, not chickens. While everything inside them tells them to rise in chivalry to be the priest, prophet, provider, and protector,[24] many have submitted to the voice of the feminist movement that tells them abortion is the right of the mother only. This stealing of the *action* of males has caused more PTSD (pain, trauma, sorrow, and despair) among the men of our nation than we realize.

It is time to make room for valiant males again. They must reclaim their identity as fathers who hover over their descendants like an eagle and fiercely protect their children from harm. They must remember who they are, and it is up to us to remind them.

The prophet Malachi predicts that one day God will "restore the hearts of the fathers to *their* children and the hearts of the children to their fathers, so that [He] will not come and smite the land with a curse."[25] I can only imagine "their" is italicized for good reason: the children being aborted in our society *are their children*. For us to restore our name *woman*, we have to begin by honoring the male's rightful place in the human family.

In the language of Genesis, a male is not just XY chromosomes or the one who produces sperm. To be male is a *verb* meaning to protect, provide, rescue, and release. His calling is to carry on his name through his descendants, but he doesn't even need earthly children to do this. Jesus was single, and so was Paul. Daniel was possibly a eunuch, and John lived on a deserted island. Nevertheless, every one of them lived up to the name male by managing the sword of the spirit ⌐, the hands that receive Ɯ, and the head that bows low ᔭ. That is the male's calling; that is his name.

It is a powerful identity to be male. It is a challenge of weaponry and responsibility, and boys will reach for it—if we teach them to. But if we teach them their voices and feelings don't matter, they won't have anything to rise to. By continuing to funnel multiple "identities," misogynistic stereotypes of "women," and lies about women's "rights" into their minds, we are doing boys and our nation a great disservice. As they become disconnected from the reality of their maleness, they might think they are "empowered" by pretending to be women or being dominated and silenced by them, but this only weakens them. A man can never replicate the DNA of a woman and will never understand the concerns, the cries, and the calling God deposited inside of our name. His calling is to protect her and his descendants; that is all it really takes to be a valiant man in God's eyes.

The Differences between Us

When a mother told psychologist Jordan Peterson that she was concerned her child's school was teaching gender as a social construct, he whipped out some differences between men and women off the top of his head:

> Men have wider jaws; larger teeth; thicker skulls; are more powerful in the upper body; can punch a lot harder; and can throw more naturally. They tend to weigh more and be taller . . . and women have finer bones. Women have a subcutaneous layer of body fat that men don't have. Women are more pain tolerant; they also have very high levels of stamina. Women tend to have a little edge in verbal ability; men tend to have a little edge on spatial ability. And apart from the straight physiological differences, there are psychological differences. Women are more enthusiastic; men are more assertive . . . men are higher in withdrawal and in volatility . . . women are more agreeable and more polite. Men are slightly more industrious, and women are more orderly . . . women are higher in openness; men are higher in interest in ideas.

He points out these psychological differences aren't huge and then names the hugest difference between men and women:

> Men are more prone to be interested in things and women are more prone to be interested in people. And that's quite a large difference by psychological standards. And there isn't any evidence that is socially constructed. The counter evidence is that

as you make societies more egalitarian, those differences actually get bigger rather than smaller, which is one of the most well-established findings in all of the social sciences.[26]

Definitively, when men and women are honored as equal partners, their differences get bigger, not smaller, which means they *soar*. They expand and increase—rather than decrease. By capitalizing on male and female strengths at the highest level, we achieve the *fulfillment of the command* to be fruitful and multiply. By elevating instead of diminishing our differences, males have an exponentially more positive impact on the culture—and that includes women and children.

Male and female are not at all the same, yet we both have magnanimous strength to amplify God's heart in the world. This is a truth we must never let go of as we light the way forward.

Chapter Six

I Am a Life-Giver

What Does It Mean to Be Female?

*If sex isn't real, the lived reality of women
globally is erased. I know and love trans people,
but erasing the concept of sex removes the ability
of many to meaningfully discuss their lives.
My life has been shaped by being female.
I do not believe it's hateful to say so.*
—J. K. Rowling[1]

To answer the "What is a Woman?" question, I didn't need to look
any further than our mothers, grandmothers, aunts, sisters, and
friends. Women tell our stories. In circles of women around the world,
you will hear our voices:

- Little girls hoping the bad man won't come in their rooms
  tonight because *they are female*.
- Stories of girls in China disposed of like trash *because they
  are female*.
- Stories of women sitting in pews next to their abusers, told to
  "submit" instead of "run" *because they are female*.
- Stories of in vitro fertilization, miscarriages, and infertility
  because they are female.

- Periods and pap smears, menopause and mammograms, endometriosis and hysterectomies, cancers of the breast, ovum, uterus, and cervix *because they are female.*
- Stories of joy-filled, fearful mothers holding sick or dead children in their arms *because they are female.*
- Stories of women who ache for time to go backwards, how the sound of the vacuum reminds them of the sucking away of their babies they never got to hold *because they are female.*
- The voracious silent killer of chlamydia that leaves women's fallopian tubes ravaged and too scarred to bear children *because they are female.*
- Stories of girls starving, harming, and turning on their bodies because they don't measure up to the media *because they are female.*
- The two hundred million girls and women alive today who have undergone female genital mutilation in thirty countries in Africa, the Middle East, and Asia, leaving them without sexual enjoyment. We could hear their cries of depression, mental illness, and suicide *because they are female.*
- Rape, incest, sex trafficking, domestic violence, and abuse *because they are female.*
- We could tell the story of the news reporter gang raped by a mob in the middle of a road in Afghanistan or innocent girls sold as child brides to Antifa *because they are female.*
- Women who are demeaned, choked, and raped on Pornhub, where the category "teen girl" charts *a billion* views a month *because they are female.*[2]

The Female Experience

Real women know that being female can feel like a wonder or a curse.

We are usually weaker, smaller, and more vulnerable—and to deny that is to deny the truth of our existence. One in three girls has experienced sexual violence *because she is female*, and 90 percent of rape victims are *female*. In her eye-opening book *The Case against the Sexual Revolution*, Louise Perry points out an adult women's upper body strength is half as strong as that of an adult man's and two-thirds as strong in the lower body. Men can punch two and a half times harder than women. Ninety percent of females have weaker hands than 95 percent of males. Perry writes, "The unwelcome truth will always remain, whether or not we can bear to look at it; almost all men can kill almost all women with their bare hands, but not vice versa. And that matters."[3]

If we took all our stories around the world and told them so they could be *lived*, so they could be *felt*, so they could be *experienced* by males—*men who pretend to replace women would be struck deaf and dumb*. Our lived experiences of violence, ache, and longing would echo around the world in a reverberating, cacophonous, astounding roar.

Deafened by our voices and muted by the name "female," the males who dare steal our name would fall to the ground in horror, shocked by their own insolence. They would be humbled by God Himself—for they have blasphemed our name.

As Jordan Peterson points out, the biological markers are *relevant*. We have XX chromosomes. We menstruate. We carry life and sometimes lose it; we lose hair and breasts and friends from fighting women's cancers with strength and vitality—and only some of us survive that battle. Do these confused men who walk onto the battlefields of our sporting competitions think they can take our name and that we are going to congratulate them as they steal our trophies? Do they really think we are going to sit down and shut up?

They've got another thing coming.

As Matthew Arnold says: "If there ever comes a time when the women of the world come together purely and simply for the benefit of mankind, it will be a force such as the world has never known."[4]

That time has come. It is NOW.

A Setting for a Precious Stone

Returning to the *beginning*, the Hebrew word for female is *nᵊqēḇâ* or *neqevah*, which means *to make a hole by piercing*.[5] While the male is pointed like an arrow ♂ she is bored through like a circle ♀. Her name literally means *hole, or pierced through, as one who is designated like the setting for a precious stone*. Her name is not just physical; it carries purpose. Like the male, the female is not just form, but *function*. Just as her body represents one who encompasses the man like a circle, so her function is to encompass, protect, and keep the boundaries.

- **Female: nᵊqēḇâ** [6] נְקֵבָה
  - **Noun Feminine**
    - **Woman, female child, female animal**
  - **Root: nâqab**
    - **To perforate/ set firmly**
    - **To make a hole by piercing; bored through**
      - **To puncture, literally or figuratively**
      - **To strike through**
      - **To hollow out**
    - **As a setting for a precious stone**
    - **Female, designated one**
      - **Appointed, specified, singled out, named**
    - **A boundary keeper**
  - **Pictograph (read right to left): 𐤑𐤄𐤏𐤋: Breath | House | Continue | Seed**
    - **The female is the continuation of life in the house and the one who brings perception, life, and revelation.**

According to Skip Moen in his incredible book *Guardian Angel*, "the Arabic cognate [of *neqevah*] not only means, 'to pierce, to make a hole,' but also 'single out' and 'appoint as leader.' These meanings are found in Hebrew Scripture. Could it be that the *neqevah* (female) is *appointed* to an office of distinction, a role that carries a special identity and bears the mark of that identity in her gender?"[7]

As the one who is "bored through," the female's inner cavity *literally* encompasses the male. Yet on a spiritual level, her function is to hold the boundaries for the family and community, just as the setting for a precious stone creates a purposeful boundary.[8] Imagine the setting for an engagement ring, showcasing a diamond—the function of the female is to encompass others and hold them as precious gifts. Spiritually, she acts as a protective shield for the male; she prays for him, and sometimes redirects him.

This concept is revealed in a mysterious verse which no one truly understands: "How long will you go here and there, O faithless daughter? For the LORD has created a new thing in the earth—A woman will encompass a man."[9] This verse means, *"A female shall encircle, surround, protect, or encompass a man."* It suggests she will march around the nation as a guardian shield. Perhaps the daughter in this verse represents God's beloved daughter, Israel. Or perhaps it means there will be time when a woman commands a nation to turn it around. The "man" in this verse represents *an army of warriors*, and we know Deborah did that very thing. In the Book of Judges, she directed Israel's army to attack, and the Lord sold the enemy's commander Sisera "into the hands of a woman."[10] The point is, a female's role can be to enclose, envelop, surround, or cause to turn back. It is the men who are strong warriors on the battlefield, yet it is the *female* who turns them around to go another direction to take out the enemy.

As we open the doorway of *neqevah*, we will find gold in her name. We will discover what females are naturally appointed and designated to do.

Nun: A Seed, a Son, and a Savior

The first letter of *neqevah* is the *nun* (n) ‫נ‬ which represents the seed planted within her. The pictograph looks like a tadpole. This letter is in the word for son. It means "sprouting seed" and eventually developed into the image of a fish. A fish is a symbol of life and fertility, and early believers used the fish to represent themselves since Jesus called them "fishers of men." First-century believers also identified themselves by the fish because the five letters that spell the Greek word for fish form an acrostic, standing for "Yeshua, Messiah, God, Son, and Savior."[11] Fishing has long been a symbol for sharing the Gospel; as we "throw out our line" into the deep, we offer the good news to the lost. For those that bite, they come out of darkness and into the light.

Whether we call the *nun* ׆ a seed, tadpole, or sperm, it represents *life*. The letter that follows the *nun* in *neqevah* is the *kof* (k) ־•־, which means *the continuation of time and the circle of life*. It is easy to see that the sperm planted within the female will bring children into the world. She is the one who continues life—just as Eve's name means the "mother of all living."

The arrow ♂ meets circle ♀—and bam! We have new life.

Nun can also mean "*son, descendent, heir to the throne*." As prophesied in Genesis 3:15, redemption would come through *the seed of a woman*. Joshua was called "The son of Nun." Joshua means "God saves" and Jesus means "Salvation."[12] Joshua was blessed with God's presence and given the appointment to defeat the enemies of God, which is precisely what Jesus did on the cross. Even in the first letter of the word female, we see prophecy fulfilled.

After the fall, God says to the serpent:

> I will put hostility between you and the woman,
> and between your seed and her seed.
> He will strike your head,
> and you will strike his heel.[13]

Jesus was a promise for God's people to be redeemed through *one willing woman, who bore the seed of one willing man*. The female is designated to be the continuation of life in the family.

Remember in the 1828 dictionary, "woman" means "man + womb." The number of eggs a woman has for a lifetime is determined *at her conception, in the womb*. Males, on the other hand, produce millions of sperm in their lifetime. Sperm meets egg. *Zakar* meets *neqevah*. Male meets female, and only through this union do we find life. So simple. If only today's gender charts made it that easy to understand. This is the truth we were raised in, so are we going to remain silent while the world funnels multiple gender identities into young people that are impossible to attain?[14] No. In good faith, we cannot.

Hostile to Life

Just as predicted in the Garden of Eden, the fact that females are life-givers is now met with extreme hostility. No longer does our society treat unwanted pregnancy as a gift, but a hindrance for women "who want to do their own thing." The feminist movement treats life as a curse and problem to be eliminated. Teen girls are put on birth control before they even become sexually active—something completely unnatural, and fertility rates are rapidly declining for young women. According to the Pew Research Center, fertility for young women reached an all-time low in 2020.[15]

Instead of teaching girls that sex is about *bonding to a mate for life, being fruitful and multiplying, carrying descendants into the world—* the sexual revolution taught women that sexual union should have no consequences. Because we are body, soul, and spirit, this is a lie with painful consequences. Girls get their hearts broken and get pregnant out of wedlock, where there is no male "to carry the boats." Fooled by these lies, they often have abortions, not understanding the meaning of their name. Even worse, men don't have to be responsible for their sexual choices. As the ultimate lie, our society places the life of the child squarely on the woman's shoulders. It is a yoke much too heavy for her, a burden she was never meant to bear.

Neither men nor women in this sexually-charged culture are taught how to cover one another and cover the life of a child—because that involves *sacrifice*. Only when a child is *wanted* does our culture celebrate it, but how many *unwanted things in our lives turn out to be blessings in disguise? Is everything we want good for us? Or does God sometimes allow things we don't want to move us into another season of our lives—the one He destined for us from the beginning?*

The abortion-loving culture regards her descendants as disposable, unimportant, and inconvenient. If that *living child* requires either parent to bow low, die to self, or give up their lives to bear new life, that is treated as *a burden and a hindrance to freedom* by abortion proponents. Women literally scream at the top of their lungs for the right to end the lives of their own children and make it look like a colorful party of flags and parades, when in truth this is painful for both men and women.

Even "Planned Parenthood" is a misguided sequence of words. Do they teach young couples about the responsibilities of parenthood? A budget? A home? A wedding? Familial support and job searches? No. They teach *nothing* about parenthood. They don't even provide diapers. They teach lies: the baby is not a human being and the woman's life is more important than the new life God is weaving within her. How easily do they forget Mary, the mother of the Messiah, was around twelve to fifteen years old and single? Yet she *made the choice* to lay down her life for her Son, who in turn laid down His life for her. This is the reciprocal nature of the female-male relationship which bears fruit for life.

Female marchers yell, "Abortion is health care! It's my body, my choice!" While they carry their nasty signs screaming, "Get your paws off my drawers," "I am not a human incubator," and "Abortion is my right!" they completely miss their God-given dignity. They miss the meaning of their s*hem*, because their name means *"one who will continue the cycle of life."*

If you try to tell these protesters that God is weaving a child in their mother's womb—they believe their *own* life matters, but *others'* do not. At the March for Life rally, Ronald Reagan said it best: "We're told about a woman's right to control her own body. But doesn't the unborn child have a higher right, and that is to life, liberty, and the pursuit of happiness?"[16]

Abortion-rights activists are truly convinced that making females—who woke ideologues call "period-havers and birthing people"—into gods who determine the destiny of another life is in their best interest. They esteem themselves as superior to males, rather than equals in decision-making. They dismiss God and end up paying for it with the pain of losing their children. I have witnessed women in their forties and fifties *still weeping* over abortions from their teens and twenties. Thankfully, Christ came so everyone in the family can be redeemed.

The *nun* at the beginning of our name *female* represents *humility*. Either we bow low or are brought low. Many of us have to break first. Jesus *chose* humility. Because He knew what it would mean to us, He descended from the highest place to the lowest place. Check out the steps Christ took to lower Himself—and see how God exalted Him, below:

As Paul reveals in Philippians 2:3–11, Jesus descended so that God could be lifted high. "Being in the form of God . . . [He] emptied Himself . . . Taking the form of a bond-servant . . . Being in made in the likeness of men . . . He humbled Himself . . . Becoming obedient to death . . . Even death on a cross. . . ." In return, "God highly exalted Him, and . . . Bestowed on Him the name which is above every name, so that . . . At the name of Yeshua every knee will bow, of those . . . in heaven . . . And on earth . . . And under the earth . . . And every tongue confess that Yeshua the Messiah is Lord . . . To the glory of God the Father."[17]

Do you see how he bowed low to be lifted high? This is the meaning of the "Son of Nun." As we wrap up the lesson of the *nun*, we can understand yet another feature of modern Hebrew. Some letters have what's called *beginning* and *final* forms, depending on where they are in a word. The beginning form of the *nun* is bent over—symbolizing a man bent low in humility—but the final form stands tall. The sages say this means that when we live a life of servanthood, we will stand tall on the day of judgment. Like the *zayin*, the final figure looks like a sword with a crown on its head—but the *nun's* sword is elongated.

Zayin   Nun

In this picture, we see that the *zayin* stands tall as the king, but the *nun* is even taller.[18]

Coming Underneath

In the order of creation, the head of the male is God, and the head of the female is the male. The male lifts the female, the female lifts the male—and they both flourish. I use the word "lift" here to help you imagine submitting as coming underneath. My wonderful mentor Devi Titus once showed me a picture of a table and asked me which was stronger, the legs or the top?

"The legs?" I guessed.

"Yes," she nodded. "It takes a lot of strength to come underneath someone and lift them up." That day she planted a picture of submission in my mind that I will always understand. The male is not to press the female down or force her to submit, since God does *not* do that with us. Christ models for the male a King who descended to the lowest place, so that God would exalt him to the highest place. Just as the father's strength is in his willingness to submit to existing demand, it takes enormous strength to come underneath others to hold them up. In her relationship to the male, that strength is also the woman's role and responsibility.

We go down in order to go up. The way of Christ is the way of going lower—and this is a good lesson for females. We are powerful, but when we lay down our swords and come together with men in unity, we multiply. "Be fruitful and multiply" is not just a physical thing God commanded the male and female to do; it is a spiritual union of the sexes coming together to bring out the best in each other. As Jordan Peterson reminds us, when we do this, we excel; we do not diminish our power—we become *at the top of our game*.[19] Just as the final form of the *nun* has an enlarged sword, so a female's life, when she walks with God, will be enlarged.

This leads to the last meaning of *nun—to continue, propagate, and multiply*. It is interesting that the first letter of the words *male* and *female* depict a scepter with a crown—but the *nun's* crown is slightly higher. Why would this be? I can only imagine that Christ lowered Himself so His Bride could be lifted high. In turn, she lowers herself to lift Him high. This is the *healthy* relationship between male and female that our culture is missing—and this is the one that empowers us to fulfill our calling to represent God in the earth. Only in the unity of the sexes do we enlarge.

This is the lesson of the *nun*: a Seed, a Son, a Savior. There must be less of us and more of others. When our natural life is reduced, we will expand. It is the opposite of what the world teaches women—but it is true.

When we put the words male and female together in the ancient language of Genesis, we see that the last letter in the male is the *resh*, which signifies humility or poverty of spirit, bowing his head under the hand of God—and the first letter for female also is a mark of humility. If humility is at the center of the male-female relationship, he will humble himself to her and she will humble herself to him. One of the most wonderful marriages I have ever known was between my mentor Devi and her husband Larry. They had a game they played with each other: "Always be the first to submit." Their ministry spread around the world.

This is the opposite of the feminist movement, which taught women that if we lift ourselves higher than our Creator, diminish our seed, and dominate men, we will expand. Quite the opposite. Taught this way, womanhood has self-destructed. Even the dictionary can't define her.

Kof: Life-Giver

In *neqevah*, after the *nun* ﬤ comes the *kof* (k) ⊶ which is the continuation of time and the circle of life. Early pictographs look like a picture of the setting sun. As the rising and the setting sun symbolize the passage of time, so the *kof* signifies the continuation of the generations that will come through the female. In Jewish culture, this letter also represents holiness.

Just imagine if the Western world taught girls that their calling to bring life into the world is holy. Like the earth circling the sun, we are invited to participate in furthering the generations; our womb is a *gift*.

The feminine word for womb in Hebrew, *beten*, is spelled ﬤ⊗ﬤ: *bet (house)*, *tet (basket, surround, contain)*, *nun (seed, son, heir)*: the House that Protects the Seed Within Her.[20] The *thet* ⊗ symbolizes life or death—because if something isn't protected, it will die. It also symbolizes a snake and is shaped like a snake coiled in a basket. So here we are: The enemy destroys the life within women, devouring her seed and calling it "good." But we have an opportunity to tell girls the truth: Your womb is a miraculous basket of protection for the life growing within you.

What if we got back to basics? Back to truth? The fetus is a *child*. It is a son, a seed, an *heir* who will continue life in the family—and it is a gift and a calling to be a mother. *God's children are running through the fields of Heaven right now.*

Bet: Guardian of the Home

The third letter in female is the *bet* ﬤ, the house. In the story of Abraham and Sarah, we discover a little-known secret: Abraham was head of the family, but Sarah was "head" of the tent. Western culture often calls the man the "head of the house," but Judaism teaches otherwise. A close look at the Proverbs 31 woman shows the husband is present "at the city gates"—the world outside the home—and the woman is intentionally managing her household. The Valiant Woman is efficient in matters of real estate, interior design, home and financial management. She brings good and not harm to her husband as long as he lives, provides nourishing food and carefully chosen clothing for her family, and contributes to the family income. Outside the home, she speaks on behalf of justice and reaches out to a world in need of her help. This is the Woman Wisdom. We see a beautiful mystery hidden in the similarity between the Hebrew words for *daughter* and *house*. When the *yud* (representing the masculine) is placed in the middle of the word *daughter* בת, it becomes the word for *house* בית . With the addition of the man, she becomes the heart of the home, a wife and mother.

In the New Testament, women are called the doorkeepers of the home. It is the woman's responsibility—in unity with her husband, of course—to watch over what people, influences, and activities come into the home; she is its spiritual guardian and manager. When Titus 2:5 is translated, "the older women must teach the younger women to be 'busy at home,'" I scratch my head. There is not a woman on the planet who needs to be *taught to be busy*. Women are busy, period. The Greek word *oikourgos* actually means *watcher or guardian*, clarifying that the woman is to *be a watcher or guardian who is aware* of what goes on in the home. The home is where the female carries her greatest authority and responsibility. She can be a great influencer outside the home, but her most lasting and meaningful legacy is centered on life within the home.

This is what Devi and her daughter Trina teach in their book *Home Experience*.[21] While being a worldwide minister, Devi's primary focus was always her home and family. When she spoke to women around the world about how to change their marriages and families, she focused their energy on a singular calling: the home.

We find this secret as woman as the head of the home in biblical Hebrew, because the language reveals masculinity and femininity. In the case of Abraham and Sarah, when he made decisions for the family, he used the masculine word for home; but once he relocated their home, he called it "Sarah's house."[22]

In matters that affected the whole state of his household, Abraham had to exert his authority—perhaps even vis-à-vis

Sarah. Not so inside the home; his house (אָהֳלוֹ) was really Sarah's house (אהלה.) In external matters, the man is in charge; in internal matters, the woman is in charge. Ensuring the household's commitment to God's Will—there the man is the authority; but in all other matters of the home the woman has precedence. This is a guiding principle of Jewish family life, and its origin is in the tent of Abraham.[23]

Paul teaches this in 1 Timothy 5:14: "So I want younger widows to get married, have children, *manage their households*, and not give opponents of the faith any occasion for slander." This phrase is the Greek *oikodespotéō*[24] and it means:

1. to be master (or head) of a house
2. to rule a household, manage family affairs
3. to guide the house

Likewise, in Titus 2:5, we are told that we are to be "workers at home." The root of this word is the same, *oikourós*, which means *to guard with great care; to keep watch over the affairs of the house*. It goes far beyond housekeeping; we are the keeper of the gates of the home.[25]

In God's design, the female is the guardian and master of the home environment. It is her domain. Does this mean she disrespects the male's role as prophet, priest, provider, and protector? No. And does this mean he can't vacuum and do dishes? Not at all—we love a man who does that—and helps with cooking and grocery shopping or whatever he is good at. They are a team, and they do it together! But ultimately, she is *responsible* to keep the home running smoothly, and she guards the atmosphere—beginning with her own attitude.

Devi always said, "the home is where the human heart is formed."[26] Creating a home where love and peace reign is primarily within the power of the female.

She selects wool and flax
and works with willing hands.
She rises while it is still night
and provides food for her household . . .
She sees that her profits are good,
and her lamp never goes out at night . . .
She is not afraid for her household when it snows,
for all in her household are doubly clothed . . .
She watches over the activities of her household
and is never idle . . .
Give her the reward of her labor,
and let her works praise her at the city gates.[27]

As far as I can tell, the head of the man is Christ, the man is the head of the family, and the woman is the head of the home. It's a simple, straightforward order—and there is no need to mess it up. But some women did. Feminists taught women that they would "enlarge" and "find their true selves" by revolting against men. They promised that rebellion, fortune-building, and ladder-climbing outside the home would bear fruit. But the opposite is true. When a woman puts her husband, home, and children first—they flourish, and so does she. When the priorities of the home are strongly set in place like a setting for a precious stone, she is rewarded for her labor in public.

"This is what the LORD says: Put your house in order. . . ."[28] When a woman does this, everybody wins.

Hey: Life, Breath, Revelation

The fourth and last letter of female is the *hey* ♀, the letter of femininity that means *breath and revelation*. You will see this letter in female, woman, and mother. The shape of the modern version of *hey* (ה) is said to be a picture of the womb—the symbol of creation and birth.[29]

The female is appointed to be the setting for the family; she continues the cycle of life. As the source of life, she brings insight and sensitivity to her relationships. While the male takes hold of the weapon or plow, risking his life to provide, protect, and nourish the family, so the woman beholds the seed growing within her, and her womb is a protective shield. God appointed the female to be the life-giver and life-bearer; her role is to nurture life, create purposeful boundaries, and create order. Womanhood is about perception. She is the "eyes looking out the windows" that reveal what others may not see. This is a precious gift and an extraordinary privilege and responsibility.

What women are created to do, men are not. It is *harder than hard* to take the role of both man and woman in the family. Due to some unfortunate circumstance, perhaps a mother or father *has to be both*: the protector, provider, organizer of the home, and spiritual leader at the same time. Being a single father or mother is the most difficult job in the world—because it takes two to do the job.

Yet there is only one of the sexes who is designated to bring life—and that is the woman. This is why we will not give up our name. We are the life-givers in the community, church, and nation.

Chapter Seven

I Am a Guardian

A Cry for Help

"She's Always a Woman to Me."
—*Billy Joel*

In 2021, a thirty-five-year-old father of four traveled around the world asking strangers, women on the street, and men in Africa what a woman is. In his book and documentary *What Is a Woman?: One Man's Journey to Answer the Question of a Generation,*[1] Matt Walsh shares his conversations with gender theorists, most of whom can't answer the "What is a Woman?" question. They either don't want to talk about it, get offended, or are very confused by the concept. The only ones who seem to know what a woman is are the Masai tribal warriors in Africa who laugh and tell Walsh exactly what a female is. They had never heard of such a thing as a man claiming to be a woman and decided to stay in the bush.

As the Cowboy and I watched the film, I sat on the edge of my seat. "I know the answer!" I said like a schoolgirl with her arm raised high. "I can answer that question!!!"

People who believe in God should have no problem defining what a woman is. She is a *verb*. She is an *action*. The office of the *ezer*, God's first word about women, is to shield another. It is to rescue a person in their time of need.

The Creation of Woman

There is only one creation story that documents the creation of woman. There are some Near Eastern creation stories written around the time the Jewish people penned the Book of Genesis, but the biblical narrative has one distinct difference from all the others.[2] In every other creation story, woman is either nonexistent or she is so easily conquered that she is more like a subordinate weakling than a strength for mankind. As Kristi McLelland says, "It is only in the Bible that we find the story of the Creation of Woman in such a way that she is vital to the story, esteemed in the story, honored in the story, lifted in the story, and has an important role to play in the story."[3]

Since the Bible is the only literary source that documents an empowering creation of woman, it's worth looking at. Since gender theorists are so "open" to an ever-expanding definition of gender, perhaps this will inform them about who we are—and why we won't give up our name.

In the biblical narrative, there is *six times more detail* given to the creation of woman than the creation of man, equaling seven verses, the number that represents completion. Where did woman come from? She originated from man. And where did man come from? He came from the soil. We best understand the *action* of woman by looking at the *action* of man. In Genesis 2:7 we read: "Then the LORD God formed man of dust from the ground and breathed the breath of life into his nostrils, and the man became a living being."

Elohim shapes Adam from the clay of *adamah*, meaning *ground*. In the most intimate act of creation, God bends low to fill man's nostrils with breath, bringing his soul to life. The word for breath, *neshamah*, is feminine. Similar to *neqevah* (female) it begins with *nun* ׆ and ends with *hey* ⚥.[4] We find this word in Proverbs 20:27 (NASB): "The spirit of man (*neshamah*) is the lamp of the LORD, searching all the innermost parts of his being."

The Spirit brings life to man. When I picture God bending low to breathe life into Adam, I think about kissing my husband or looking into his eyes and telling him I believe in him. When I breathe life into him, he is filled with what he needs to accomplish his purpose. As Kristi McLelland says, women are "light-bringers and life-givers."[5] Who do we bring life to? Both *man* and *mankind*, the same word for Adam.

In 2018, Purdue University issued a new handout to university students called "Stereotypes and Biased Language."[6] This widely-used grammar resource for college students suggests that students don't use words with "man" in them—including "mankind"—in their writing because they claim it is sexist. Apparently, such words could "offend groups of people based on sexual orientation, ethnicity, political interest, or race."[7]

Does the following definition of mankind seem sexist to you? Let's explore it and find out if what they say is true. Let's give this "lie a good hearing." Remember that mankind is *not just form, but function*. It is an *action*.

- **Man: 'âdâm אָדָם** [8]
  ○ **Noun Masculine**
    • **Man, mankind, human being**
    • **Adam, first man**
  ○ **To be red, to look ruddy, like the soil**
  ○ **Pictograph (read right to left): ᴍᴍᴛᴅ𝄃 Water | Doorway | Strength**

Adam, *man*, and *mankind* are the same word that mean *earth* or *red*, like the soil or the blood flowing through our veins. The letters of *Adam* deepen our understanding. The *aleph* (a) 𝄃 means strong leader or "in God's image." The *dalet* (d) ᴛ means doorway or movement. The *mem* (m) ᴍᴍ means water or blood. Together ᴛᴍᴍ means blood or likeness. So *Adam* or *mankind* means: a strong leader made in the likeness of God, flowing with blood and water. He is the man of the red earth, created to serve the earth. What is his function? Is he just a "he"? Or does his name carry the weight of *action*?

The LORD took the man and placed him in the garden of Eden
to work it ['âbad] and watch over it [shâmar]. (Genesis 2:15)

To work (abad) is to serve or tend to, as in working for another and
making oneself a servant.[9] To watch (shamar) is to keep, guard, treasure, preserve, protect, beware, and serve as a guardian.[10] Abad is about
servanthood, and shamar is about stewardship. His calling is to serve
and steward—not only the earth, but his family, legacy, community, and
nation. Adam is the first watchman.

Eat Eat or Die Die

God places a vast array of fruit in front of the first man, telling him to
freely eat. But then He warns him not to eat from the tree of the knowledge of good and evil. In Hebrew, the root of the word eat is repeated to
emphasize enjoyment. Freely eat reads like this: eating you shall eat. But
this isn't about food. It's about self-regulation, self-control, and denying
his carnal instincts. The pictograph of eat means the strength to control
what is allowed.[11] Similarly, die reads like this: dying you shall die. "Eat"
is emphasized, and so is "die." As Skip Moen writes in Guardian Angel:

And the LORD God commanded the man, "You are free to
[eat eat] from any tree of the garden, but you must not eat from
the tree of the knowledge of good and evil, for on the day you
eat from it, you will certainly [die die]." It isn't eating until I am
stuffed. It's eating for enjoyment and delight. This is not an "all
you can eat" buffet. This is a gourmet meal. The act of consuming acknowledges our responsibility to control what God allows.
We can feast because He gives us permission, but we are still
responsible for how we consume.[12]

So would Adam stuff himself or would he show control? "Adam is not to be
driven by his desires," Moen writes, "He is to be guided by God's word. He is
to remember what God said, and act accordingly"—the meaning of male.[13]

Either he will obey God and be fully satisfied or disobey God and be fully empty. It's feast or famine. Either enjoy the abundance under God's protective umbrella and thrive, or distrust God's goodness, make his own decisions, and experience emptiness, shame, and misery. This is the test of mankind, the choice before us: *Eat eat* or *die die*. Eat and live and live of eating—or eat and die and die of overeating.

So, God makes a woman to help man with this.

> Then the LORD God said, "It is not good for the man to be alone.
> I will make a helper as his complement [ezer kenegdo]."[14]

She comes on the scene immediately after the prohibition and warning to control himself. These first two words about woman tell you exactly who woman is. As we will see, *ezer kenegdo* means *a vital helper who will help man in a way he cannot help himself*. But first we must understand the problem of aloneness.

Aloneness Devastates

The Hebrew word for alone is literally *bad*.[15] "To be alone" means *to be destroyed and separated from the whole, like limbs cut off from a human body or branches severed from a tree*. When man is alone, it means suffering and death for him. Separateness is a place of ruin; he will *not* flourish. Alone, he will covet; alone, he will lust; alone, he will follow the selfish inclinations of his heart; alone, he will forget his name and be driven by his appetite. *Eat eat . . . Die die*.[16]

Remember *Elohim* is an "us." As soon as He gives Adam a temptation to resist, He says there is something vital missing in the Garden of Eden. Something is suddenly *not good*, and that has to do with *aloneness*. Author Kristi McLelland asked a seventy-something-year-old rabbi why God created woman at this exact moment. He told her: "There was an enemy in the Garden; and it was always going to take man and woman together to contend against the enemy and for the way of the

Lord. Woman was made to *contend*." As Kristi says, "He's not talking
about our form; he is talking about our function."[17]

Woman is the answer to the very first problem faced by man—the
problem of aloneness. She fills his need by helping him walk in obedience to God and not in the lust of the flesh. Not only will man need
companionship and love to keep him alive, but he will also need someone to hold him accountable. In this moment, God *commands* him to
deny himself. He must understand he is a servant and steward who
will lay down his selfish desires for the life of another. The temptation
to *eat, eat* will be strong. He will not be able to withstand alone.

The word for "evil" in the tree God warns him about is *ra*, meaning *misery, sorrow, affliction, distress,* and *calamity*.[18] Knowing this,
you would think he wouldn't go near that tree. But how many of us
"take and eat" the thing we know we shouldn't? Whether it be alcohol,
drugs, overconsumption of social media, pornography, sex outside of
marriage, gluttony, greed, betrayal, jealousy, selfishness, violence—we
know these things aren't good for us. When driven by lust or loneliness,
we are prone to *eat, eat, die, die*. Only then do we cry out to be saved
and rescued from ourselves; we cry for help.

Where should an addict trying to kick his addiction *not be*? Alone.
This is the key to Alcoholics Anonymous: No one resists alone. It takes
community and comradery. As Scripture says, "Two are better than one
because they have a good reward for their efforts. For if either falls, his
companion can lift him up; but pity the one who falls without another
to lift him up."[19] Why did so many people lose their minds during the
COVID-19 lockdowns? Separateness brought ruin. People lost their
bearings and became distressed. Aloneness created division in the mind,
destruction in relationships, and death.

Moen writes:

Adam doesn't need an assistant or co-laborer. The assignment to
[rule and reign], be fruitful, multiply and take stewardship over
the earth is given to *both* male and female. They equally receive
God's prime directive. But the command prohibiting eating of

the tree of the knowledge of good and evil is given to Adam alone. It is not Adam's productive energy that needs assistance. It is his faithfulness to God's instruction. He needs a *protector, encourager and spiritual director.* He needs someone assigned to keep him on the straight and narrow. He needs one who comes alongside for the express purpose of guiding his obedience.[20]

The authority to govern the earth and everything in it is given equally to both sexes. But right here, Adam needs someone to help him. Adam needs a woman. Adam needs a helper, shield, and guide. As Tiphani Montgomery says:

The wife is a little more important than you think. He sent a wife to you as a front line. The wife is supposed to be an intercessor, a battle ax—that nothing gets past the wife cause I'm the rib, baby, I cover the heart. You can't get past this piece of bone. I might look I'm bone, baby but I pack some weight! Don't play with it, cause looks are deceiving.[21]

Just as Man is the priest and prophet of the earth, so Eve (*Havvah* in Hebrew, meaning "life") is the priest and prophet of Mankind. Moen explains:

Eve (Havvah) has a role to play, but it is not the role of domestic companion, production assistant, or Vice President for Public Works. Unless we recognize this aspect of the description about the Tree, we will not acknowledge that her role is the role of priest and spiritual guide for Adam! She is designed to make sure Adam stays faithful to God. She is the one who stands between God's command and Adam's obedience, watching over him so that he will not go astray. Adam guards the Garden. Eve guards Adam. The help she brings is the help of reminding, rescuing, and demonstrating trust. In this role, she parallels God's ultimate relationship with Israel.[22]

When God is called *Ezer*, the name given for woman, he is rescuing, aiding, and abetting Israel as a shield from its enemies. Most Bibles translate *ezer kenegdo* as "helper suitable, helpmeet, helper who is just right for him." *Ezer* does mean help. But these translations do not fully tell us the extent to which we are designed to help mankind. Perhaps male interpreters over time have not painted a fully loaded portrait of woman's worth. So we are going to look closely at the original language to grasp the meaning of the incredible gift God is giving man in this moment.

The Power of *Ezer Kenegdo*

The words *ezer kenegdo* are repeated twice: once when the Lord acknowledges the need for woman, and second when He shows Adam what he truly needs. After naming all the animals, Adam can see there is none like him. The animals will never satisfy him. He needs a woman, an *ezer*.

Ezer is a *masculine* word meaning to help or rescue someone with great strength. It is derived from a *verb* which means to *surround, defend, and protect*. It is a military term that describes God's relationship to the people of Israel.

- **HELPER: 'êzer עֵזֶר** [23]
  - ○ **Noun Masculine**
    - **Concentrating help and assistance**
    - **Help in a manner that reduces another's responsibilities**
    - **Strength**
  - ○ **Often used in a military sense, indicating strength and power**
    - **Root: 'âzar**
      - □ **To surround, protect, defend, or aide**
      - □ **To rescue or save**
      - □ **To ask forgiveness**
    - **Noun form: azara**
      - □ **Enclosure**
      - □ **Courtyard surrounding a building that serves needs**

- • Other related words: limit and hold together; restrain; collect; gird; hold back; progress; enclose; enrich
  - ○ Pictograph (read right to left): ℜ☈⌾ Head of Man | Weapon | See

The biblical name Ezra means "Helper." That's what a woman is. *Ezer* is a combination of the root *azar*, meaning *to rescue or save*, and the first two letters of her name, which mean *strong*.

We deepen our understanding by looking at the letters. She is the eye, or *ayin* (o) ⌾, the one who watches, shades, knows, and understands the needs of man and mankind. She is his first line of defense, the *zayin* (z) or weapon ☈ who nourishes, protects, and redirects him. The last letter is the *resh* (r) ℜ, the head or chief of the tribe. She is a frontline defense, a weapon who will contend on behalf of mankind.

Women are *ezers* in all of their relationships. While the story of the Garden is often framed as an emblem of marriage, every woman is an *ezer kenegdo*. First, she is female. Second, she is woman. Third, she is wife and mother. Before she is anything else, woman is designed to protect and defend mankind. *Ezer* is the definition of "all women, everywhere."[24] Variations of this word occur over two hundred times in Scripture, most often referring to God as a "help" in times of trouble. This exact word appears twenty-one times; nineteen of those refer to God while the other two refer to woman.

In every instance, *ezer* acts as a *guardian protector, strengthener, and rescuer.* She displays masculine and feminine characteristics—but this does not make her male. This makes her someone who will war on your behalf. The root of *ezer* is *to surround as a protector—to encircle.* This is the essence of the female, who protects the womb and protects her husband and family, especially through prayer. She is designed to "circle," to surround man with *military-like strength and power.*

In almost every instance where God is called *Ezer*, He is rescuing Israel from the onslaught of their enemies. Would we call God a "suitable helper?" Or would we call Him a strengthener and rescuer? When we see God as *Ezer*, He is a warrior who hears our cries for help and swiftly answers—the same definition is the meaning for the word *woman*.

What do women do with babies? Friends? Husbands? Families? We encircle them. We protect them. We answer their cries for help and come to their side to assist them in a way they cannot do for themselves. Godly women contend for man, for marriage, for life, for family.

From volunteering in nurseries to feeding the hungry to helping our college kids set up their new homes, you will find women doing the activity of the *ezer* everywhere in the earth. Women are dressing themselves in strength, rising in difficult times, feeding their families, earning a living, and counting dollars and cents. Women in the U.S. Senate are contending for our nation right now. PTA moms are showing up, not only to help, but to contend when necessary. Grandmothers are helping their granddaughters as you read this. They are teaching, training, preparing young women for life, for family, for community. Young women are helping their little brothers, their best friends. They are teachers, nurses, doctors, lawyers, politicians. They serve in our military, and they welcome men home with kisses and hugs. They fight for family, lead prayer teams and Bible studies, and help one another. *Ezer* is what we do; it is what we are made for; it is who we are.

Yet history tells another story—that woman was created to serve man in a subordinate role. Yet we must ask this: Is God a secondary, subservient figure in the life of Israel? Or is He a warrior with a strong hand, a powerful rebuke, and a compassionate heart, fully able to deliver them from the onslaught of their enemies?

To truly know who woman is, we must first understand who God is. This is precisely the problem in our society right now. Too many have turned away from God as their *Ezer*. Too many have rejected His help. Because they don't know who He is, *they don't know who they are.* They can't answer the "What is a Woman?" question—because they don't know God made woman in His image—and He is our *rescuer when we cannot help ourselves.*

Our Brother's Keeper

Woman is the one we cry for, call aloud for—the one we desperately need. In oneness—not in separateness—man and woman have the strength to rescue a nation in distress. A school in distress. A marriage in crisis. A son and a daughter crying for help. When we see God as *Ezer*, we understand how woman relates to those she is created to help:

> [He] rides across the heavens to **help** [ezer] you.
> and on the clouds in his majesty.
> The eternal God is your **refuge**,
> and underneath are the everlasting arms. . . .
> He is your **shield** and **helper** [ezer]
> and **your glorious sword.**
> Your enemies will cower before you,
> and you will **tread on their heights.**[25]

This is the companion man needs in the Garden—a warrior who will stomp out the enemy out of love and devotion to him. Here we see the *action* of woman: She is a *help, support, and protector—and she holds a sword and a shield.* When God's people Israel are afflicted and needy and surrounded by enemies, they cry for help as a child cries for his mother:

> Our soul waits for the LORD; He is our **help** [ezer] and our shield.[26]
> But I am afflicted and needy; Hasten to me, O God! You are my
> **help** [ezer] and my deliverer; O LORD, do not delay.[27]

When the great men of WWI and WWII fought the battles of their lives, what letters did they read by flashlight in the dark of the night? What pictures did they tuck in their chests? Who did they long to return to? Who did they want to hold in their arms? Woman.

The most remembered psalm that speaks of God as our Help is Psalm 121. Here is a combination of two translations to see more deeply into our identity as woman:

THE LORD OUR PROTECTOR

I will lift my eyes toward the mountains
Where will my **help [ezer]** come from?
My **help [ezer]** comes from the LORD,
the Maker of heaven and earth.

He will not allow your foot to slip;
your Keeper / Protector will not slumber.
Indeed, **the Protector of Israel**
does not slumber or sleep.

The Lord is your **Keeper / Protector**
the Lord is your **shelter right by your side** . . .
The Lord will **protect** you from all evil;
he will **keep** your soul.
The Lord will **guard** your going out and your coming in
From this time forth and forever.[28]

The word "Keeper / Protector" of Israel is *shâmar*. This is the same
word God uses when He tells Adam to "keep" the Garden. It means
watchman—one who saves life. The *actions* of woman are to *keep,
watch, guard, shelter, save*.

Excavating the roots of *azar* helps even more. The word *azara* is
derived from the same verb, meaning *enclosure*. It indicates *social
and moral support, deliverance, salvation, protection, and assistance.*[29]
She is like a "courtyard surrounding a building that serves its needs."[30]
Skip Moen writes:

> To be the *ezer*, she is to play the same role with her man as God
> plays with his people. That includes deliverance from oppressors,
> rescue from danger, assistance, support and reinforcement, shield-
> ing from death, blessing within a covenant relationship, provision

in difficult times, trustworthiness, hope and forgiveness. No wonder she is the capstone of creation.[31]

By calling woman an *ezer* to Adam, God is giving us our charge: Keep
watch over *man* and *mankind*. Guard them. Save them. Serve them.
Deliver them. Help them! Usually, men are culturally bound as the
guardian-protectors of the family. They are our weapons. But we are
their spiritual weapons. We have their backs. When there is an enemy
to contend with, man needs woman by his side.

This is what women already know. We may not be aware this is the
original definition of woman, but we know we are the ones who guard
the soul of the family, protect our husbands, and give help to the children and community. We don't have to be told that we protect the spirit
of the house, or that we shield man with our prayers. This is who we
are. This is what we do naturally.

A Supporting and Opposing Force to Mankind

Devi Titus used to say that if man was made in the image of God,
woman was made in the character of God.[32] When someone calls a
woman for help, she will rush to their side despite their unworthi-
ness. This is how women are wired. Likewise, God rescues us when
we least deserve it, but He doesn't just come by our side. He meets us
face-to-face and shows us mercy and truth at the same time. When we
are naked before Him, He *sees us*. He *knows* us. He *deeply* respects
us. The word for this is *yâda'*—the same word God uses for sexual
union with Adam and his wife Eve.[33] It means he understands us.
He cares. He knows what we need—and sometimes what we need is
hard to hear.

We see this most powerfully in the root of woman's name, *azar*,
which can also mean "to ask forgiveness."[34] Inside our name is the
strength to forgive, our most nourishing manna. The most influential
women in my life have modeled both loyalty and forgiveness. A woman
who does not forgive is a poison to herself and others. The women

I respect most have helped me in my time of need, but also sat face-to-face with me in the crucibles of my life and told me the truth.

This is the meaning of the second part of woman's name: *kenegdo*.

Translators say *kenegdo* is difficult to interpret, but it's really not. That sounds like a coverup to me. It occurs twice in Scripture, only for woman. The root, *neged*, means *one who is in front of; before your face; opposite, parallel or corresponding to*. While an "ezer" is side-by-side with you, a "kenegdo" is face-to-face.[35]

Ezer is man's first line of defense. *Kenegdo* is the opposing force for his energies. Imagine man as a river, and woman as the riverbanks. She channels his arrow-like force.

- **KENEGDO**
  - Prepositional phrase
  - Neged[36] נֶגֶד
    - In front of oneself; conspicuous; straight forward; in sight of; before your face, in your view or purpose
    - Corresponding to; parallel to; similar to
    - Opposing; opposite to
  - Root Verb: nāḡaḏ[37] נָגַד
    - To give an account to another
    - To be conspicuous, tell, make known
    - Declare, show, utter, expound, report, announce, show, inform
    - To publish, declare, proclaim
    - Messenger
  - Pictograph: ⊐ᴸˠ = Tell
  - Related Word with the addition of the *yud*: ⊐ˠᴸˠ = Noble, One who tells orders; ruler, prince, leader (the one in front).

Looking at the real definition of the root verb in *kenegdo*, we see the function of woman. She is to be face-to-face with man, oppose him if he goes the way he should not, and tell him what she sees. *Kenegdo* is a compound of two prepositions, *ki* and *neged*. *Neged* means *before, in*

front of, corresponding to, against, opposing, and opposite. Ki means
like or as. When we add a suffix meaning "him," the translation of ezer
kenegdo is: "I will make a vital helper similar / opposite / equal to him."
She is a *helper or rescuer that is face-to-face with him, and who opposes
or is against him at the same time.* The Torah Study for Reform Jews
states, "In Genesis 2:18, God calls woman an *ezer kenegdo,* a 'helper
against him.'"[38] This sounds like a contradiction. How can a force *for*
him also be *against* him?

Rabbi Shlomo Riskin explains:

> The literal translation is help-opposite. Other translations are
> "help meet" or "a help to match him" or "compatible helper";
> terms which do not fully reflect the inner tension of the concept.
> [The Hebrew commentator] Rashi, in explaining the phrase,
> writes, "If the man is worthy, then his wife will be an 'ezer' (a
> helper), and if he's unworthy, she'll be a 'kenegdo', (against him,
> an opposite force)."[39]

Isn't this how God is with us? As the brilliant Kisha Gallagher puts it,
"When we are walking uprightly, He is our help, but when we stray, is
He not against us?"[40] Even when He opposes what we are doing and
how we are living, isn't He still *for us*?

Woman will oppose man if he is headed in the wrong direction and
use her voice to do it. At times, she will help him best by speaking the
truth he may not want to hear. Devi often did this for me. With gentle
words, she could break my bones with the truth. One time she told me
I had a hard time submitting to my husband because I had "an elevated
view of my own wisdom." *Ouch.* One night in a parking lot, she held
my shoulders and looked at me with eyes as calm as fresh water. "Only
speak words that build him up," she commanded, putting her finger
over her lips. If only I had taken that to heart earlier, we could have
avoided a lot of pain. A *kenegdo* tells us the truth that we desperately
need to hear. Like the Holy Spirit, she warns us of what is coming,
shields us from danger, and confronts us when we need confronting.

Skip Moen describes it like this:

> She is both advocate and chastiser. She is *perfectly suited* to act
> as the intimate guide for a man to stay connected to the Lord.
> And she is *perfectly opposed* when her man is tempted to have
> his own way. She is his ultimate weapon against unrighteous-
> ness, even when that unrighteousness is found within him. . . .
>
> She is his intercessor. She is to guard his relationship with
> the Creator, support him when he embraces God's direction and
> oppose him when he does not. She is the helper-opposite in the
> only arena where he needs additional attention. Not work, not
> world-changing assignments, not dominion, not stewarding—
> but spiritual awareness and obedience.[41]

The truth is, a woman does all of these things for the man she loves.

A Correct Translation

We can easily translate *ezer kenegdo* as "I will make a power [or
strength] corresponding to, parallel to, face-to-face with, and in opposition to the man."[42] The best translation I've seen is: "I will make a
vital helper similar to him,"[43] which comes from the Septuagint, the
earliest extant Greek translation of the Old Testament from the original Hebrew. The question remains why it was ever changed. Yet it still
does *not* include the part of her that *opposes* him when he needs it—a
distinction male translators have perhaps thwarted out of fear, and
unnecessarily so. It also misses the point that she is "the one in front,"
his protective shield between him and the enemy.

Most men will tell you their wives keep them in check—and that is a
good thing! Women in the Church should do the same. When men fear
women's loving yet open challenges to their behavior in order to protect themselves, they lose the value of her perceptions that will prove
to be life-giving. In the roots of her name, we find that *neged* comes
from *negad*, which means "to make known," similar to the *hey* ✝ in her

name. This word means *to tell, announce, show, utter, inform, publish, proclaim, and declare*. It literally means "Messenger."

The risen Christ first revealed Himself to women.[44] He charged them as the first messengers to make the Gospel known. Likewise, He first revealed his identity as the Messiah to a woman, who went and told everyone she had met the Lord.[45] The wisdom of Proverbs charges us to speak up for those who cannot speak for themselves. The Wise Woman "speaks with wisdom, and faithful instruction is on her tongue."[46] Women were created to speak. It is the hidden manna of our name. Churches who silence women are limping along because their definition of woman does not come from the *rule of first mention*. This must be corrected.

Since our role is to help mankind, we cannot do this without opposing sin. The Church is the only place in our society where women most often do not have equal say—even though our first charge is to "rule and reign" alongside men. The *ezer kenegdos* in the Western Church should be allowed to call out sin, redirect men, share their insights, and speak their mind without fearing oppressive men who insist "submitting" is only the woman's role. By claiming that blind submission is woman's primary directive, they completely miss who we are created to be. In the Garden, God Himself tells the man to leave his father and mother for her. He gives up his life first, *on her behalf*.[47] Jesus was the first male who modeled the submission of the Father *first*.

When a man submits to God, it is easy for a woman to submit to him; she doesn't even have to try. She naturally follows this lead. But when he is in rebellion, she doesn't have to submit. Her first allegiance is to God's righteousness. Since "vital helper in front | opposite | equal | to him" is the most obvious translation, it is time woman's name is defined correctly. In a world that doesn't know who we are anymore, we can right the tide.

The world is in desperate need for *ezer kenegdos* right now. It is time for translators to live up to their name and "remember." We must revisit the ancient language of Genesis and get this right. It is time to make room for woman to rise to the meaning of her name. We can pass this on to future generations, who will need her vital breath:

1. Woman is a vital, strong helper to man / mankind
2. She is man's first line of defense against the enemy
3. She will use her voice to oppose sin and redirect those who are going the wrong way

A woman will *do* what we are naturally inclined to do: Help when you need help; and tell you the truth when you are not living up to your name, your *shem*, which is your character and reputation.

We can now return to the verse: "How long will you go here and there, O faithless daughter? For the LORD has created a new thing in the earth: A woman [female] shall encompass [turn back and shelter] a man."[48] This is a military action in which woman marches around an army of men to turn them around and protect them from the enemy. We turn men around best with wisdom and love. We win them through forgiveness. We woo them to protect, provide, and nurture the life within us.

It will take Wise Women to turn the feminist movement around. Right now, this world needs *ezer kenedgos* who will answer humanity's cry for help, oppose a movement that is going the wrong way—and turn it around in the right direction. Women have the power to course-correct a nation in distress. We must turn mankind back towards their purpose, to help them remember.

Out of God's incredible love for man, He creates woman who is fully his equal and fully his match. In this way, mankind will not have to contend with the enemy alone; together they will rule. Unless, they get divided, which they do.

Chapter Eight

I Am a Wife

More Precious Than Rubies

He is bone of my bone, flesh of my flesh—
I get behind him till the day of his death.
I am gentle grace—the softness at his side.
I will lift my face—and serve him like a bride.
—*The "I Am a Wife" poem[1], written for my husband*

The transgender movement talks about men "passing" as women, saying that if they dress like a woman, they are one. Is this possible? Only if womanhood is surface-based; yet even then, womanhood is not an outfit. Womanhood is a verb; it is a *being*; it is a *doing*; it is not a *looking*—and although *ezer* is a masculine word, it is embodied by the female. Men need women; they don't need to *be* women.

You cannot create an *ezer* or a *neqevah* with a scalpel. Our purpose as women is woven into our DNA. The meaning of our name is in what we are made *to do*—not in how we *appear on the outside*. The *ezer* is appointed to remind man of his identity, assist him in his calling, and be his spiritual guard who squashes his enemies under her feet. As *neqevah*, she maintains healthy boundaries for the gift of their sexuality. It is not only the *form* of the female that makes us woman; it is our *function as a life-giver and guardian* that make us who we are.

No One Dominates

When men hear about women's empowerment, naturally they often fear they are being told to take a back seat. But in God's design, this is not the case. As Skip Moen writes:

> When we discover that the Bible empowers women, men fear dominance. They react to this empowerment by resisting change. In our society, men have been so beaten up over their "failures" as husbands and fathers that they are not likely to warm to the possibility that the Bible portrays women as spiritual guides. . . .
>
> But the *full* picture of the biblical revelation isn't a threat to men or women. Yes, women are empowered. They are uniquely, divinely designed to play a significant role in protection, direction, and correction. But dominance is not part of the picture. In the biblical model, *no one dominates!* Each operates *interdependently*. One without the other diminishes the image of God in the world.[2]

From His Side

Let's look deeper at the creation of woman to uncover secrets hidden in her name.

> So the Lord God caused a deep sleep to fall upon the man, and he slept;
> then He took one of his ribs (*tsêlâ'*) and closed up the flesh
> at that place. The Lord God fashioned into a woman (*'ishshâh*) the
> rib which He had taken from the man (*'îysh*),
> and brought her to the man. The man said,
>
> "This is now bone of my bones,
> And flesh of my flesh;
> She shall be called Woman (*'ishshâh*),
> Because she was taken out of Man (*'îysh*)."[3]

Traditionally, the word *tsela* has been translated as "rib," but Hebrew scholars are well aware it means *side*. *Tsela* means *side*.[4] The same word is used to reference the *side* of the Ark of the Covenant, the *side* of the temple, and the *side* of the altar. Had she just come from a single bone, he would not have called her "bone of my bones and flesh of my flesh."

This misunderstanding that woman came from a single rib may have contributed to the historical diminishing of her worth. It is much more meaningful to understand that man gave half of himself for woman than it is to imagine her coming from a single rib, which he could live without. She was not built from a *piece* of Adam. She was built from *half of Adam*. She was built of the exact same substance, fashioned according to plan.[5]

The *entire* rib cage would have been included in his side. As the side of man or mankind, she will *stabilize* him. *Stand beside* him. *Balance* him. The ribs protect the heart, lungs, and essential organs of the body. Likewise, woman protects the heart and soul of mankind. She guards the interior, delicate parts of man that may seem insignificant to some, but that are essential to his flourishing.

This wasn't taught to men throughout history. They were taught she was under his feet; he was the head that could boss her around, or they could use her like a piece of flesh and discard her. Historically, both men and women have been taught that woman was a subservient creature, suggesting that like the animals, Adam had authority over her; she was beneath him. But this is found nowhere in the creation of woman. She arrives on the scene as a similar, opposite counterpart. She is not part of the animal kingdom; she is entirely equal to him.

Unfortunately, slews of men since antiquity—church-going men included—have modeled that they can degrade and silence women, and women should still show allegiance to them. Not so. Men destabilize themselves when they abuse women. They break their own ribs, and their hearts get wounded too. Plus, their prayers hit the ceiling.

Both in Malachi and 1 Peter, we see that when a man deals treacherously with his wife, is unfaithful to her, and does not value her as a priceless gift from God, his prayers, offerings, and blessings are *cut off*.[6] Why would this be? Because she is the Apple of God's Eye—and when you hurt her, you poke the pupil of *Elohim* and *Av*, her Creator and Father.

Eve was created from the emotional side of Adam, the tenderest place of his heart. Yet, she is strong like bone. Bone is strong on the outside but soft on the inside. Deep within marrow, the lifeblood of mankind flows. In the soft, rich center of the bone are stem cells that are so powerful they can heal the sick. Likewise, woman is the lifeblood of mankind and a conduit of its healing.

We bring mankind balance, structure, protection, and life. While man is to "tend and keep" the Garden, woman is to "tend and keep" man. Made from the earth, man is the guardian-steward of the earth. Made from man, woman is the guardian-steward of man, created to stabilize him as she serves as his defense and shield.

The Name of Woman and Wife

When God splits Adam into two, we first see the word *woman*: *'ishshâh* (אִשָּׁה), which is the same word for *wife*. This is no coincidence, I assure you. The letters of her name have a secret meaning. Her name means *Breath of Fire*.

Living up to the meaning of our name, a woman brings vitality or destruction to every environment she is in. Like the Holy Spirit, she sets the tone of the atmosphere, revealing what is unseen. Since God calls woman "Helper," the same title Jesus gives for the Holy Spirit, my mentor Devi used to always tell me, "You are to the atmosphere what the Holy Spirit is to you."

The woman is the life-breath of the family. She is the one who helps everybody flourish. She doesn't put her needs first; she honors her husband by coming underneath him and lifting him up, like the strong legs of the table. She uses her voice to bless and not to curse. Yet if she is unfaithful to protect her man, she will be the voice that tears everything down. A woman has the power to build or destroy with her words and her attitude.

- **WOMAN: 'ishshâh אִשָּׁה** [7]
  - ○ **Noun Feminine**
  - ○ **Woman, Wife, Female**
    - • **Opposite of man**
    - • **Wife (woman married to a man)**
  - ○ **To Create Material**
    - • **Being; existing**
    - • **Fire-shaped material**
    - • **Supporting pillar**
  - ○ **Related words: nourish; create; withstand**
  - ○ **Pictograph (right to left)**
    - • **אשׁה Breath | Devour | Strength**
    - • **שׁא = Fire**

Ishshah means female, woman, and wife, the opposite of man—simple and clear. Within the ancient meaning of her name, she is a creator, nourisher, and supporting pillar.

The spelling of woman is *aleph, shin, hey* אשׁה. Like the man, she is a strong leader א who teaches with the authority God provides. While man is the "head" held accountable for the state of affairs, *both* men and women are called to leadership; *both* are designed to lead with *strength and gentleness*, as God leads us. In fact, the first letter of *mother* and *father* is also the *aleph*; they are both given the mandate to shepherd the flock.

In the center of woman's name is the *shin* שׁ, a picture of two front teeth that symbolize devouring or consuming. This letter is symbolic for the power of her words. As Proverbs remind us, a gentle word can break a bone and a word aptly spoken is like apples of gold in settings of silver.[8] The *shin* or teeth that reside in the middle of woman's name are guarded on either side by the symbols that represent God 𐤉 and the Holy Spirit 𐤔. A woman's greatest temptation is to be driven by her emotions. When she is out of control, she may use her strong, sharp words to devour the life entrusted to her.

This was my biggest test—and the one I failed most often—in the midst of my crucible. Out of anger, victimhood, or contention, I often insisted I was right—and even if I was, it didn't matter. My biggest strength became my greatest weakness. I used my "way with words" to jolt words through the air I later regretted. Through pain and testing, I had to learn to submit my emotions to the Holy Spirit and clamp down on the pearl guards in front of my tongue.

As women, we must be *very careful* with our words. We can use our words to breathe hope into seemingly hopeless circumstances or deliver a sucker punch to the gut. We must guard our tongues between the strength God provides and the *hey* 𐤔 on the end of our name, the symbol of life and revelation. The letters of woman's name mean *Breath of Fire*, reminding us that our words have the power to *create or destroy*.

Women, Watch Your Mouth

Just as God's breath either grants life or removes it, so a woman's words have similar power in the life of her husband.[9] As Proverbs 12:4 says, "A capable wife is her husband's crown, but a wife who causes shame is like rottenness in his bones."[10] A wife is like the marrow, the lifeblood. If she brings her husband shame and dishonor, she will be a cancer to him and literally rot his bones. He will not be able function in his purpose; he may even forget who he is.

If a woman is contentious or argumentative, a man would rather live on the corner of a rooftop, with no shelter, no warmth, and no food, than live with her. As the Proverbs say, "Better to live on the corner of a roof than to share a house with a nagging wife."[11] If she is quarrelsome or finds fault in everything he does, her husband will not be able to stand to live with her. But if she holds him up like the setting of a precious stone, making her home a place of love and peace, he will love her for it.

In a marriage, a man's greatest desire from his wife is praise. When she uses her words to build, strengthen, and encourage him, he remembers why he fell in love with her in the first place. Because she believes in him, he is motivated and finds success in his work. Kisha Gallagher writes:

> The strength of a wife or woman is in how she expresses the praises of both YHVH and her man. With words women reveal the will and Word of God to their husband and children. Words can encourage, inspire greatness, and motivate others. Words can bind up wounds and brokenness. Words can uncover the heart of a matter or situation. . . . There's a reason women are known for "talking."[12]

Through words, women come to understand ourselves and our relationships better. Most importantly, we breathe life into one another's families. I am picky about this. I refuse to surround myself with complaining, nagging women. My best friends speak life into my marriage and family, as Devi did. Because of her influence, I have completely changed how I talk to my husband, and because of that, the Cowboy and I are closer than ever.

Remember: "There is one who speaks rashly, like a piercing sword; but the tongue of the wise brings healing."[13] We are face-to-face with man to breathe life with our words; this is the *action of womanhood*—and the sooner we learn this, the better.

Men, Watch Your Hands

Woman is *ishshah* (אִשָּׁה), Breath of Fire. Man is *ish* (אִישׁ), Hand of Fire. When a man's hands are used for productive labor and building rather than destroying, he lives up to the meaning of his name.

- **MAN: 'îysh אִישׁ** [14]
  - ○ Noun Masculine
  - ○ Man, Male (in contrast to woman, female)
  - ○ Husband
  - ○ Human being, person (in contrast to God)
  - ○ Withstand, Exist
    - Man with Proven Character
    - Servant, champion, great man
    - Good, great, mighty
    - Steward
    - Worthy
    - Warrior
  - Pictograph (right to left):
    - ᄂᄂᄀᄼ: Devour | Hand | Strength
    - ᄂᄂᄼ: Fire

Ish means man, male, or husband. Once again, his name has character in it: *servant, champion, good, great, mighty, worthy, warrior.* These are the words of identity we speak into sons, and when we do, we call men higher.

The spelling of man is *aleph, yud, shin,* ᄂᄂᄀᄼ the hand in the center of the flame. Together, the *aleph* and *shin* ᄂᄂᄼ spell *fire, 'êsh.*[15] Just like woman's breath, man's fire can provide peace and protection, or destruction and war.

The first son of Adam couldn't control his fire; he murdered his brother out of jealousy and fear. Yet God had sternly warned Cain that if he could not *control the fire within him,* it would be his ruin—and it was. When driven by desire, a man's hands can *take and eat,* the same pattern that caused the fall and the flood. It was the sinful nature of man, taking and eating from the daughters of God, that angered God to the point of flooding the earth and starting over. The same sin led to the burning of Sodom.

When man uses his clenched fist to suppress rather than uphold woman, he suffers and dies, and the Lord's anger burns against him.

Too many women's fathers, grandfathers, brothers, uncles, and husbands burned without control; they took and ate without permission, and women bear those scars. The first command was for man to *eat with the strength to control what is allowed*. When men use their hands to punish and terrorize, they miss out on the opportunity to nurture the soil of the family. They are to be the palm that receives ש, the head that bows low א (*zakar*), and the warrior and steward (*ish*) ר. Men are the gardeners of the family, and their hands are very powerful.

Man's hands are designed to nurture his family and then release them, not control them. Ideally, man's hands promote security and not fear. Just as God used His two hands to create Adam, so man's hands till the garden of the family. It is not true that women are the only nurturers. Men nurture also. When a man understands this, He reflects the original male, Christ.

The fire inside of man must be channeled, and God uses woman to channel it. If he has a woman to work for, he will channel his energies into creating a life for her. Kisha Gallagher explains that a man's (or husband's) greatest strength is found in what he does with his hands:

> The "hand on fire" or the man has great potential. Those fiery fists can accomplish mighty things. If they are fueled by the cool heavenly flames, his hands will become calloused and strong by putting food on the table, building the house, leading and blessing his family, and sometimes even wielding a rod that gently corrects the children. All feel safe, secure, and loved by the large worn hands that create and protect a home that is warmed by his fire.
>
> But as you've already surmised, this great strength is also a man's or husband's biggest test. Hands that strike and abuse, hands that withdraw when they should caress, hands that fail to work, hands that deal under the table, hands that touch what is forbidden . . . all these things are a misuse of a man's fire, but are no less powerful. No one is safe, secure, or loved

by a man that gives his fire to these destructions. It won't take long before his house turns to ashes and all of his labors are consumed.

The good news is that we always have a choice to change fuel sources. A man that finds himself wearing sack cloth and sitting in ashes can rebuild. And if he stays the course, those very ashes will make the ground doubly fruitful. There is always hope. YHVH desires reconciliation. And He loves even the fallen.[16]

Man, Woman, Fire

The letters that spell fire are central to the names man and woman, yet equally important are the differing letters in our names. These letters are critical in understanding the distinctiveness in our gender. Man is Fiery Hands ⊱ and woman is Fiery Breath ⚇. We usually don't think of people as fire, but when we do, we realize the power they have. In Scripture, we often find God guiding His people by a pillar of fire, speaking in a burning bush, or sending fire from heaven. On Mount Sinai, His people saw him as a "devouring fire."[17]

When we remove the *yud* ⊱ (the letter of masculinity) and the *hey* ⚇ (the letter of femininity) from the names man and woman—and put them together, they spell YaH, ⚇⊱ the shortened name for God.

But once YaH is removed from their names, all that is left is fire, *esh* ⊔⅃⅃. Without YaH, man and woman are only beings of fire. So the scribes say that without God at the center of their relationship, man and woman will consume and destroy one other. Once we remove God from the equation, we are a fire burning out of control. We are *fire-fire*.

Without God, man will beat the ground, break the rib, bruise his own side, and destabilize himself. His life becomes lopsided and though he may try, he cannot live up to his name, *champion, mighty, steward*. When his fire is out of control, man can snuff the life inside of woman. As violent men do, he may take from her and wound her. But if he treasures the one he loves as precious, his hands become her safe place.

If he loves her well, he will create an environment where she can build, create, grow—and become the woman she is meant to be.

In our culture, we have removed God from the center of the relationship between man and woman. By opposing one another, "the patriarchy" and "the feminists" annihilate the beauty of sex and gender. As masculinity and femininity have been demeaned, we must ask ourselves, "What could unity behold?" As Gallagher states, "The man and woman each have a piece of the name and authority of God, but only when they come together as one flesh, can we see the Creator's name. . . . The question is, what will you do with your fire?"[18]

Fire can transform dead soil into a fertile environment. Fire can bring warmth and heat, comfort and light. Fire can cleanse new land for sprouts to grow, or fire can annihilate an entire forest. Gallagher writes, "If we are fueled by the motives and desires of the flesh, we will burn and consume ourselves and our relationships with a destructive heart. Even if we manage to put the flames out, irrevocable damage and scarring is left in our wake. We must be very careful and intentional with the power the Creator has granted unto us.[19]

Without God at the center of the relationship between the sexes, we are a fire burning out of control. Driven by our carnal desires for power and domination, we will only hurt one another. Our best choice is to turn towards one another, appreciate one another's gifts, and speak life.

The Gift That Gives

When we read in Genesis 2:22 that "God fashioned into a woman the rib which He had taken from the man," the word "taken" means she is a gift he gives himself. The recipient of the gift—man—provides the giver—woman—with the opportunity to accomplish her calling as stabilizer and rescuer, and this is a gift to her. In Hebrew thought, to give is to receive. To receive is to accept, and to take is to give. In the Garden, man understands that woman is a gift to him, and to receive her is to know her worth. *For a wife [woman] is more precious than rubies,* a phrase used for Lady Wisdom:

> Wisdom is **more precious than rubies**,
> Nothing you desire can compare with her.
> She offers you long life in her right hand,
> And riches and honor in her left
> She will guide you down delightful paths,
> All her ways are satisfying.
>
> Who can find a virtuous and capable wife?
> She is **more precious than rubies** . . .
> Her husband can trust her, and she will greatly enrich his life.
> She brings him good, not harm, all the days of her life.[20]

This gift God has given man is supposed to be *protection and security* for him. If she is wise, she will bring him good and not harm. She will keep him from getting his feet caught in a snare.

> For this reason a man shall leave his father and his mother,
> and be joined [*dâbaq*] to his wife; and they shall become
> one flesh.[21]

In God's design, man gives up his life for woman first. He breaks ties with his former life and follows hard after her. His new life is *with her*, not his parents—and *she* will be the one to walk alongside him as they choose the direction of their family. She will help him in a way that he cannot help himself.

Knowing who she is, it is easy to leave everything for her. He *holds fast* to her. The word for this is *dabaq*, to pursue closely; adhere to, join to, follow close (hard, after); abide, pursue, stick. Phonetically, this word means "source, well, or fountain."[22] For man, she will be a life-giving fountain he can draw from. If they both understand what she is created to do, she will be a well of love and belonging. Yet if woman rejects wisdom and doesn't use her power for his benefit, she will be a noose and a trap.

Drink water from your own well—
share your love only with your wife.
Why spill the water of your springs in the streets,
Having sex with just anyone?
You should reserve it for yourselves.
Never share it with strangers.

Let your wife be a fountain of blessing for you.
She is a loving deer, a graceful doe.
Let her breasts satisfy you always.
May you always be captivated by her love.
Why be captivated, my son, by an immoral woman,
Or fondle the breasts of a promiscuous woman?

For the LORD sees clearly what a man does,
examining every path he takes.
An evil man is held captive by his own sins;
they are ropes that catch and hold him.
He will die for lack of self-control;
he will be lost because of his great foolishness.[23]

This is why the feminist movement that revolted against the "patriar-chy" created more perpetrators. In a godly patriarchy, the man gives himself on behalf of his wife. Marriage turns out to be a shield of protection for them both. Oneness is a strong help to him; it will aid him in living up to his name by channeling his energies towards loving and enjoying the beauty of woman. When a man understands his calling and hers, his life is directed towards the positive goal of nurturing his wife.

It is not good for man to be alone. That is why God gave him a woman he would deeply respect and cherish. The desire to be seen, known, and loved is fulfilled through a relationship with God and our husbands. We see this word, *yada*, in the sexual union in Genesis

4:1. They don't just "have sex" or even "consummate the marriage."
Yada means he knows her, he understands her, and he is deeply connected
to her emotionally. He respects her.

Loveless Sex Is Not Empowering

As Louise Perry points out in *The Case against the Sexual Revolution*,
feminist mantras that told young women to "have sex like a man"
caused nothing but pain for both sexes.[24] Liberal mantras declaring
"sex work is work" deny the emotional component of sex for both
partners. In the name of "consent," they tell girls to have as much as sex
as they want, which is a lie with serious consequences. Not only does it
harm emotionally fragile young women, but it often results in abortion,
turning women against their own makeup to protect life. It is a culture
which has created irresponsible men and damaged women.

In her powerful book, Perry unveils the failure of liberal feminism
to protect girls from the pain caused by their promises of "sexual freedom." After working in a rape crisis center, Perry let go of liberal feminist ideas about sex. It turns out that loveless sex is not empowering.
She writes:

> [Liberal feminists] have made the error of buying into an ideology
> that has always best served the likes of High Hefner and Harvey
> Weinstein, his true heir. . . .
>   This fact becomes clear when we look at the twenty-first cen-
> tury university campus, where the gospel of sexual liberation is
> preached loudest and where BDSM societies[25] and "Sex Weeks"[26]
> are the new normal. . . . Few liberal feminists are willing to draw
> the link between the culture of sexual hedonism they promote and
> the anxieties over campus rape that have emerged at exactly the
> same time.[27]

On college campuses, where young women are prescribed boatloads of
pills for depression and anxiety, liberal feminism refuses to link their

pain to loveless sex, abortion, and the pain and loss these behaviors result in. Emotionally, they get pillaged. Not only do they have to suppress their natural instincts for monogamy, but girls have to pretend no-strings sex doesn't hurt.

Perry describes hook-up culture as a rotten deal for women, framed by liberal feminists as the path to liberation.

> They have done a terrible thing in advising inexperienced young women to seek out situations in which they are alone and drunk with horny men who are not only bigger and stronger than they are but are also likely to have been raised on the kind of porn that normalizes aggression, coercion, and pain. But in liberal feminist circles you're not supposed to talk about the influence of online porn, or BDSM, or hook-up culture, or any of the other malign elements of our new sexual culture, because to do so would be to question the doctrine of sexual freedom. . . .
>
> Liberal ideology flatters us by telling us that our desires are good and that we can find meaning in satisfying them, whatever the cost.[28]

Chivalry's Not Dead

Recently, our daughter Olivia shared an analogy she learned from a wise woman. When a woman gives her body, she gives the man everything. But when a man gives a woman everything, he gives her his wallet. Young women who sink their teeth into feminist lies about sex cannot figure out why they date the men they love for years, and yet he does not propose. *Stop having sex with him and you'll be engaged in six months*, the wise woman says. This is the easiest analogy for a young woman to understand. As long as she gives an unmarried man everything, he will not be in a hurry to give her everything, which is access to his wallet. When she respects herself enough to wait for marriage, he will *yada* her; he will respect her too. And he will give himself up for her *first*.

What would be better than teaching girls they can have sex without painful emotional consequences? We could teach them that being driven by desire is not always good; that's how people get hurt. We could teach them that loveless sex is not empowering. We could tell them that being loved by one man is better than giving themselves to ten. We could warn them about emotional wounds from hookup culture. We could model for them that sex is sacred because it is.

For boys, we could model that chivalry's not dead. We could teach them to channel their desires into productive labor. We could teach them to dig ditches instead of throwing women into the ditch. We could teach them to be princes and prophets, kings and leaders with a calling not only to protect women but to guard their spiritual beings.

When we teach boys that a wife is the riverbanks to channel his masculine energy, we inspire chivalry inside of him. A return to chivalry will produce fruit for women and bring lasting happiness and love for both sexes. As Perry charges us, we must teach young people to prioritize virtue over desire.[29] When we read the Song of Solomon, we blush and get hot in the face. It is the most beautiful love affair the world has ever read. This physical, emotional, and spiritual union between a male lover and his female bride is filled with pleasure and longing. From the woman's voice we hear her say, "I belong to my love, and his desire is for me."[30] By loving him wholly and completely, she has channeled his energy towards *her*. As Honore de Balzac says, "The motto of chivalry is also the motto of wisdom; to serve all, but love only one."[31]

Right now, we have the opportunity to course-correct an entire generation and teach them the truth of their worth and the power of oneness. As one flesh, husband and wife are the picture of Christ, our Groomsman, and the Church, His Bride. Through us, young women could learn the meaning of our name: I am a wife, and I am "more precious than rubies."

Dressed in Compassion

In the name of liberal feminism, woman revolted against mankind. Instead of calling men back to their true name—the benevolent protector we are created to guard—they left women exposed and vulnerable. In doing so, they tore away the gift of their assignment in the earth: to stabilize men. When woman fails her mandate to uplift and challenge mankind, people are driven toward carnal desires that war against their own good. This has happened between feminism and the patriarchy. As Moen writes, "Feminism is as misguided as male chauvinism. Both attempt to rewrite the biblical design in their own image."[32]

They *eat eat, die die,* and *blame blame,* unless they turn back to YHVH, who brings *Life! Life!*

The first woman failed her post. She didn't protect the one she was made to help. The first man failed as well; he didn't remember the command. In spite of their misdeeds, their names never change. Adam is still *Adamah,* the Image-Bearer. Eve is still *Chavvah,* the Life-Bearer. They are still man and wife, *one flesh.*

After they eat the fruit, shame enters the Garden. They hide. God calls on Adam first and asks him three questions: *Where are you? Who told you? Did you eat?* For the woman, He asks one pointed question that every woman must ask in her relationships: *What did you do?* They both try to blame the other, but that would bear no good fruit.

Many try to say the first couple was cursed. This is a myth. God cursed the ground and cursed the serpent, but He never cursed His children. Yet their sin was equally sad. She listened to the wrong voice; she misquoted God's command; she didn't guard; she didn't help. He forgot his allegiance to the One who made him; he dismissed God's warning; he was passive instead of protective; his sin was not remembering.[33] What is frustrated in the fall is their *function.* They will struggle in their role as *zakar, neqevah,* and *ezer kenegdo.* But their identity is still fixed. She is still Strong Help who holds the borders; He is still the Arrow Warrior meant to pass on his name and shoulder the family.

God curses the serpent first, predicting the gift of His Son who will bring them back to the Garden again: "And I will put enmity between you and the woman, and between your seed and her seed; he shall bruise you on the head, and you shall bruise him on the heel." Then he tells the woman, "I will intensify your labor pains; you will bear children in anguish. Your desire will be for your husband, yet he will rule over you." He then tells Adam the ground will be cursed because of him. "By the sweat of your face you will eat bread, till you return to the ground, because from it you were taken; for you are dust, and to dust you shall return."[34]

They have eaten from the tree of *ra*, which brings calamity.[35] For men, this is about their identity, how they use their hands. The Hebrew word for sorrow is *'âtsab*. It means anguish, vexation, frustration, and lament. It is emotional turmoil marked by grief.[36] Adam will be *so frustrated* as he attempts to fulfill his divine commission. No matter how hard he works, some part of the earth will still be unresponsive. His productive effort will no longer guarantee fruitful results. As Moen writes, "He will be alienated from the very thing that made him, the *'adamah*.'"[37]

For women, this is about their relationships. What used to come easy will be simple no more. Just as Adam is alienated from the earth, Eve will be alienated from Adam. Her relationships with her children will be marked by sorrow. The turning away from God and towards the serpent will make her weary. Pregnancy, childbirth, and childrearing—the womb of *neqevah* will bring vexation and lament.

In her relationship with man, trust has been lost. What woman is meant to do, what she knows she can do, will be met with his resistance. This *stinks* for her. He will no longer see her as lifesaver, lifegiver, and life-bearer. Instead of treasuring her strong help, man will seek to dominate her. This will cause *so much pain* for women—a generational anguish. The fall would wreak havoc on what she values most, her relationships. She would hate the devil for this—and that animosity would serve her well. Because one day, through the womb of a woman, Jesus would crush the snake on the cross.

Elohim didn't want them to live this way forever, so he sent them outside those Garden gates.

When Adam and Eve leave the Garden, "The Lord God made garments of skin . . . and clothed them."[38] This phrase "to clothe" and "garments" is found elsewhere in the Word as coverings for the garments of priests.[39] When they walk out of the Garden to face the world together, they are the world's first priests.

These merciful garments represent the compassion of a loving God who will never turn His back on them. Their identity, their calling, and their assignment never change.

The most passionate book of love in the Bible is written from a woman's perspective. She says to her lover:

> Place me like a seal over your heart,
>   like a seal on your arm.
> For love is as strong as death,
>   its jealousy as enduring as the grave.
> Love flashes like fire,
>   The brightest kind of flame.[40]

Passionate oneness between man and woman will shield them both from harm. Like a hearth around a fire, oneness brings light, warmth, and heat. Marriage will channel their desire toward love that is safe and free and filled with possibility. They are un-alone this way. To fulfill their mandate, they must walk in gracious companionship. If they do, they will find lasting happiness and enjoy the fruits of their hands.

Despite our misdeeds, God still calls us *ezer* and *zakar*, a Cry for Help and the One who Needs Her. When man and woman leave the security of the Garden, they are still Hand of Fire and Breath of Fire, and their love is a mighty flame. They are still the first daughter and son of the Most High God. They are still faithful, chosen, and called; meant to subdue, rule, and take dominion. Adam and Eve will always be the world's first father and mother who led us to the Christ child.

Together, they will wrestle to steward the earth as one. Not only are they called to steward the earth, but they must steward one another. They must steward their names, their *shem*, and pass the meaning of their names to every generation forward.

Chapter Nine

I Am a Mother

The Glue

Mom, you are the glue that holds this family together.
—Zachary Glen Allen Strickland

Every time a woman is used as a biblical symbol, she represents a system of beliefs that influences people. Mothers are the greatest influencers in our homes and in our nation. I wrote this book because I am a mother, and the destruction of masculinity and femininity is happening on my watch. As the gatekeepers of the family and the spiritual guardians of the home, community, and nation, it is our responsibility to take back our name. This is not to be left upon the shoulders of the daughters. They are called to carry on the family legacy, and young women are figuring out how to do that now. The calling to take back our name is the call of the leaders, the mothers specifically. But we cannot do this while being silenced by fear.

The Bride and the Harlot

Just as there are two women the Word speaks of—the Wise Woman and the Foolish Woman—so there are two women who represent two distinct ideologies: the Bride and the Harlot. Whether the ideology is represented by a political movement, a religion, a people group, a nation, or a language, we can be one kind of "she" or another: the Wise or the Fool, the Bride or the Harlot. First, we can choose to be part of the set-apart Bride of Christ, represented by the nation of Israel. As believers grafted into Israel through the blood of Christ, we are part of God's chosen people, His Bride.

But in the Book of Revelation, we see another woman who represents world systems, the Harlot. Many young women in our culture know very little about her; they follow her ways like a baby deer caught in a barbed-wire fence. The promiscuity of our culture proves to be a tangled and bloody noose. Yet they have no idea they are following the voice of the Harlot. It is primarily the responsibility of mothers to teach them the difference between the sound of the voice of the Bride and the hunger in their ears that gives in to the slippery tongue of the seductress. The Harlot destroys men, women, and children—so they must understand what she looks and sounds like.

In the Book of Revelation, we find her drunk, reveling in the wine of sexual immorality, glorifying herself with riches and power, indulging her sensual and excessive ways. She sits upon the back of a scarlet beast, which represents the government systems of the world. John's vision of her is reminiscent of the adulterous woman of Proverbs: "Come, I will show you the judgment of the notorious prostitute who sits on many waters. The kings of the earth committed sexual immorality with her, and those who live on the earth became drunk on the wine of her sexual immorality." John saw this adulterous woman riding the beast:

[She is] dressed in purple and scarlet, adorned with gold, precious stones, and pearls. She had a gold cup in her hand filled with everything vile and with the impurities of her prostitution. On her forehead a cryptic name was written: BABYLON THE GREAT, THE MOTHER OF PROSTITUTES [HARLOTS], AND OF THE VILE THINGS OF THE EARTH. Then I saw that the woman was drunk on the blood of the saints and on the blood of the witnesses to Jesus. When I saw her, I was greatly astonished.[1]

I bet he was astonished! The woman riding the beast is sitting upon the waters which represents "people, multitudes, nations, and languages."[2] She is wasted drunk, dressed provocatively, and wearing expensive gold and pearls, filled with the impurities of her sexual fetishes. The verse that closely follows beams from the page like the north star: "This calls for a mind that has wisdom."[3] What is the beginning of wisdom again? The fear of God. As Revelation foretells, the world system of false religion that rides upon the beast is a woman who will make war upon the Lamb. "But the Lamb will conquer them because He is Lord of Lords and King of Kings. Those with him are called, chosen, and faithful."[4]

Notice how God names His people: *chosen, faithful,* and *called.* The world system that exalts promiscuity is a false religious system being worshiped throughout the world. But God identifies those who are a part of His chosen Bride by our blessings and gifts, not our sexual prowess. When universities throughout America exalt sexual immorality, they train young people in the language of the Harlot. When we oppose the language of gender ideology, we may be persecuted, called old-fashioned, or even cut off from the people we love. But we must remember *we are not in a battle against flesh and blood*—our war is *not against people.* Instead, we are in a war against the *world forces* represented by the Harlot, which represents a false religious system that does not speak the language of God.[5] God's language is one of love, unity, truth, light, and justice.

Mother: The Glue and the Strong Water-Giver

In Hebrew, the mother's name *'êm* means *glue.* In Jewish thought, the mother is the light of the house and the point of departure separating the family, community, and nation from evil influences. As the glue, she is the strong arm that holds the family together through her work and love.[6] As the Spirit influences the environment, so the woman is highly influential. Just as the feminist movement shifted our nation away from the heart of the family, so mothers have the power to shift our focus as women back to the home. We can counter-influence the culture with our voices, our Breath of Fire. We have enormous power to bring both physical and spiritual renewal to a nation and world in distress.

- Mother: 'êm[7] אֵם
  - Noun Feminine
    - Mother of humans
    - Point of departure or division; a dam or parting
    - Glue
      - Binding agent
      - The bond of the family
      - Arm that holds everything together
      - Of Deborah's relationship to the people
  - Root: אמם (amam)[8]
    - Be dependent upon
    - Giving physical and spiritual life
    - Tribe; people; ethnic entity
    - Related words: serve; limit; glow; develop
  - Pictograph (read right to left): ᴍᴧ𝖞 Water | Strength
    - Strength Over Chaos
    - The Strong Water-Giver

The pictograph of her name, em, ᴍᴧ𝖞 means Strong Water-Giver or Strength Over Chaos. Like the Father, ᴍ𝖞, her name begins the aleph 𝖞 , which means strong authority. The second letter of her name is the mem ᴧ, symbolizing water, blood, chaos, or the deep. Like the Spirit hovering over the deep in Genesis 1:2, she moves. She stirs the air. She brings order to chaos.

Not only is God pictured as the Father in Scripture, but He is also pictured as a mother. As Isaiah writes, "Can a woman forget her nursing child, or lack compassion for the child of her womb? Even if these forget, yet I will not forget you. Look, I have inscribed you on the palm of My hands; your walls are continually before me."[9] "As a mother comforts her son, so I will comfort you, and you will be comforted in Jerusalem," He says.[10] When His daughters are in distress, He cries out, "I have kept silent for a long time, I have kept still and restrained Myself. *Now* like a woman in labor I will groan, I will both gasp and pant."[11]

Today is the day to gasp and pant for this generation of children. Now is the time for mothers to no longer be silent but to speak! In the word for mother we also see that she represents a tribe of people. She is the giver of spiritual life. In Judaism, the mother is the primary role model for a religious upbringing. As the light-bearer, she is the one who lights the *Shabbat* candle. She is deeply honored in Jewish culture, as she turns "meat into milk" to feed her family physically, emotionally, and spiritually.[12] In Judaism, the mothers feed their families with spiritual milk, while they eat the meat at their father's table. The mother is the glue, or binding agent of the family. She is also a *dam*, separating children from harm's way and showing them the right road to take. She guards all the influences in children's lives—at home and in her community. Women do not have to physically bear children to do this; as leaders, we are all the *glue* and *strong water-givers* for mankind, those we are called to protect and redirect.

A mother is the "Strength Over Chaos" who brings order to everything she touches. Conversely, an emotionally chaotic mother will affect the entire family. In my work with incarcerated women, I have seen that the absence of a healthy mother at home causes painful heartache. Her pain of being separated from her children is devastating, and the family feels like it is unraveling without her presence. We have seen this happen in our society. When mothers were driven out of the home, the heart of the family suffered tremendous losses. Divorces rose, children turned to drugs and alcohol, and the daughters followed the voice of the Harlot instead of the tempo of the Bride.

Women of the Western Church have been traditionally taught that *men* should be the spiritual role models of the home, but this is not the teaching of the Torah, the ways of Judaism. Due to this teaching, many Christian women resent their husbands when they are not behaving like the "true spiritual leader of the home." But instead of expecting him to take our post, we should just do the work of *real* biblical motherhood, which is to be a light in the home and a spiritual guardian. Even if she works outside.

the home, the domain of the home is woman's post to guard. Likewise, we have to guard and redirect our sons and daughters from the lies of the sexual liberation movement, which will only cause them heartache.

As L. Grant Luton told me, "God designed marriage so that the husband could model God's devotion to the wife, and the wife to model the church's devotion to God. In this way, children can see both of these important roles portrayed daily in the home. *All* of us are to be lights. When Yeshua said, 'You [plural] are the light of the world,' it was to a crowd of men and women."

Femininity Enlarges

When Abram and Sarai were wanderers in the desert, God gave them a promise. Through Sarai, who was ninety years old, they would bear a son, and their descendants would be as numerous as the stars in the sky. When Abram was ninety-nine, God said to him, "I will establish My covenant between Me and you, And I will multiply you exceedingly."[13] At this moment, God changed their names from Sarai to Sarah and Abram to Abraham, adding the *hey*, ה the symbol of *femininity* to their names.[14] The sages say God gave half of His holy name (YHVH) to the chosen couple. Shaped like the womb in modern Hebrew ה, the infusion of the *hey* brings expansion; it multiplies and expands.[15]

As the funny saying goes:

> Whatever you give a woman, she will make greater. If you give
> her a sperm, she'll give you a baby. If you give her a house, she'll
> give you a home. If you give her groceries, she'll give you a meal.
> If you give her a smile, she'll give you her heart. She multiplies
> and enlarges what is given to her. So, if you give her any crap, be
> ready to receive a ton of. . . .[16]

I'll let you guess what that last word says. The lesson is that we will multiply, but what will we multiply? Resentment? Bitterness? Pain? Sexual promiscuity? The demeaning of men? The demeaning of the womb? Or will we teach our daughters to protect and shield our sons from evil influences and lead others into the ways of the Wise Woman, who receives life to the full?

The Name of Eve

The first Mother, Eve, or *Chavvah*, has a name that is similar to the meaning of the word for Spirit, the *ruach*. They share two of the three letters in Eve's name.

- **EVE: Chavvâh** חַוָּה [17]
  - **Proper Name Feminine**
  - **Life or Living**
    - **Life-giving**
  - **The First Woman**
    - **Wife of Adam**
  - **Root: châvâh**
    - **To tell, declare, show, make known**
    - **To breathe**
  - **Root: chăvâ'**
    - **To show, interpret, explain, inform, tell, declare**
  - **Pictograph (read right to left): ** Breath | Nail | Wall

Eve's name means *the mother of all living*. How does she give life? Through her *breath*. She *tells, declares, shows, interprets, explains, informs, and interprets*. The first letter of Eve's name is *chet* ח.., symbolizing abundant life.[18] This letter represents a dividing wall and protection from evil influences. Looking at the second letter, the *vav* Y, she is a uniting force like a cross, symbolized by the tent peg. The last letter is the *hey* , meaning "Behold." The roots of her name are *chavah* and *chava,* both of which mean *to declare or announce.* She was created to reveal and make known through the power of her voice. There were many prophetesses in the Word who did just that, including Miriam, Deborah, Huldah, and the wife of Isaiah, to name a few.

Eve's name means: *to declare, to tell, and to make known*. Jesus knew this. That's why He revealed the resurrection, His Messiahship, and His healing power to women. He knew they would spread the Gospel like no one else. Instead of muzzling and demeaning them as religious leaders did, He released them to speak. The moment he said, "Woman . . . Go and tell," He redeemed the voice of Eve.[19]

Talking is as natural for women as breathing—and He gave us an assignment in line with our *identity*. This is why the enemy always wants to steal women's voices—from little girls being abused to grown women called to preach, to Christian women who use their voices to tear down instead of build up. Sadly, the devil often partners with the Church to silence us. As a result, young women are suffering from not hearing the women of God speak clearly about gender, self-image, relationships and all the things that matter most to them. If they don't hear from women in the Church, they turn to social media instead.

In most churches, the entire congregation rarely—if ever—gets to hear from a woman. While we regard our fathers in the faith as the chiefs of the tribe and greatly respect their wisdom, our culture desperately needs the voice of the mothers right now. One way to redeem woman is to remember her name. Women who have been afraid to speak up about their husbands' abuses or who have a message to declare must be set free to go in the leading of God.

Silencing Women

The letters in the word *woman* mean *voice of fire*. Why doesn't the Church teach this? Because if they did, some men would have to admit they mistranslated God's word for woman. For a world in a quandary, the Church can no longer avoid defining the name woman correctly. This is our responsibility to shoulder. It is not the responsibility of the world, the gender theorists, or the ideologues who change our name in the dictionary. It is our responsibility and privilege—and we are the only ones who can do it.

The Apostle Paul knew what woman meant; he was a Hebrew of Hebrews who likely memorized much of the Old Testament. As a Messianic Jewish rabbi, he knew the root of *kenegdo* meant *to tell, announce, report, utter, show, declare, inform and proclaim.*[20] He knew the root of *Chavvah* is *to tell, declare, and make known.* Pauline verses that have been interpreted to say "women should not speak" do not call upon his understanding of the Torah, from which he drew his definition for woman: one who would release revelation through the power of her voice.

Like Jesus, Paul knew the right women should speak, lead, and teach alongside the men, which many valiant women did in his churches. He knew the Jewish mother was the spiritual teacher of the family. He also knew woman's name meant *breath of fire*, and too much talking could get them in trouble, so in a culture where women weren't educated, he made a radical declaration that they should *learn* and released them to share the Gospel as led by God, just as Christ did.[21]

But Paul also knew *the wrong women*, the *harlots*, would try to dominate men. Their prideful, flaunting ways and takedown of authority could rule over weak-willed men and lead them to forget their mantle to walk with God. But two of the statements he made to warn us about this issue have been interpreted to make broad claims that *all women* shouldn't preach. So—as much as oppressive men won't like it—we must reclaim these two verses.

To do so, we will first ground ourselves in the anchor of Paul's philosophy: "There is no Jew or Greek, slave or free, *male or female*; for you are all one in Christ Jesus."[22] We have to remember his teaching that "We have different gifts, according to the grace given to each of us," including prophesying (speaking), serving, and teaching.[23] As he wrote, "Christ himself gave the apostles, the prophets, the evangelists, the pastors and teachers, to equip his people for works of service, so that the body of Christ may be built up until we all reach unity in the faith."[24] These statements made by Paul are not gender-specific; they apply to all believers, so that *must be* our foundational understanding to interpret the troubling verses that follow.[25]

In 1 Timothy, Paul writes a personal letter to help Timothy with disruptions in his ministry. In the letter, he tells Timothy he doesn't want men to be controlled by anger or arguments, also known as the need to be "right" (hint, hint). Then he says he wants women to dress appropriately during the prayer service (in which *everyone* prays out loud). He doesn't want them to come into church with "elaborate hairstyles, gold, pearls, or expensive apparel" but with good works, like women who profess to worship God.[26] But why is he worried about what the women are wearing? In Texas, I can go to church wearing big hair, gold, and pearls; so what's the big deal? My mentor Devi was the most glamorous preacher I've ever seen—and she wore elaborate jewelry and clothing to say the least—yet her heart was incredibly pure, both in her marriage and ministry.

Biblically, clothing is synonymous with the position of a person's heart. For example, God puts jewelry on the daughter of Ezekiel 16 to imprint her worth; but he rips it off the women of Zion because they flaunt it as a source of pride.[27] The attire Paul warns Timothy about is worn by the *cult prostitutes* of Ephesus, who reside in the Temple of Artemis right next to Timothy's church.[28] These women dress seductively and flaunt their "gold and pearls" (*chrysos* and *margarites* in Greek), which are the *same exact bedazzlements* worn by the Scarlet Harlot in Revelation 17:4.

In 1 Timothy 2:9–10, Paul starts out using the plural Greek word for women (*gunaikas*), but in verse 11 he shifts to the singular (*gune*), referring now to *a particular woman* who should not "teach or exercise authority over a man, but to remain quiet."[29] English translators adjust the text to refer to *all women*. But in the Greek, this doesn't fly. It is clear he is talking about a singular woman in a specific situation and not making a broad-sweeping statement about all women. (If he were, we'd have to tell Texas church-going women to stop with the big hair—something *they will not do*!) This "authority" Paul is talking about is domineering and forceful, not submissive. So this *deceived woman* has a spirit of seduction and domination. Paul doesn't want *that woman* speaking and ruling in church. Amen to that!

Not all women, but *that woman* is the picture of the Foolish Woman. For the Wise Woman who honors God with the position of her heart, gold and pearls are not a problem—and neither is speaking to men. The Wise Woman doesn't dominate or usurp authority; she honors and submits to godly authority. If Paul was really saying all women shouldn't speak, he would have been opposing Jesus who *sent the women to tell the men* He had risen, and when they didn't believe the women, Jesus rebuked them sternly for their stubborn unbelief.[30] Yet *we still have this confusion* propagated by much of the Western Church—that *all* women should never speak from pulpits. Hogwash. The godly women in Paul's church were not the ones he was warning Timothy about. We are not all domineering seductresses. We are messengers called by God to share the Gospel.

When we read Scripture, we have to do so through the Spirit of the text. We have to start with *ezer kenegdo, neqevah, ishshah (woman), Chavvah (Eve) and Em (Mother).*

Let's look at the other verse people cite to silence women. Once again, Paul is writing a letter to the church in Corinth to address certain disruptions during worship services, in which he exhorts *all attendees* to prophesy and speak, but in an orderly fashion. Then suddenly we read: "Let the women keep silent in the churches; for they are not permitted to speak, but let them subject themselves, just as the Law says."[31] In his book *Guardian Angel*, Moen writes:

> The biggest problem with this verse is the obvious fact that the Torah (the Law) does *not* say anything like this. . . . Women took an active and *outspoken* role in the community . . . They are not only mothers; they are judges, rulers, priestesses, leaders, guides, prophetesses, organizers, directors, teachers and *talmiydim* [students and teachers of the Word] . . .
>
> Paul speaks to particular issues. He is not making a general ruling here. He is not inconsistent with his own heritage and religious beliefs. Women in Paul's Scriptural heritage and in his personal experience take whatever role God directs them to take.[32]

It is improbable that Paul would claim something was written in the Torah that does not exist; neither does he quote it in his usual manner, since *there is not a single verse* that says women must be silent in the synagogue.[33] So is Paul confused here? That's unlikely. In *Beyond Sex Roles*, Gilbert Bilezikian suggests Paul is quoting the claim of his *opposition*—since in the verses prior he is exhorting *everyone* to use the gifts of prophesy.[34] If Paul actually did say this, how can he instruct all people to prophesy and then tell half the congregation to shut up? This is a double-minded statement inconsistent with the Law. Paul emphasizes that spiritual gifts are given to both genders and removes all distinctions between us in his anchoring theology "male nor female, slave, nor free." Moen pontificates:

> The propagation of the idea that women are to be segregated to roles different than men flies in the face of biblical teaching, including Pauline teaching. It is inconsistent with equality under Christ; it ignores the Hebrew role of the *'ezer* and it is in opposition to the interpretation of the church fathers. Church tradition after 250 AD invented this misogynist idea. It's time to get rid of it. Translations of the text that propagate this bias verge on heresy. They reveal the misogyny of the translators, not the intent of the Most High God.[35]

The rest of the New Testament is full of female leaders, including Junia, who as Moen explains, is clearly "outstanding among the apostles."[36] Philip's four daughters are prophetesses (which Paul calls "the most desirable gift");[37] Euodia and Syntyche are evangelists; Phoebe is a deacon, leader, or president (which male translators call "a servant"); Priscilla is a pastor-teacher whose ministry is more prominent than her husband's (the minister at Devi's funeral preached on her!); Mark's mother, Lydia, Nympha, and Chloe led churches in their homes; and John addresses a letter to the "chosen lady" in 2 John, writing to a woman who appears to be a house church leader or pastor.[38] The Gospel radically altered the position of women in first-century society.

As Margo Mowczko writes:

It would be wonderful if the Church as a whole would recognize that, according to the New Testament, women did function as ministers and leaders—as apostles, prophets, evangelists, and pastor-teachers—and that they were respected and valued in these roles by such people as the apostle Paul. In short, it is biblical for a woman to be a church leader. Moreover, if we deny gifted women the opportunity to exercise their ministries, we reject some of the very people Jesus has appointed and given to his church. The church's mission can only be enhanced and made more effective when gifted men and women minister together using their complementary skills and abilities. Men and women should be united in the cause of the gospel and in building up the body of Christ, as well as in equipping the people of God to reach the lost. (Ephesians 4:11–12)

In Acts 21:17, we read in all caps (which feels like being yelled at by God): "'AND IT SHALL BE IN THE LAST DAYS,' GOD SAYS, 'THAT I WILL POUR FORTH OF MY SPIRIT ON ALL MANKIND; AND YOUR SONS AND YOUR DAUGHTERS SHALL PROPHESY.'"[39]

My prediction is that future generations will understand this—and as mothers, we will teach our sons and daughters that they will prophesy together, and this will cause the Church to expand and multiply like the stars in the sky. The daughters are the pillars of the home, nation, and community. We see this concept in this verse: "Let our sons in their youth be as grown-up plants, And our daughters as corner pillars fashioned as for a palace."[40] Just as sons are likened to fruitful vines that grow from the soil, the daughters are a strong, essential, and supporting pillar to the Church. Without the feminine side of YHVH, the structure falls down; she is the corner piece of the structure that holds it up with strength. But as long as women are held back, so will the ministry of the Church be held back; it will be lopsided and fall. The divine directive has not changed: "He created them male and female. God blessed them and God said to them, 'Be fruitful, multiply, fill the earth, and subdue it.'"[41]

Sister, Speak

If the Church righted this wrong, so many good things could happen:

1. Women would be released in their calling to spread the Gospel.
2. Women would be held accountable as to *how* they used their voices.
3. The Church would experience the fullness of male and female ruling and reigning together.
4. The daughters would hear from the mothers in the house of God.
5. Women's concerns would be addressed from the pulpit.

The woman's voice carries the wind of the Spirit. As the mother of the Messiah, Mary spoke the Magnificat, lifting her voice in some of the most beautiful poetry the world has ever heard. When village life ceased in Israel, Deborah arose as a mother. With her words she redirected an army of men, and God sold the enemy into a woman's hands.[42] Jael finished the job, taking a hammer and driving a tent peg into the meditations of an evil ruler. Esther used her influence to save a nation. And Mary Magdalene was the first evangelist. These brave soldiers worked in concert with men to accomplish these daunting assignments. No one flourishes alone—not one sex. It is only in concert that we win, take dominion, and conquer.

When godly women rise up to take back our name, men will follow, and together we will stand, side-by-side, our faces like flint. Godly fathers will fight to protect the perceptions of the mothers. Right now, mothers, daughters, and Deborahs across this nation are rising up and using their voices as a purifying fire.

By keeping godly women down, the cult of prostitution has risen. A spirit of domineering femininity that is not in God's likeness is dominating the narrative about women. It's time for the true mothers, the priestesses and prophetesses of God, to speak. And when we do, we must speak in the language of love, remembering that nobility—not nastiness—is at the center of our name. When we speak on the topic of gender, we can be truthful. We can be bold. But we do not need to demean trans people or the homosexual community. We can—and we will—speak in the language of love, which is the universal language all hearts yearn to hear.

Chapter Ten

I Am from the Land of the Free and the Home of the Brave

The Warriors

Our innate femininity is being demonized. The innate masculinity of boys is being demonized. Our identity is under attack. They are trying to actively dismantle our natural identities and undermine this notion that every child is born in God's image.
If they can remove that belief system, they can introduce any idea.
—Landon Starbuck[1]

"Binary is bullsh**!" the pale girl stated. "This idea that the body is either male or female is totally wrong." When *Teen Vogue* with their two million subscribers slipped this teaching into teen girls' minds in 2019, it worked. Using a variety of voices to tell us about sex and biology—none of whom belong to doctors or biologists—*Vogue's* YouTube video presented this as the new truth:

Most of us are taught that if you have a vagina, you're a girl, or if you have a penis you're a boy, but, like, many simple binaries break down, when you start to really get into the nitty-gritty.[2]

Over history, the location, or the idea of what determined one's true sex shifted a hundred years ago. It used to be whether or not you had ovaries or testes, then it shifted to what kinds of chromosomes that you had, but the body doesn't just have one place where we can sit there with a microscope or something else and say, "Hey, wait a second this is really who you are; this is your true sex." In fact, *who you are is who you say you are.*

A fully grown woman—whose body is made up of trillions of cells that read "female," says:

Too many people still believe that there's such a thing as a true sex and that it comes from your chromosomes. It's not the case. Science has known this for decades and it's actually a consensus in science and uncontroversial.

Cross-dressing males then tell teen girls:

When I say I am a woman, I don't just mean that I identify as a woman. I mean that my biology is the biology of a woman, regardless of whether or not doctors agree.

Trans women are not biological men. We should never talk about any woman who is trans as a man; not a biological man, not a natal man, not really a man. This is used to target trans women and make us out as predators, especially when it comes to bathroom bills. The reality is that a trans woman's biology is a female biology.

A trans woman is a woman; she's not tricking anyone. All of her body parts are female body parts.[3]

Teen Vogue closed comments on the post, so healthy psychotherapists, parents, teachers, and detransitioners cannot question the narrative. No debate is allowed. If you question the idea that a "trans woman" is truly a biological man—which is the truth—you will be called *homophobic* and *transphobic*. Other people will slap that identity on you, even if your only concern is *the health and safety of teen girls*.

1828, 1984, and 2024

How do we go from the 1828 Webster's dictionary to *Teen Vogue*? It actually works a lot like George Orwell's fictional book *1984*, based on life in Communist Russia in 1948. First, the powers-that-be limit the information you receive. Second, they repeat the same mantras over and over and over and over and over again. Third, they demonize those who question the narrative. Fourth, they elevate their ideology over personal experience that contradicts it. Fifth, the beliefs of the group are absolute and perfect. Anyone who disagrees is faulty by nature. Sixth, the patterns of behavior appear to have arisen spontaneously from the environment, when they actually have been carefully orchestrated. Seventh, the world becomes sharply divided between the absolute good (the group ideology) and the absolute evil (everything outside the group.) Eighth, those outside the group must be sinful, intolerant bigots who have yet to admit their intolerance. Once a person has experienced this total polarization of good versus evil, the person under thought reform has great difficulty regaining a more balanced view of the complexities of human morality.[4]

As Orwell writes, "Freedom is the freedom to say that two plus two makes four. If that is granted, all else follows."[5]

After I left my first church, which turned out to be a cult, the International Churches of Christ (ICC),[6] I studied mind control with a man who also knew Greek and a little Hebrew. As a gift from my parents, I attended a cult recovery center called Wellspring Retreat and Resource Center near Athens, Ohio. When I arrived, I refused to believe I was in a cult. *Impossible*, I thought.

The big residential house had cooks and counselors. But I posed a problem. I had recorded to memory the entire handbook of the ICC. I knew their teachings so well that my tattered Bible highlighted *only* the things they taught me, while verses that spoke against thought reform were untouched. My mind filtered *everything* I saw through their mantras.

What are we going to do with this Word girl? Paul Martin, the director, thought, so he called his brother Stephen, who had developed a study about thought reform and the power it holds on those in its shadow.[7] For two weeks, Steve unfurled the original languages of the Bible to me that speak against false teachers. I discovered I had in fact been under mind control. I could hardly believe it. I *loved* the people in the church. They played guitars in the park and acted like a tight-knit family. Worse, I had taught college girls their booklet. I had baptized women into the group—which is precisely the problem. We baptize people in Christ, *not* in group ideology.

I will never forget the moment that tipped the scales. I was standing at the bathroom sink in the apartment I shared with girls in the ICC. I asked my "discipler" (mentor) what she thought would happen if I left the church. She told me she thought I would go to Hell. I basted my face in scalding hot water and opened my eyes. I was in trouble. Frantically, I opened an email my aunt had sent me two years prior, which the church claimed was "persecution" and told me *not to read*. (Usually, the most important information you need is the exact thing they tell you not to look at.) Finally, I clicked on the links my aunt had sent me and paid attention to their warnings. The truth was, this movement was hurting people and dividing families.

At Wellspring, I stayed up all night writing down what I learned. Determined to help my friends in the group, I wrote a 125-page letter to the church, dismantling their teaching.[8] The pastors and young people in this movement needed the truth. This information could help them; it could free them! They could learn how thought reform works, how cults prey on the unsuspecting and confused. I could help them see how we all got sucked into this.

But it was to no avail. When I returned from Wellspring, I came back to an empty apartment. The only things left were my shivering dog and the trash. Dirty dishes were piled in the sink, with flies buzzing around the debris. My roommates had vanished like ghosts in the wilderness. Astounded, I stood on the linoleum floor and cried. Where had they gone, the people who claimed to love me so much?

With my mother at the wheel, we drove from apartment to house to apartment, leaving my letter on doorsteps. Sometimes a person would answer the door, but quickly shut it when they saw my face. Multiple calls to the leadership were met by echoes of silence. The only communication I received was a letter in the mail from the woman who baptized me: the story of Judas in cut-and-paste.

I heard through the grapevine that the pastors told the congregation I was to be treated like a branch cut off from the vine. The leadership had everyone turn in their letters and burn them in a heap on the altar of their ideology. The smoke rose from a massive campfire on the beach where I had been baptized.

How Thought Reform Works

Psychiatrist Robert Jay Lifton was one of the early psychologists to study mind control. He called it *thought reform* and identified eight criteria that are used to change people's minds. His study was based on the psychology of totalism and brainwashing in China. He writes:

> Any ideology—that is, any set of emotionally-charged convictions about men and his relationship to the natural or supernatural world—may be carried by its adherents in a totalistic direction. But this is most likely to occur with those ideologies which are most sweeping in their content and most ambitious or messianic in their claim, whether a religion or political organization. And where totalism exists, a religion, or a political movement becomes little more than an exclusive cult.[9]

Because I was in a cult and have studied these movements closely does not mean that I negate the experience of those involved. Like me, most are innocent. So by unveiling the tenets of thought reform, I am only doing what Orwell did: showing people how it works. We should never be afraid to look more deeply into movements that sweep young people off their feet.

Is learning about thought reform threatening to those who embrace gender ideology? It should not be. Any environment which discourages the attainment of knowledge is unhealthy. As Thomas Campbell says: "The truth is not delicate; it will stand up to vigorous testing."[10] Only fools run from knowledge; the attainment of wisdom begins with seeking understanding, not running from it. At first, I vehemently denied looking at the underpinnings of the movement I was a part of. But doing the painful work of looking at it square in the face was my best choice. Truth actually does set people free.

Lifton's criteria for thought reform are eight psychological themes *against which any environment may be judged.* He writes, "In combination, they create an atmosphere which may temporarily energize or exhilarate, but which at the same time pose the gravest of human threats."[11] *1984* is still required reading in public high schools. Let's pray that remains. If they burn that book for future generations, *make your kids read it.* How do totalistic environments change people's minds about sex and gender? The first tenet of Lifton's criteria I will introduce is called "loading the language."

Loading the Language[12]

- New words and language are created to explain the new and profound meanings that have been discovered. Existing words are hijacked and given new and different meaning.
- Black-and-white thinking is embedded in the language, such that wrong-doers are framed as terrible and evil (as defined by the group), whilst those who do right (as defined by the group) are perfect and marvelous.
- The language is characterized by thought-terminating cliché (thought-stoppers)
- The group repetitiously centers this new language on all-encompassing jargon.

- The meaning of words are kept hidden from the outside world, giving a sense of exclusivity—and those who do not use the words according to their "new" definitions are punished.

The *Teen Vogue* video is a perfect example. If you believe in biology and are grounded in reality, you might say a "trans woman" is a biological man. But the ideologues will claim you are bad for saying this; you are "fueling violence" towards "victims," which are trans women. The term used to be "transvestite" or "transsexual," and it clearly meant a biological man dressing like and wishing himself to be a woman—while retaining the fact of his male biology. Today, the language is loaded with new meaning. *Vogue* tells us that trans women (males dressing as females) "are women, and have a female biology"—and to question them is an "act of violence." This mantra is repeated over and over, enforcing the new rules of language.

In the book *1984*, this is called "Newspeak"; characters are evil even if they *think* differently than the new language. Canadian youth would greatly benefit from understanding this, since speech about LGBTQ+ persons is now legally regulated in Canada.[13] Language is how we communicate our thoughts, so if a government can control the language, it can control the thoughts of the population. As Orwell explains, once you limit the words, you limit the parameters of thought.[14] Today, judges (who have no business being judges) are *denying parental rights* to those who call their trans daughters "she." Calling a biological girl *a girl*—even your own daughter—is now considered "family violence" and labeled "misgendering."

Even teachers, administrators, and bosses must play by rules that are cognitively impossible. In 2013, Harvard researchers looked at live brain scans to discover that within 200 milliseconds of seeing a face, the brain recognizes two things: sex and race. In a flash, our brains say: male or female, black or white. This is why emergency alert systems say white male, black female, and so forth—because *everyone's brain registers what that is.* We would never in a million years expect a parent or teacher to call a black person white; yet these new "rules" are now being forced on people whose brains distinguish between male and female instantaneously.

Harvard seems to have forgotten their own scientific discovery. In 2022, "students at Harvard University were told that failing to use a person's preferred pronouns could be a violation of the university's sexual misconduct and harassment policies during a mandatory online Title IX training." Harvard now claims that using the grammatically correct pronouns to address someone is *abuse*. Even though it is the most natural thing in the world to call a female "she," they claim this is an "attempt to limit a person's sense of self based on identity."[15] All the power of someone else's identity is based on pronouns *others use*? Now that's a stretch. When rational people are blamed for others' mental and emotional distress for believing they are "born in the wrong body," we are in an impossible situation for healthy relationships.

If you don't use Newspeak, you may be accused of discrimination, abuse, and sexual harassment. Those who equate gender ideology with the new gospel will punish you, banish you, and treat you as a threat.

But I am a woman, and I know what a woman is, so I'm not going to be intimidated by a thought reform tactic that I can see a mile away. In this book, we are staying grounded in *reality*. We are going to "Give this lie a good hearing," as Orwell challenged writers to do.

In this new language, a female can be a male, but a black person cannot be white. Young people are forced to lie, and they are taught it is brave and good to choose their gender from a growing menu of options. When a young person wants to do this, they should be affirmed and celebrated, because they "decide who they are." Not parents. Not biology. Not God. *Children*—who cannot legally drink a glass of wine, own a gun, vote, get a tattoo, buy cigarettes, get their ears pierced, or travel alone—are being encouraged to self-identify. If the parents do not agree that the child should start taking hormones to attempt to change their gender, they are labeled as "unsupportive."

Trans activists encourage young, impressionable kids to "transition" without their parent's knowledge. The mantra goes like this: agree or be banned.

As *Teen Vogue* claims, gender theory is based on science and is "uncontroversial," although there are no scientific criteria for gender identity because it is marked by mental distress. The powers-that-be elevate the irrational and unscientific beliefs of the few over the morally grounded beliefs of the masses. This is a thought reform tactic called "Sacred Science." Here are its characteristics:

The Sacred Science[16]

- The beliefs and regulations of the group are framed as perfect, absolute, and non-negotiable. The dogma of the group is presented as scientifically correct or otherwise unquestionable.
- There is an aura of sacredness around its basic doctrine or ideology, holding it as an ultimate moral vision for the ordering of human existence.
- Questioning or criticizing those basic assumptions is prohibited.
- A reverence is demanded for the ideology/doctrine, the originators of the ideology/doctrine, and the present bearers of the ideology/doctrine.
- Offers considerable security to young people because it combines a sacred set of principles with a claim to a science embodying the truth about human behavior and human psychology.

In *Women's Health*, sex therapist Paula Leech assures us the "sacred science" of gender theology will bring greater clarity:

> The language we have around [gender identity] is rapidly expanding to accommodate for the wide variety of gender identities and expressions out there. The more we can expose ourselves to the diversity of gender identity and expression out in the world, the

more likely we are to find ourselves reflected back with greater clarity.[17]

So are the kids experiencing greater clarity? Or greater pain? With this teaching advancing like a fire out of control, we find the converse is true—young people are more unclear than ever.

According to a CDC study published in 2023, young people are showing worsening levels of persistent sadness or hopelessness across all racial and ethnic groups. Yet the mental health of girls has declined the most. In 2021:

- Thirty percent of girls seriously considered suicide and 24 percent made a suicide plan
- Six out of ten felt hopeless and depressed
- One in five experienced sexual violence in the past year
- More than one in ten had been raped in the past year
- One in three girls and one in five boys have been sexually abused
- More than half (52 percent) of LGBTQ+ students are experiencing poor mental health. More than one in five (22 percent) attempted suicide that year[18]

Sadly, we are teaching them that pronouns, name changes, and cross-sex hormones are the answer—all of which will not fix their waffling identity. There is so much more we can do for them than this.

Being constantly told they are defined by sexuality only decreases their self-empowerment. Equally as harmful is the culture's toxic messaging which convinces them they are victims of the "racist, misogynistic, homophobic, transphobic white supremacist, right-wing extremists" of this nation—which couldn't be further from the truth. Isolation and media brainwashing—with lie after lie being funneled into their minds—has worsened their mental state, not helped it.

The Children

In 2023, LEGO—a company that markets its toys to children ages three and up—released its "A-Z of Awesome," which it called "a colorful alphabet of identities built from LEGO® bricks, created by our incredible LGBTQIA+ fans!" The company's website reads:

> "The A-Z of Awesome" aims to present the community's vocabulary more widely through a fun and playful medium. . . .The creative inspiration for this campaign was born out of the insight from GLAAD that almost half (45%) of non-LGBTQIA+ people find conversations around gender identity confusing.
>
> "As we start Pride month, it's the perfect time for families to start new conversations about sexual orientation, gender identity and gender expression," said GLSEN Executive Director Melanie Willingham-Jaggers (they/she).[19]

Most healthy human beings do not see a need to discuss the meaning of LGBTQIA+ "identities" with children ages three and up. What do young children need to know about lesbian, gay, bisexual, transgender, queer / questioning, intersex, and asexual people? But this is not all—there are masses of children's books that are reinforcing this movement.

In public schools across America, school calendars insist that LGBTQ+ students are not merely treated equally and fairly but revered for their courage. Abigail Shrier writes in *Irreversible Damage: The Transgender Craze Seducing our Daughters*:

> The year long Pride Parade often begins in October with "Coming Out Day," "International Pronouns Day," and LGBTQ History Month; November brings "Transgender Awareness Week," capped off by "Transgender Day of Remembrance," a vigil for transgender individuals killed for this identity. March is "Transgender Visibility Month." April contributes "Day of

Silence / Day of Action" to spread awareness of bullying and harassment of LGBTQ students. May offers "Harvey Milk Day," dedicated to mourning the prominent gay rights activist; and June, of course is Pride Month—thirty days dedicated to celebrating LGBTQ identities and decrying anti-LGBTQ oppression.[20]

It is no wonder kids are announcing their gender dysphoria and trying to find their place in the "gender identity spectrum." This is what they are being taught to do. *If this is how I can get attention, then I will do it!* A typical girl who feels awkward in her body and finds herself on the fringes of society will look for her place in the LGBTQ+ acronym because she is wired for belonging.

In schools that embrace gender theory, kindergartners read *The Genderbread Person*, *The Gender Unicorn*, and *I am Jazz*, the story of the Disney star Jazz Jennings, whose parents transitioned him from "boy to girl" at five years old. This "star" is now an infertile adult on a boatload of hormones with no sexual function, but the children's book only teaches little ones that "they might have a girl brain in a boy body" and vice versa. In K-6, the California Board of Education provides *Who Are You? The Kids' Guide to Gender Identity*, which presents children with a "smorgasbord of gender options." In middle school, they get to watch *Trans 102*, which challenges kids to imagine "knowing you're a boy when everyone else tells you that you're a girl. Or knowing you're neither. Or a bit of both."[21]

In high school, it gets graphic. As Abigail Shrier painfully documents in her book *Irreversible Damage*, the most highly respected health curricula that include gender identity and sexual orientation[22] are so radical and explicit she thought they were actually trying to arouse the kids. The material found in these programs promotes anal sex, oral sex, and fisting—and most parents haven't even read it.

"What is the cumulative effect of all of this LGBTQ education?" Shrier asks. "'I think what it does is it normalizes us,' Dr. Chiasson offers, including herself in the LGBTQ. And presumably, it does."[23]

My concerns are two-fold: Number one, sexual activity that truthfully harms people is being lauded as healthy and normal. No wonder kids are feeling hopeless. It's no surprise Planned Parenthood is a booming business that now provides cross-sex hormones. According to this new religion, Abstinence Is No Longer Best—which is why we all need to be aware of the sex ed programs our schools are teaching.[24] I read every single word before I sign off on it.

My second concern is that this increases bullying. By singling students out and focusing relentlessly on their gender and sexuality, same-sex-attracted kids are harassed more, not less. Straight kids get tired of hearing about queerness being equated with courage. LGTBQ+ students should be respected like everybody else and taught to develop the *character traits* that make them strong. According to LEGO's "Alphabet of Identities," B is for Bi, G is for Gay, and T is for Trans.[25] In my identity poetry, B is for beautiful; G is for grateful; T is for telling the truth in love.

Censorship

It is almost unbelievable that people who openly oppose the exposure of divergent sexual behaviors to children are *censored*—something we couldn't have imagined ten years ago. While Google and YouTube funnel links into children's iPads that offer "Are you Gay?" quizzes, outspoken people like me are accused of "violating community standards" on Facebook when we oppose males in female sports—something that leads to serious harm. This leads us to another tenet of thought reform, called "Milieu Control."

Milieu Control [26]

- The most basic feature of thought reform is the control of human communication within an environment. If the control is extremely intense, it becomes internalized control—an attempt to manage an individual's inner communication.

- Control over all a person sees, hears, reads, writes (information control) creates conflicts in respect to individual autonomy.
- Psychological pressure often through a sequence of events, such as seminars, lectures, and group encounters, which become increasingly intense and make it extremely difficult for one to depart from the group.
- Sets up a sense of antagonism with the outside world; it's "us against them"
- Closely connected to the process of individual change (of personality); they make themselves "the engineers of the human soul)"
- Their conviction is that reality is their exclusive possession.[27]

Liberal media either ignores or criticizes the stories of desperate detransitioners who have been mutilated by the medical community on the altar of gender ideology. Liberal news will not report on the barely dressed men wearing leather bondage gear who expose themselves to children in the Pride parades, or the Drag Queen story hours where children curiously listen to stories about gender identity told by adult men dressed as prostitutes. Any pushback from right-thinking people is called "anti-trans rhetoric."

We are not talking about mild news stories; we are talking about the bodies of children in Canada, Europe, and the United States being mutilated beyond repair—and they deserve to be heard. Instead of exposing this as thoughtful journalism would do, the media lauds the powers-that-be. They celebrate President Joe Biden saying "transgender people shape our nation's soul," as he stands in front of the White House with a massive Pride flag behind him, hanging center stage and symmetrically equal to the United States flag.[28] As Judicial Watch President Tom Fitton put it, "To advance revolutionary transgender agenda targeting children, Biden violates basic tenet of US Flag Code and disrespects every American service member buried under its colors."[29] As Biden called the LGBTQ+ community the bravest and most inspiring people, an example for the United States and the entire world, those in our armed forces looked on. We have literally changed the meaning of courage in our country. It used to be those who ran headlong into the blazing twin towers; now it's gender and sexual identity.

But liberal news media says nothing of the Tavistock gender clinic in the United Kingdom, which closed its doors due to lawsuits that proved they had irreparably damaged children by fast tracking them to gender transition.[30] When a school shooter is trans, the news media covers it up—instead of investigating the effects of gender medicine on depressed teens that will influence them towards violence. Our governing authorities are limiting the information we receive—and the most catastrophic effect is on the children—because in their innocence, they believe what they see and hear.

If we tried to define the "+" in LGBTQIA+ for children, we'd have to explain BDSM; "attraction to minors," which is pedophilia; polygamy; leather fetishes; and bestiality. If we wanted to show them all the flags the + represents, we could show them Volvo's website that promotes the "abrosexual" flag, among many others. Abrosexual means "a person's sexuality may change more frequently over the course of hours, days, months, or years. They could be 'gay one day, then be asexual the next, then polysexual the next.'"[31]

Universities nationwide now provide college students with an LGBTQ+ glossary of "helpful terms," all of which are alarmingly the same, under the terms "Diversity and Inclusion." They list over one hundred terms; when I was in college, I was familiar with fewer than five of them.[32] According to Brown University in Providence, Rhode Island, "the terms BDSM (Bondage, Discipline/Domination, Submission/Sadism, Masochism) refer to deriving pleasure from inflicting or receiving pain in sexual context." I quote: "These practices are often misunderstood as abusive, but when practiced in a safe, sane, and consensual manner, can be part of a healthy sex life."[33]

When the twenty-something author Megan Lasher, who uses "they" pronouns, writes an article for *Seventeen* magazine called "A Brief History of the LGBTQ+ Acronym," "they" fail to mention the real meaning of the plus symbol. Instead, they name over thirty sexual preferences and gender identity terms that teenagers "should be familiar with." This writer, who also specializes in astrology, quotes the *New York Times*, which claims "the symbol '+' represents all non-cisgender and non-straight identities that are not included in the acronym, or 'everything on the gender and sexuality spectrum that letters and words can't yet describe.'"[34] If there are sexual behaviors beyond those thirty, why should *Seventeen* magazine encourage impressionable teenage girls to know about them?

When we were well-adjusted teenagers, there was no such vocabulary. Even if there were, sane adults weren't "educating" us about them, because most adults can't fathom what they are, or how this list of "identities" could possibly be considered gospel truth.

What happened to Mr. Rogers's singing?:

Boys are boys from the beginning; girls are girls right from the start. Everybody's fancy. Everybody's fine. Your body's fancy and so is mine. Only girls can be the mommies. Only boys can grow up and be the daddies. Everybody's fancy. Everybody's fine. Your body's fancy and so is mine.[35]

When LEGO tells three-year-olds, "C" stands for "Coming Out" and "I" stands for "Intersex," we *must stop and think*.[36] Are we using China's brainwashing techniques to convince children to identify themselves with sexual urges before they have had a single sexual encounter? Or are we teaching them *who they really are* by calling out *the character traits* that make them awesome? In my poetry, "C" stands for Courageous and "I" stands for Impressive. "V" doesn't stand for *victim of sexual violence*; it stands for Virtuous.

Are sexual choices as varied as American cereal boxes really a great idea for kids from kindergarten to college? Or are we leading them the way of Lady Folly, to the den of death? Are families more solid than ever, or are parents reeling from the grief of this indoctrination of their children into multiple "identities" that seemingly show up out of nowhere?

What on earth are we doing to the kids?

Wisdom Takes a Stand

If this disgusts you as much as it does me, good. It should. Part of woman's name is *guardian-protector of humanity*. Lady Wisdom "calls out in the streets; she raises her voice in the public squares. . . . At the crossroads, she takes her stand" (Proverbs 1:20, 8:2). We are at a crossroads in our communities, nations, and world. Now is the prime opportunity to take a stand. In the Book of Revelation, Jesus rebukes the churches who tolerate the woman Jezebel, who teaches and misleads His servants into sexual immorality. I quote Him: "All the churches will know that I am He who searches hearts and minds, and I will repay each of you according to your deeds" (Revelation 2:20–23). Your stance against this evil being indoctrinated on God's children will be rewarded with the crown of the faithful.

Pray for the kids. Speak at a school board meeting. Do *something*. Anything.

If that means homeschool, homeschool. If that means challenging the government, do it. If that means saying NO, say NO. Anything else is of the devil—and he masquerades as an angel of light (2 Corinthians 11:14).

Let's not forget—in fact, let's remember—the rainbow came after the biggest storm humanity had ever encountered—a storm that drowned the earth due to sexual deviancy, among other perversions (see Genesis 6:9–17). Today, that rainbow surrounds the throne (see Revelation 4:3). The devil has seen it, and he wants it for himself.

But he can't have it. Not on our watch. I am from the Land of the Free and the Home of the Brave. I am a mother. I am a life-giver who brings order to chaos, and I am called to protect the children no matter the stakes.

Chapter Eleven

I Am an Advocate

Summoned to Your Side

When you have something to say, silence is a lie.
—*Jordan Peterson*[1]

As the number of detransitioners who condemn gender interventions for children continues to rise, we must listen carefully to what they are saying. Their heartbreaking stories show the shocking consequences of medicalizing minors for gender confusion. Parents, doctors, and therapists impacted by thought reform are leading children like sheep to the slaughter.

With soft feminine lines shaping his genderless face, twenty-year-old Kobe tells his story on Fox News.[2] Framed by a pink and white leather chair, he looks straight at the camera, baring the medical abuse he endured in the guise of "gender-affirming care." You won't see it on liberal media. They must suppress information that raises questions about trans activism that supports gender "transition" for minors. They claim that anyone who questions it is transphobic—even the kids themselves. As you read Kobe's story, you'll see this is not a left- or right-wing issue. This is a humanitarian issue. Children's lives are at stake.

Stuck Somewhere in Between

As a child, Kobe liked pink and played with Barbies, a typical characteristic of boys who grow up to become gay. Dr. Richard Green, an American doctor and lawyer who spent much of his career in gender medicine, says, "Most of these effeminate little boys, who rejected their maleness and wished ardently to be girls, were not future transsexuals, but future gay men."[3] Studies confirm these findings, as Helen Joyce points out in her riveting book *Trans*.[4] But gender medical practitioners tell boys who feel like girls in childhood that they were "born in the wrong body" and guide them down a pathway to medicalization. If they walk that road long enough, they become eunuchs and *cannot go back*.

At age eleven, Kobe discovered male-to-female transition on YouTube and decided it was a way out of the shame he felt over his same-sex attraction. He felt unlovable as an effeminate boy in society, and instead of dealing with his feelings, he received coaching from older trans activists he met online. They told him he'd be better off as a woman and taught him to manipulate his parents with suicide threats. It worked. Kobe threatened to kill himself, and at thirteen, his parents allowed him to start dressing as a girl. A psychiatrist started him on puberty blockers that suppressed the natural production of testosterone in his body during the most developmental stage of his life. This permanently stunted his growth and had catastrophic effects on his mental health.

"If I was never indoctrinated into this stuff," Kobe says, "I would have never been suicidal over being biologically male. . . . I think I would have just stayed a feminine boy, and there's nothing wrong with that. . . . It made me feel like there was something wrong with me."[5]

The most highly acclaimed transgender specialist in the world, Dr. Steven B. Levine, warns that encouraging children or adolescents towards life as a transgender person raises major red flags. He states that hormonal and surgical procedures may enable some people to "pass" as the opposite gender, but these procedures carry multiple long-term physical, psychological, and social risks. Some of these are listed below:

> Sterilization (whether chemical or surgical) and associated regret and sense of loss; inability to experience orgasm (for trans women ["male-to-female transitioners"]); physical health risks associated with exposure to elevated levels of cross-sex hormones; surgical complications and life-long after-care; alienation of family relationships; inability to form healthy romantic relationships and attract a desirable mate; and elevated mental health risks.[6]

As Levine articulates in his expert submission on March 12, 2020, transgenderism is a painful disorder that causes *extreme* mental anguish. The person is disassociated with their biological sex, and that calls for *truthful* therapeutic environments that delay the medicalization pathway until full-grown adulthood. At that point, there are still greats risks socially and medically. For his firm stance on this, LGBTQ+ organizations claim that Levine, who has worked with hundreds of trans patients throughout his career, including caring for transgender inmates, has actually "made his life's work the denial of trans and gender-nonconforming people's healthcare."[7] Health care is now a loaded term, and Levine has been canceled for warning the world about the need to protect the kids.

Confirming the lies Kobe learned on social media, Kobe's "gender-affirming care" doctors began talking to him about sex reassignment surgery (SRS) when he was only fifteen. While suppressing his testosterone through puberty blockers, they flooded his body with estrogen therapy. This destroyed his developing libido, and to this day he suffers pain upon arousal. The estrogen caused brain fog, memory loss, and uncontrollable weight gain. He spiraled into an eating disorder and lost his drive to do anything. Estrogen therapy in boys can also result in bone density loss.[8] He now lives with severe back pain up his spinal cord and fears he has osteoporosis—*at age twenty.*

Youth and Brain Development

In ten years, the prefrontal cortex (PFC) of Kobe's brain would finish developing. The PFC regulates decision-making, emotional balance, and intuition that enables a realistic vision of the future.[9] This part of the brain embodies the capacity for complex planning, problem solving, personality expression, memory, and social regulation. It helps manage intense feelings and suppresses emotional urges for sex, food, and drugs. The PFC is responsible for good decision-making; in short, it regulates behavior.[10] According to the National Institute of Mental Health, the prefrontal cortex is one of the last parts of the brain to mature. It finishes developing in the mid-to-late twenties.[11]

Since this part of the brain isn't fully developed until about twenty-five years old, it is illegal for teens to own property or carry a gun. But somehow the left-wing medical community has abandoned the "Do No Harm" mandate and decided minors are able to make decisions about their bodies that will affect their *entire lives*. This is something European countries have pulled back from as they awaken to the dire consequences of "transing" adolescents.

Tavistock, the largest gender "affirming" care center in the United Kingdom, closed its doors due to lawsuits for "rushing children into taking life altering puberty blockers without adequate consideration or proper diagnosis."[12] Many children realized they had made an irrevocable mistake and did not have the cognitive ability to give informed consent. A lawsuit settled in their favor in December 2020: "There will be enormous difficulties in a child under 16 understanding and deciding whether to consent to the use of puberty blocking medication." Furthermore, the court said it was "doubtful that a child aged 14 or 15 could understand and weigh the long-term risks and consequences" of this treatment.[13]

According to multiple studies, there is a very high level of desistance in children with gender dysphoria if they are offered psychological support and alternatives to "affirmation-only" treatment, such as *the passage of time*, called "watchful waiting." A 2021 study showed that 87.8

percent of people who experienced gender dysphoria in childhood no longer experienced it in adulthood, when *no social transitioning and medical intervention had taken place.*[14] As Levine asserts, the psychological needs of these children call for therapeutic intervention that is based on truth, not lies. The role of a good therapist is to look under the surface at the pain an individual is experiencing, not to collude with delusional thinking.

When a therapist treats a girl with anorexia or bulimia, for example, she does not pretend the girl in her office should be a size 2 instead of 4, hand her fat-burners, and tell her to starve herself more. If being a size 4 is not healthy for her, the therapist's role is to tell her the truth: She would be healthier as a 6 or 8. If a size 14 woman believes herself to be a Barbie doll, that is not healthy either. Simply put, there is no therapeutic process by which self-diagnosis that must be affirmed is the norm. Any good psychologist worth their salt knows this, but gender-affirming care doctors that operate on children deny it completely.

America and Canada are diving headlong into these procedures, ignoring the studies from Sweden and the United Kingdom which prove this is a heart-breaking and damaging pathway for minors.

A "Happy Medium"

Kobe's story proves this to be true. He says that multiple psychiatrists, doctors, and therapists depicted his male genitalia as a problem to be eliminated. Since the time he was fifteen, they spoke about sex reassignment surgery like it was a lifesaver. But through a twist of fate, his insurance denied him for SRS, which saved his penis at nineteen years old. Instead, his doctors convinced him that an orchiectomy, the removal of his testicles, would be a happy medium until he could get the surgery. If his insurance had approved SRS, doctors would have inverted his male part to mold a fake "vagina"—which they'd keep open through dilation for the rest of his life—as if being a "woman" reduces us to a *hole*.

A procedure normally reserved for full-grown men with testicular cancer, the orchiectomy is being used on young feminine boys under the guise of gender-affirming "care." Without testicles, Kobe now no longer produces testosterone and is reliant on sex hormones for the rest of his life. He has barely any sex drive. He has hot flashes like a woman in menopause.[15]

Doctors promised him this pathway would enable him to live a normal life, but all it did was make him a life-long medical patient. He says with heartbreak in his voice, "I'm trying to reclaim my manhood now. It's hard. I have breasts, I have the hip development of a woman, because I started the estrogen so young. I have no gonads." His skull never masculinized; he has no Adam's apple, facial hair, or muscular definition like a man. His voice didn't deepen, and he will have no descendants. Due to ureteral dysfunction caused by the surgery, urine often drips down his leg. His endocrine system is shot. When he wanted to get off estrogen, the gender clinic didn't help him. He weaned himself off of it alone, a brutal, painful experience that wreaks havoc on the body and the mind.

Kobe is literally a human experiment that failed—but he is a survivor and a voice for the voiceless. He says:

I did everything they told me to do and I still had that trauma and personal self-hatred that was driving everything else. I hated myself. I wanted to die. I was constantly trying to become someone I wasn't. If they had allowed me to invert my genitalia, I don't think I'd be here [meaning he'd commit suicide]. . . . I should have never been estrogenized. I should have never had my puberty blocked. They glamorize things . . . they tell you you'll become a woman . . . it means nothing. I'm stuck in this middle body. Not completely male, not female—it's just this weird in between.

When he shared his story, he received an onslaught of messages from trans people telling him he should kill himself. They told him he "passed" as a woman in society and should have stayed that way, that he was prettier as a "girl," and threw it all away. His trans "friends" have abandoned him. He destroys their narrative.

As of this writing, his Twitter profile calls him "God's Favorite Eunuch."

The Helper

When God first introduces us to the actions of woman in Genesis 2:18, He uses the Hebrew word *ezer*, which means to give vital, strong, and lifegiving help. This is similar to the word Christ uses for the Holy Spirit, *parakletos* in the Greek. He calls the Holy Spirit our Helper, the same word for woman. More literally it is "one who is called or summoned." It also means to plead the cause of another.

- **"Helper" in Greek: Parakletos[16]**
  - **Noun Masculine**
  - **Summoned, called to one's side, especially called to one's aide.**
    - **One who pleads another's cause before a judge; a counsel for defense, legal assistant, an advocate.**
    - **One who pleads another's cause; an intercessor.**
      - **Of Christ at God's right hand, pleading with God the Father for the pardon of our sins.**
    - **A helper, succorer, aider, assistant**
      - **Of the Holy Spirit, who leads us into a deeper knowledge of the gospel truth, and gives us divine strength to undergo trials and persecutions on behalf of the kingdom.**

When people need emotional, legal, or spiritual help, we are called to come to their side. Not only are we summoned to help, assist, aid, and plead for them, but we are also called to legally defend them. Wisdom tells us not only to pray for others, but to speak up for their rights and ensure they get justice.[17] This is who we are as women: We are helpers, strengtheners, and defenders of the vulnerable. Both men and women can and should be advocates for victims of gender ideology—regardless of their political beliefs. Jesus said the kingdom belongs to the children—not the right-wing children or the left-wing children—the *children, period*. It is our responsibility to advocate on their behalf.

The *action* of womanhood is to lead others into a deeper knowledge of the truth, to pray for them and advocate for them—emotionally, spiritually, and legally. It is to come to their side, in a hurry when they call. This is the meaning of the word that came from Christ's lips as He echoed God's first word spoken about woman.

The Pathway for Girls

The identity of *loved, chosen, and redeemed* sons and daughters far outweighs the one hundred paranormal terms colleges are presenting to young people as a menu of identities. As universities are brainwashing young minds with the sacred science of gender ideology and denying the harm it causes, they are drawing young people into an unstable community that is not healthy for children who are questioning their gender.

What happens when a young girl who prefers to play with trucks, ride bikes in the mud, and wear basketball shorts has to "choose her gender identity"? Let's say she is repelled by Barbies and bikinis and selfies?

The truth is, she is "awesome" already—a girl who loves the outdoors. She is a tomboy. Maybe she'll grow up to be a carpenter, a marine, or an artist if she focuses on her *talents*. But the LGBTQIA+ club at school will want to know, what's your label? Trans? Bi? Lesbian? So let's say she chooses trans, since that's the fad. Then what? Should she start going into boys' locker rooms?

If her parents don't "support" her new gender, they will be labeled transphobes and told she'll kill herself if they don't comply—which the American College of Pediatricians describe as "emotional blackmail" that many parents have succumbed to.[18] As Swedish child and adolescent psychiatrist Sven Roman, who is far from conservative, sums up the research, there is "no scientific support for gender-corrective treatment to reduce the risk of suicide." [19] Psychologists Dr. J. Michael Bailey of Northwest University and Dr. Ray Blanchard from the University of Toronto agree. [20] But the left-wing medical community will clap their hands over their ears because they are the ones medicalizing the children. They demonize those who speak the truth and claim *they* are her savior. They will help her "transition" without telling her *transitioning is impossible*. They will frame parents as enemies, which is a trait of cults and Marxists and Communists. They will claim that pausing her puberty while her brain is developing is no big deal.

Gender-affirming doctors or Planned Parenthood (can you see the thought-stoppers in those titles?) will block her natural hormone production and put her on testosterone, which will give her a huge surge at first, but then result in increased aggression, foggy thinking, and depression. She will grow facial and body hair, and her voice will deepen like a man's. The next step is "top surgery," the loaded word for double mastectomy. Doctors will cut off her healthy breasts which are composed of glandular tissue, fatty tissue, blood vessels, lymph nodes, connective tissue, and ligaments. They will behave as if breast removal is the answer to her confusion. If her wounds don't heal, then that's her problem, right? This is what happened to Chloe Cole, whose double mastectomy at *fifteen years old* was a huge mistake. She is now a leading voice to protect minors from gender-affirming "care." She recently testified before the House of Representatives, saying, "My childhood was ruined." [21]

The question is this: Should our government allow doctors to block puberty to fix girls' dysphoria—or should they align with "Do No Harm" and wait until puberty does its miraculous work? Should we teach girls like Chloe that masculine characteristics don't take away her femaleness? Should we call out their talents, and teach them to focus on serving others rather than staring at a body that will always change? Should we help them become more comfortable with themselves? Yes, we should do that and more. We should teach young women that their identity is fixed; it doesn't change. Girlhood is beautiful. Womanhood is awesome.

Most girls struggle with their bodies, so self-diagnosing gender dysphoria for teen girls is a muddy path. Let's take Sadie, for example,
whose doctor blocked her puberty, put her on testosterone, removed
her breasts and uterus, and attempted to turn her into a man. In this
"care" to affirm her cross-sex "identity," they destroyed her body.
Sadie is now in her twenties and has woken up from the nightmare,
which she calls "indoctrination." She realizes *she was always a woman*.
But now she is a woman with a neo-phallus, a dangling piece of flesh
between her legs that hangs like dead skin. The skin of her forearm
from the skin-graft is the ultimate symbol of self-harm. She has constant pain. She has smiley-faced scars where her breasts once were.
She is infertile. She has a man's voice. She will be deformed for life—
only in Heaven made new, where the God of justice will judge those
who dismembered her perfectly healthy body. Sadie is deeply grieved
beyond words. She calls herself a eunuch, and there are *many* like her.[22]

If trans activists won't listen to the experts that condemn the insanity
of medicalizing minors for gender confusion, you'd think they'd listen
to trans people who underwent these procedures in adulthood. Blaire
White, a male-to-female trans person who *knows he is not a woman*, is
one of the leading voices against woke lies about gender, with 1.24 million YouTube subscribers.[23] Shape Shifter, who cried on Blaire's show
about the botched surgeries that destroyed his sexual function, says:

> I 100% feel like I was part of some cruel medical and social
> experiment. I wish somebody hugged me a few years back and
> said, "You know what, you can present feminine. You can wear
> heels, hair, whatever you want, but the sad reality is we don't
> have the technology to make you an actual woman". . . . My
> penis is gone and I forever regret it. They didn't protect me from
> myself.[24]

These young people's voices deserve to be heard. Shape Shifter's
story will wreck you. It should be shown to every parent considering
"transitioning" their child.

Blaire, who underwent transitional treatment in adulthood, calls the story of Jazz Jennings "monetized child abuse."[25] TLC made a fortune on Jazz, whose parents started "male-to-female transition" in preschool, all on camera for an adoring world to applaud. Barbara Walters came to their home to interview the family, introducing Jazz as a "brave soul born in the wrong body." Jazz's mother said on the show, "We tell her, God made you special, because there aren't too many girls out there who have a penis." At seventeen, Jazz underwent a vaginoplasty, but his male part was so shrunk from puberty blockers started at eleven that it was a total failure. The doctors admitted that the experimental surgery caused complications they didn't expect.

Jazz says, "I haven't experienced any sexual sensation. The doctor is saying an orgasm is like a sneeze. I don't even know what she's talking about." Later episodes of the show display the mother trying to figure out if her daughter is axesual or demisexual. The program has been running on TLC for years, documenting the brainwashing, gaslighting, and medical abuse Jazz has grown up with, while producers, directors, writers, lighting and set designers, makeup artists, stylists, camera crews, and doctors don't put a stop to it. Meanwhile, elementary school teachers who promote gender ideology read *I Am Jazz* to little kids, a cute book for toddlers about how cool it is for a boy to be a girl. The fairytale makes no mention of her eating disorder, one-hundred-pound weight gain, depression, urinary complications, and sexual numbness. Jazz cried on the show, "I just want to be happy. I just want to be me, but I never feel like myself."[26] This child was sacrificed on the altar of a lie.

Could this be the greatest atrocity against potentially same-sex attracted youth the world has ever seen?

When we speak out against the genital mutilation of children, the left frames our objections as having to do with homosexuality, when the truth is quite the opposite. We are concerned about *protecting* masculine girls like Sadie and Chloe and feminine boys like Shape Shifter and Jazz from irreparable harm. We are speaking up for their worth as vulnerable young people deserving of protection. As *Advocates,* women are called to plead for humanity. We are to be the *dividing wall and dam* between them and the enemy who steals, kills, and destroys young lives. The shocking truth is, we believe their sex organs are valuable, no matter how they use them.

Canceled

When Sadie woke up from her indoctrination and questioned the narrative, the gender-affirming clinics had no answers for what to do for her mutilated body. The hospitals took no responsibility and neither did the therapists. But she was a child! She believed them! So she turned to the LGBTQ+ community for support—the ones who cheered her on every step of the way. But they blackballed her and called her a traitor because she no longer uses their lingo. "Trans" was her identity. Now she has none.

Steve Martin told me in an interview that this is a clear example of brainwashing techniques, including the "Demand for Purity," "Loading the Language," and "Dispensing of Existence" wrapped into one. What I hear Sadie trying to say is, "I am a woman, and I always was one," but she is left feeling like it is all her fault—*that she ruined her own life.*

When a group negates the real-life experiences of those harmed by their narrative, this is called "Doctrine over Person," according to Robert Jay Lifton:

Doctrine over Person [27]

- The importance of the group and its doctrine are elevated over the importance of the individual in all ways. The group's ideas are superimposed over what is real.
- If one questions the beliefs of the group or the leaders of the group, one is made to feel that there is something inherently wrong with them to even question—it is always "turned

around" on them and the questioner/criticizer is questioned rather than the questions answered directly.

- The underlying assumption is that the ideology is ultimately more valid, true, and real than any aspect of actual human character or human experience and one must subject one's experience to that "truth."
- One is made to feel that doubts are reflections of one's own evil.

Like Sadie, if a girl does everything the "affirming care" pit tells her to, her mental health disintegrates rather than thrives. As the Tavistock clinic finally admitted, "young women who had begun the process of hormonal transition had shown 'no overall improvement in [their] mood or psychological wellbeing using standardized psychological measures,'" as Abigail Shrier noted in her book.[28] The promise is this: *Let us remake you into another image than the one God made you in*—and you'll be all better. You'll be "free to be you!" But it's a lie.

When Tavistock closed its doors and an investigation proved gender treatment does not improve the mental health of confused teens, Shrier points out that *The Times of London, The Observer, The Economist,* and *The Guardian* hailed this as a landmark case. But the U.S. legacy media acted like it didn't occur. Meanwhile, Planned Parenthood, one of the largest suppliers of testosterone to biological females—begun opening on-campus medical clinics at public schools across Los Angeles, the second-largest school district in America.[29]

When young women like Sadie wake up infertile, suicidal, and with no sexual sensation, who will "care" then? What happens when they awaken to the fact that they were butchered by the adults around them and given prescription drugs to "fix" them? What if they speak out? What if Sadie says, *This was wrong! I have been permanently damaged at the altar of a lie:* I WAS ALWAYS A GIRL?

This leads us to the fourth tenet of thought reform, one of the most painful: "Dispensing of Existence." Not only does the LGBTQ+ move-

194 I AM A WOMAN

ment distinguish between "believers" and "non-believers," using cancel culture as a punishing rod for those who don't align with their beliefs, but trans activists throw away those who dissent like rubbish.

This is the reason why so many people who are gay and transgender *do not* support this movement as a whole. They want nothing to do with it and are instead exposing it. Gays Against Groomers, Professor Kathleen Stock, and Blaire White are among them.[30] *Don't these kids' experiences matter?* These advocates demand. *Since when is self-ID a thing for kids? Why are we experimenting on them with no scientific proof that it even helps them? We are causing irreparable damage!*

When they speak up, they are no longer called "trans allies," but *enemies—even though they are friends.* They are a voice in the wilderness, to whom the religious zealots of trans activism shut their ears. These liberal activists are trying to help kids who are different, who feel out of place in society, who struggle with same-sex attraction and hate their bodies. *So am I.* Is the doctrine so superior to a person's experience that it cannot be questioned?

Like the ICC, when people leave the group and expose the false ideology, they are deemed no longer important, and their feelings don't matter. They are publicly maligned and crucified. This is called "Dispensing of Existence," a theme of cancel culture. According to Lifton:

Dispensing of Existence[31]

- The group draws a very sharp line between themselves and the outside world. Insiders are to be saved and elevated, whilst outsiders are doomed to failure and condemnation.
- The group's ideology is more important than personal beliefs and values. The beliefs, values and words of those outside the group are equally invalid.
- Since the group has an absolute or totalist vision of truth, those who are not in the group are bound up in evil, not enlightened, not saved, and do not have the right to exist.

- People who leave the group are singled out as particularly evil, weak, lost or otherwise to be despised or pitied. Rather than being ignored or hidden, they are used as examples of how anyone who leaves will be looked down upon and publicly denigrated.
- People thus have a constant fear of being cast out, and consequently work hard to be accepted and not be ejected from the group. Outsiders who try to persuade the person to leave are doubly feared.
- The group is the "elite"; outsiders are "evil" and "unenlightened."

Being rejected by one's peers is a teenager's worst nightmare. They long to belong. So on top of losing sexual function—a nightmare we cannot imagine—they lose their community, the people they trusted and believed.

If we do not change the laws that protect these children, if we just stand by and say, "Christians should stay out of politics," we are not living up to our name, *woman*. Our role is to advocate for the legal rights of those who are being crushed. If they do not repent, today's doctors, judges, and cult leaders will have hell to pay when they meet God on judgment day. For Jesus says *the kingdom of heaven belongs to the children, and anyone who harms a child would be better off drowned in the depths of the sea, the darkest place on earth*.[32] The government should *protect* the vulnerable—but too often they *deny* their experience, which causes even more pain. These kids will have to be deprogrammed from this ideology to understand nothing was ever wrong with them in the first place. As detransitioner Cat Cattinson puts it, "My body was never the problem."[33]

We can only hope detransitioners—the eunuchs of our day, which includes people who identify as transgender who have not yet had an encounter with Christ—find a healthy community that will love them for the long road. May that community listen to their cries as they heal. And may their stories never be forgotten.

Chapter Twelve

I Am a Friend

A Shepherd

*You tell people that you love how to avoid the road to hell.
And you don't do that because you're shaking your finger at them,
or because you're a moral authority. You do it because you don't
want them to burn. The more love you view other people with,
the higher the moral demand that's placed on you. That's why it's
so important to be truthful.*
—*Jordan Peterson*[1]

While there are many Christians who either side-step, ignore, or angrily judge people in the LGBTQ+ community, let's be real: Historically, Christians have done a pretty shoddy job of loving people who struggle with same-sex attraction.

Jesus's call to not judge our brother rings truer than ever before. Becket Cook's mother is a great example. During her son's years spent living the homosexual lifestyle, she treated her son as a *best friend* and prayed for his conversion to Christ. Jesus rescued him from himself, and Becket now has an incredible podcast with over two hundred thousand subscribers, and most of all, a very fulfilling ministry.[2] Caleb Kaltenbach is a pastor who grew up attending Pride parades. In his book *Messy Grace*, he tells the story of how his church served his parents with such tremendous love that they gave their lives to Jesus.[3]

Christ rescues people when they are suffering. As Romans 5:8 (NIV) says, "God demonstrates His own love for us in this: While we were still sinners, Christ died for us." And while a relationship with Jesus requires repentance from sin, no entrance to Jesus requires that we clean ourselves up first. The cleaning is what happens after, and that's God's job, not something we can do in our own power. (See Matthew 3:6; Acts 2:38; 1 John 1:9; and 1 Corinthians 6:9–11.)

On a personal note, I love people who are in the LGBTQ+ movement. I love because that's who I am. Let's get something crystal clear: Kindness is the only thing that changes people's lives. Arrogance repels. Pride stinks. Self-righteousness is the ugliest outfit we can wear. People who struggle with sexual and gender identity *struggle*, period. They have their crosses to bear like we all do.

In order to help and not hurt people in the LGBTQ+ community, we will need to run towards them and not away from them. When people are searching for gold, we will intersect their paths. Sometimes we will be summoned to go a way we hadn't planned to go, but when we hear God's voice telling us to move, we will need to *move towards them*, in a hurry.

The Ethiopian Eunuch

Castration, in whatever century or whatever context, eliminates a man's ability to bear children to carry on his family name. There is a story about a castrated man in the Book of Acts. How is he portrayed? Trans? Or as a male without testicles?

When we come to Acts 6, we meet Stephen, a man full of God's grace and power. Stephen gives the sermon of a lifetime in Acts 7, to which religious zealots "put their hands over their ears and began shouting." Picture it. The synagogue leaders can't *stand* to listen to the incredible wisdom by which Stephen spoke, tracing the life of Christ back to Abraham. The high council of religious leaders refuse to face the idea of Christ's death on their bloody hands. So they persuade people to lie about Stephen and get everyone riled up against him. With Stephen's face bright as an angel's, they drag him through the streets and stone him to death, approving his massacre. He dies while asking God not to charge them with their sin.[4] This leads to a great wave of persecution that sweeps over the church, and all the believers are scattered throughout Judea and Samaria—where they spread the Gospel like wildfire. People are healed of demons that scream as they leave their victims. The lame are healed, and warlocks abandon their sorcery for the power of God to break every chain.

Philip, one of the original twelve disciples who walked with Jesus, is summoned by an angel to travel down a desert road all by himself. There, he meets a eunuch, the treasurer of Ethiopia. A man of great authority and intelligence, the eunuch guards the treasury of the queen, but would likely never know the touch of a woman. Today's woke culture might call him asexual, aromantic, nonbinary, trans, or not a man—as if his male organ determines his identity. But that is not the story recorded in the annals of history.

He is on his way back from worshiping in Jerusalem when the Holy Spirit leads Philip to walk alongside his moving chariot. Philip *runs*. He does not run away; he runs *toward* the man. The eunuch had either been castrated in childhood or chosen it for himself in adulthood. He was a man who would have no descendants—like Paul, like Jesus, like Kobe. Philip finds him reading aloud from the Book of Isaiah:

> He was led like a sheep to the slaughter,
> And as a lamb is silent before its shearers,
>   he did not open his mouth.
> He was humiliated and received no justice.
> Who can speak of his descendants?
> For his life was taken from the earth.[5]

"Do you understand what you are reading?" Philip asks.

The man replies, "Well how could I unless someone *guides* me?"[6] Another way of saying this is, *How can I understand this, unless someone shepherds me?*

We have to wonder what he felt in his soul when he read about being led like a sheep to the slaughter in humiliation and deprived of justice. He urges Philip to come and sit with him, and Philip climbs into the chariot to sit by his side. "Tell me, is the prophet talking about himself or someone else?" The eunuch asks, curious. He is probably thinking, *this looks like it's talking about me.*

Then Philip opens his mouth and beginning with that verse, tells him the Gospel.

How many of us see a trans person and turn the opposite way? How many shut their mouths when a young person needs guidance? How many are running *toward* them to come alongside them, advocate for them, and open our mouths to help them into a deeper knowledge of Jesus? How many of us hurry to their sides to love them and listen to them?

Philip does not quiz the man about his sexuality. He does not ask for pronouns. He does not recommend gender transition surgery to make him feel like a "woman." No. He tells him the stripped-down essential: the Good News.

Another way of asking, "Who can speak of his descendants?" is *"Who can relate to this generation?"* That is the question of the hour. How do we plan to reach these kids? Model and missionary Christina Boudreau, who partners with our ministry to reach young people for Jesus, puts it this way, "We are bare bones about it. The Gospel is enough."[7] As part of the *Whosoevers* movement,[8] Christina is tackling the mental health crisis among youth with one simple strategy: the Gospel. Turns out, it is more than enough. They are leading droves of kids to Christ with one simple message: Jesus loves them and gave His life on their behalf.

In Old Testament law, a man with crushed testicles or whose male organ was cut off was treated like a bleeding woman and not allowed in the assembly of the "righteous."[9] To people like this, Christ says: I was *crushed for you, to unite you to me.* "I have called you back from the ends of the earth, saying 'You are my servant.' For I have chosen you and will not throw you away."[10] In Isaiah 56:3–5 we read:

No foreigner who has joined himself to the LORD should say, "The LORD will exclude me from His people"; and the eunuch should not say, "Look, I am a dried-up tree." For the LORD says this: "For the eunuchs who keep My Sabbaths, and choose what pleases Me, and hold firmly to My covenant, I will give them, in My house and within My walls, a memorial and a name better than sons and daughters. I will give each of them an everlasting name that will never be cut off."

Now think of that. The eunuchs get a *better name than Sons and Daughters*. The "memorial" they receive is the hand of favor, strength, and power that can never be cut off.[11] That's pretty powerful—and there will be a lot of them in this generation.

As Philip and the eunuch are riding along, the eunuch sees some water and says, "Why can't I be baptized?" He commands the chariot to stop, he and Philip get in the water, and he is baptized that day. The eunuch never sees Philip again but goes on his way rejoicing. This means "God speed"; it is a verb, an *action* of his soul. He was *exceedingly glad, thriving, and filled with joy*.[12]

His real need, like everyone's, was to be seen, known, and understood. To be given a place of belonging. The family of God should be that place, where no one is ostracized, rejected, or demeaned. Being forgiven by Christ gave the eunuch an identity that would never change. That identity would last forever.

I'm Coming to Your Home Today

If you scour the Gospels, you will find plenty of instances of religious people snubbing their noses at women who society considered "sinful." But you will not find a story in the gospels of the Son of God condemning people for sexual behavior when they come to Him in search of healing. The Son is a Builder and Restorer; He is the Repairer of the breach in our souls. He is also a "Friend of Sinners," and in Hebrew that means *Shepherd to the lost*. He doesn't bash His sheep; He ushers them into the pasture and keeps them in the fold with tender mercy and care. The word "friend" is rooted in the word for shepherd.

- ■ FRIEND: rêaʿ רֵיעַ [13]
  - ○ Noun Masculine or Feminine
  - ○ Friend, companion
    - • Neighbor
    - • Fellow-citizen (who may be weaker)
    - • One another
  - ○ Root: râʿâh
    - • Tend; satisfy needs
      - □ Leading to pasture; grazing; wandering and tending
      - □ Being neighborly and concerned
      - □ Thinking; seeking spiritual sustenance
  - ○ Pictograph (read right to left): ᗡᏒ See | Head of Man
    - • The pictograph Ꮢ is a picture of the head of a man, the ᗡ is a picture of the eye. Combined these mean "man watches" as a shepherd watches over his flock.

Jesus said, "I have called you friends, because I have made known to you everything I have heard from My Father."[14] To be a friend is to watch over another with a loving eye, to show concern for others like a shepherd with his flock.

How does Jesus interact with those who feel despised and hated by their community, including their families? He moves *toward* those on the fringes of society with compassion in His heart:

- • "Jesus, *moved with compassion,* put forth his hand and touched them . . ."[15]
- • "Jesus . . . *moved with compassion* . . . healed their sick."[16]
- • "Jesus . . . *moved with compassion* . . . began to teach them many things."[17]
- • "When he saw the multitudes, He was *moved with compassion* for them because they were faint and scattered abroad, a sheep having no shepherd."[18]

He deals with outcasts *very differently* than He deals with religious people who claim to be God's elect. A perfect example is the story of Zacchaeus. As the chief tax collector, he was considered the worst of the worst, the most hated member of society. In the story, we discover Zacchaeus is too short to see over the crowd, so he climbs up in a sycamore tree to catch a glimpse of Jesus passing through his town. Jesus looks up and says, "Zacchaeus, hurry and come down because today I must stay at your house!"[19]

Just like the first word of the Bible tells the story of the Gospel letter-by-letter,[20] Jesus has a way of telling the end before the beginning. Before He meets Zacchaeus on the road, He tells a story to those "who had great confidence in their own righteousness and scorned everyone else."

> Two men went to the Temple to pray. One was a Pharisee, and the other was a despised tax collector. The Pharisee stood by himself and prayed this prayer: "I thank you, God, that I am not like other people—cheaters, sinners, adulterers. I'm certainly not like that tax collector! I fast twice a week, and I give you a tenth of my income."
>
> But the tax collector stood at a distance and dared not even lift his eyes to heaven as he prayed. Instead, he beat his chest in sorrow, saying, "O God, be merciful to me, for I am a sinner". "I tell you, this sinner, not the Pharisee, returned home justified before God. For those who exalt themselves will be humbled, and those who humble themselves will be exalted."[21]

Jesus challenges religious people not to sit in seats of honor when they throw a banquet, but to invite the poor, the crippled, the blind, and the lame. He tells them *not* to invite their friends, brothers, relatives, and rich neighbors over for lunch. Instead, He tells them to "go out in the country lanes and behind the hedges and urge anyone you find to come, so that the house will be full."[22]

Jesus challenges us today:

If you love those who love you, what credit is that to you? Even sinners love those who love them. If you do what is good to those who are good to you, what credit is that to you? Even sinners do that. . . . But love your enemies, do what is good . . . expecting nothing in return. Then your reward will be great, and you will sons of the Most High.[23]

He asks us, "Why do you look at the speck in your brother's eye, but don't notice the log in your own eye? Or how can you say to your brother, 'Brother, let me take out the speck that is in your eye,' when you yourself don't see the log in your eye? Hypocrite! First take the log out of your eye, and then you will see clearly to take out the speck in your brother's eye."[24]

If we think we have no log, we are the ones who have an incorrect view of ourselves. If we treat others as if we are better than them, we are not able to help them. God will oppose us, and *we do not want God as our opponent*.[25] We must remember Christ was misunderstood, mislabeled, bullied, and abused by *religious people*, not misfits—for He came as a misfit and died for the misfits. He arrived on the earth as a tiny flame. He doesn't snuff out the flickering lights of the hurting and broken; He breathes life in them.

When we behave as if those who believe in gender ideology are "bad" and we are "good"—we could easily put out a smoldering wick. Jesus invites them to *know* Him—and when they have an encounter with His love, they will be changed forever. As therapist Charla Janecka says, *"It's not my job to change them. My job is to speak identity and point them to Jesus."*[26]

When I look back on the fringy, disheveled street preachers who rescued me from the snubby noses of haute couture designers, I have to smile. The upper-echelon fashionistas looked down on me for my pimples or bruises or weight, while the street preachers modeled true friendship. They taught me what *living faith* looks like. They reached out to a girl who was lost and confused, and invited themselves to my house when I was living in a country where I knew hardly anyone and didn't have a friend in sight. The people at the Wellspring Retreat Center did the same for me; they cared for me and did not judge me. Because of that, I learned a tremendous amount from them about the true meaning of love. Being a Christian is not thumping your chest in zeal of your own righteousness; it's being a shepherd looking for the lost.

When Jesus invited himself to Zacchaeus's house, the people were displeased. "All who saw it began to complain, 'He's gone to lodge with a sinful man!'" But Zacchaeus was excited and filled with joy. When Jesus came to his home, Zacchaeus told Him he would give half his wealth to the poor and promised to pay back those he cheated on their taxes *four times* as much. "Today salvation has come to this house," Jesus told him, "Because he too is a son of Abraham. For the Son of Man has come to seek and to save the lost."[27]

Jesus tells us to invite hurting people into our homes because that's what He does. It makes me wonder how many sons of Abraham we are missing out on knowing because we look down on others who are different than us. Mark my words: It will be *our* pride—not that of the lost—that will hamper our ability to bring others into the kingdom like Jesus did. We will have to check judgment at the door, cast it away like a burnt cigarette, and clear the smoke out of our eyes. We will have to look at the innocence inside of people and call them by their true name.

To be a friend is not just a noun; it is an *action*. It means *to guide one in the sheepfold where they can find spiritual sustenance*. This is what Philip did when he obeyed what the angel told him to do and ran alongside the chariot to get to know the eunuch. And this is what Jesus models for us, every single time.

In order to change our lenses about God's beloved children in the LGBTQ+ community, we will need to go out of our way to show messy grace. We will need to invite people into our homes—or go to their homes—to know them more deeply. Where there is rejection, we have the opportunity to show unconditional love and acceptance. Where there is confusion, we are to offer clarity, but not with judgment.

Telling the Truth in Love

One of the biggest reasons Christians are fearful of talking about gender is that they don't want to offend anybody. But that's ridiculous. Jesus offended people all the time for telling them the truth. It's all in how you say it. Sometimes I feel like I can hear my mentor Devi's voice coaxing me through the hard parts of my life. Her voice is gentle and kind, and it always woos me to wisdom.

With all the cruel words being flung about, written on posters, chanted in the streets, and flailed at people on social media, the tone of women's voices in this hour is extremely important. The greatest mandate of all is to love. As 1 Corinthians 3:14 says, we can have all this knowledge, but if we don't have love, we are just a loud gong or a clanging symbol. Both the Lady Folly and Lady Wisdom cry out in the public square for people to follow them. But wise people sound different than fools. They listen for a long time. They honor others above themselves. And they tell you the truth.

As Paul David Tripp writes:

> To love truth, you have to be committed to love, and to love love, you have to be committed to truth.
>
> The biblical call to love will never force you to trim, deny, or bend the truth, and the biblical call to truth will never ask you to abandon God's call to love your neighbor.
>
> Truth isn't mean and love isn't dishonest. They are two sides of the same righteous agenda that longs for the spiritual welfare of another. Truth not spoken in love ceases to be truth because it gets bent and twisted by other human agendas, and love that abandons the truth ceases to be love because it forsakes what is best for the person when it has been corrupted by other motives.
>
> Today you are called to loving honesty and honest love. You will be tempted to let one or the other slip from your hands. Pray for the help of the One who remained fully committed to both, even to death.[28]

Love has to be kind, or it is not love. So as we stand for truth about the meaning of the word *woman*, we must be as gentle and patient as God is with us. We just have to live it. It doesn't matter if we know our name means "Breath of Fire" if we breathe fire on people with our words. It makes no difference to know *Elohim* means Shepherd if we are just storing up knowledge for ourselves. As the sages say, "We don't pronounce God's name with our lips. We proclaim it with our lives." [29]

The word friend means shepherd too. Now go be one.

Chapter Thirteen

I Am a Sister

The Hearth around the Fire

There is power to words with history, both good and ill.
To me, the word "Woman" has its own power,
and I do not believe we can meaningfully analyze
the harm done to women and girls without using
language that has concrete meaning.
—*J. K. Rowling*[1]

I want to be extremely clear about this, because it is important that we make this distinction: Trans activists *do not* represent the majority of the LGBTQ+ community, which includes decent people who simply want to not be discriminated against based on their sexuality. I agree they should have these rights. They are people just like us, and if they want to spend their lives loving someone in a legally bound commitment, they deserve legal protection like we all do. Likewise, no one should be fired or harassed for being gay or trans.

Trans *activists*, on the other hand, want men in women's prisons, boys in girls' locker rooms, government funding for sex change operations, and the removal of safeguards for gender transition, even for minors. Since this ideology puts girls at risk, and the government won't pay for women to get breast implants, this is where I disagree. In healthy environments, people can love one another and disagree at the same time. But trans *activists* do not practice what they preach. "Kindness, diversity, and inclusion" are bywords that mean, "If you don't agree with gender fluidity, you are *transphobic*. I will clap my hands over my ears and scream before I will listen to what you have to say." Just as there are wicked people who call themselves God's elect, so there are always bad eggs in the bunch.

This is precisely why truly pro-women people like us have banded together with feminists like J. K. Rowling, Kathleen Stock, and Helen Joyce. Suddenly, Christian conservatives and rational feminist scholars and journalists are joining arms. On this issue, we meet on common ground. We believe man and woman are clearly distinguished by sex; we believe male and female are immutable and clearly definable. Furthermore, we stand as a strong wall of protection against this movement—on behalf of the children it touches.

Brothers and Sisters Bound by Covenant

We are brothers and sisters bound by a covenant to protect the children, and no matter how much backlash we get for speaking out, we will not move. In Hebrew, the root of the words brother and sister is the same. Brothers and sisters are a "Strong Wall of Protection." Their name literally means "A Hearth around a Fire." They represent the highest calling of *Elohim*—unity.

- **Root of Sister and Brother: achach[2] אחה**
  - **Unity**
  - **Bring Together; Togetherness**
  - **Fireplace; Protect**
    - **Hearth: a dividing wall that protects the family from fire.**
- **SISTER: 'âchôwth אָחוֹת [3]**
  - **Intimate Connection**
- **BROTHER: 'âch אָח [4]**
  - **Strong Wall**
  - **One who stand between the enemy and the family, a protector.**

Brothers stand between us and anything that might hurt us. By nature, they protect. Sisters also protect, and together we are a force of unity. Unfortunately, the nature of this movement divides brother from sister, mother from father, male from female. It is divisive. And in a world where we already have enough division, we need to seek common ground. The adults in the room need to be the hearth protecting the children from the embers of this fire. When brothers and sisters stand together in unity, they are a shield of safety. This is good. And this is what men like Jordan Peterson and women like Helen Joyce, Kathleen Stock, and J. K. Rowling are doing. Their positions are not based on religion, yet together we stand.

As the *Telegraph* wrote of Joyce's book *Trans*, "A grown up has entered the room." Richard Dawkins called her book "Frighteningly necessary."[5] Yet we must be prepared for battle, because if you stand firm against the demonic language that warps our gender, you will be attacked.

When the Truth Hurts

There are few people who have been bashed so brutally as J. K. Rowling, the once-beloved author of the bestselling *Harry Potter* series, who has laid herself on the altar. When she said "woman" needs a concrete definition, her fans became her opponents. In a continuous stream on X, formerly known as Twitter, trans allies threatened to rape, beat, maim, and kill her.

Whether it be thought reform, cancel culture, or just idolatry, it is revolting to read the accounts of how Rowling and others have been treated. From burning books to nasty sexual slurs to leaving human feces at professors' doors, many of the people in this movement are driven by misogyny, the hatred of women. If you don't agree with them, they excommunicate you. Yet *any voice* whose goal is to shame and humiliate women who speak the truth is not a voice to be listened to.

Here's the bottom line: Womanhood cannot be canceled because it's in our veins. The *action* of womanhood is standing up for the vulnerable, and that includes trans people *and* the girls that trans activists' laws *do not* protect.

A longtime donor and advocate for LGBTQ+ causes, Rowling has said that female-only spaces should exclude males for purposes of protection. For this, she has been called "a cunt, a bitch, a TERF" who deserves "cancelling, punching, and death." "Hundreds of trans activists have threatened to beat, rape, assassinate and bomb me," she says.[6]

"It isn't enough for women to be trans allies. Women must accept and admit that there is no material difference between trans women and themselves," she writes in response to her book-burning.[7] Unless she repeats the thought-stopper—"Trans women *are* women"—she is met by death threats, which only confirms her concerns about this movement. In the *Witch Trials of J. K. Rowling,* her story is told by Megan-Phelps Roper, a former victim of a Christian cult.[8] It seems we have much in common. Rowling herself is a sexual assault survivor. For women like her, *men and women are not the same*. In her words:

> I stand alongside the brave women and men, gay, straight and trans, who're standing up for freedom of speech and thought, and for the rights and safety of some of the most vulnerable in our society: young gay kids, fragile teenagers, and women who're reliant on and wish to retain their single sex spaces. Polls show those women are in the vast majority, and exclude only those privileged or lucky enough never to have come up against male violence or sexual assault. . . .
>
> Trans people need and deserve protection. Like women, they're most likely to be killed by sexual partners. . . . Like every other domestic abuse and sexual assault survivor I know, I feel nothing but empathy and solidarity with trans women who've been abused by men.

So I want trans women to be safe. At the same time, I do not want to make natal girls and women less safe. When you throw open the doors of bathrooms and changing rooms to any man who believes or feels he's a woman, then you open the door to any and all men who wish to come inside.[9]

For this, she's been told she is *literally killing trans people with her hate*. In Scotland, where she lives, half of the male prisoners currently claiming a trans identity "discovered their true selves" *after* conviction. With "self-ID" laws that claim a man no longer needs a sex change operation to declare himself a woman, he can be incarcerated in a much less threatening environment, the women's prison.[10] Women in prison are no longer safe, which for me is where I stop in my tracks. I have spent a lot of time around women prisoners, and I know that the majority have already suffered enough violence and silencing in their lives. Rowling says:

Vulnerable women in Scotland are being told "their concerns, their fears, their despair, must take second place to the feelings of men who identify as women. Politicians who say there is no clash of rights have no idea about the lives of women in situations they will never face."[11]

Her crime is believing that biological sex matters in cases of law and policy. As a victim of sexual violence herself, she refuses to separate her soul from her biological reality in order to make others feel better about themselves.

The acclaimed author, researcher, and philosopher Kathleen Stock has endured similar treatment in academia, despite her self-proclamation as a lesbian feminist. As a philosophy professor at the University of Sussex in Great Britain and the author of *Material Girls: Why Reality Matters for Feminism*, she believes that people cannot change their biological sex.[12] In order to protect *all* people, she argues that biological reality should take precedence over gender identity in law.

Like Rowling and myself, when she saw "self-ID" as the only necessary criteria for men entering women's private spaces, she spoke up.
Because a man says he's a woman, he is one? we ask—*and this trans-
lates to law?* A man no longer has to go through gender reassignment
surgeries, treatments, and years of therapy to change his birth certifi-
cate and passport? With this philosophy funneling from the top ranks
of government and academia to young people at the bottom, Stock
took a stand—as most philosophers and psychiatrists worth that title
would. A rare breed, Stock has paid the penalty for her "misbehavior."
She states:

> Gender identity theory is egregiously false. It is terrible, pseudo
> philosophy and would fail a first-year essay. As a philosopher
> who cares about logic and truth at a basic level, I couldn't believe
> that all these academics were just waving it through.
>
> I'm a lesbian and a feminist. I assumed that academic femi-
> nists were covering women and girls' rights and I didn't need to
> get involved. I started to see that they were not only *not* covering
> it, but they were also actively undermining women's rights in
> the name of feminism, and there were all these knock-on conse-
> quences for lesbians.[13]

The new fad of biological men expecting access to lesbian communities deeply offends her. Women who uphold lesbian-only spaces are
now being called TERFS. In her usual bluntness, she says, "lesbians
don't have penises." Stock describes this activist movement as "unbe-
lievably narcissistic, me, me, me. . . ." Giving males who have twice
the upper body strength as females free reign in changing rooms is like
letting people flood the border with drugs and trafficking—until girls
get maimed. Once the trans activists have children who are raped or
mutilated, will they admit that feelings *don't* trump biology?

Aside from Kathleen Stock's stance on single-sex spaces, like the
rest of us she is very concerned that same-sex attracted youth are being
ushered along a road that leads to genital mutilation and sterilization.

For these beliefs, Stock was intimidated so severely by students on her campus that she had to go into hiding. The threats come from trans activists, most of whom are not even trans people.

Let's get this straight (no pun intended). She is a left-wing lesbian, part of the LGBTQ+ community, and she believes women's spaces should be female-only, which you would think most feminists would agree with—but not anymore. Crowds of students at the University of Sussex endlessly harassed her for this, requiring police protection which the university did not supply. She was told she'd have to teach from home. For believing in two genders and *not wanting to have sex with a man*, Stock has been publicly brutalized. Their intimidation put her through an awful few years, including a university investigation into "institutional transphobia."[14] She was cleared of any such claims, but the university upheld the activists and essentially muted her. After eighteen years devoted to teaching, she left, and they lost a brilliant professor. But at least she knows she's a woman. Stock wishes we could all just get back to reality.

These brave leaders are very supportive of trans people, very concerned about same-sex-attracted youth, and show no bigotry whatsoever in their speaking or writing. Their beliefs are not based on religion. Nevertheless, they are *all* called *right wing bigots and transphobes* for simply saying that biological sex is fixed and that self-ID is dangerous and misleading.

When Lies Become Laws

Although there is not a hint of discrimination in the tenor of these voices, anyone who believes what 99 percent of the people on the planet believe—there are two sexes—is punished. People are losing their jobs, awards, titles, and families over this. This kind of discrimination is so arbitrary, yet the courts are upholding it. Researcher Maya Forstater, who lost her job for supposedly "transphobic" tweets, took her case to court and asked the judge if her philosophical belief that sex is determined by biology is protected in law. The judge ruled that her beliefs were *not* protected by law and upheld her firing.[15] After years of fighting in courts in the United Kingdom, she finally won the *right to think critically about gender*.[16]

Would the United States uphold her right to think? Especially with a judge on the Supreme Court who acts as if the definition of woman is too hard to nail down? Truth be told, it doesn't seem so. A teacher in California recently lost her job for not allowing boys in girls locker rooms, a college lacrosse coach who spoke against trans athletes competing in female sports was "reassigned" to a desk job, and Google fired an engineer for questioning its diversity policies by pointing out the psychological differences between men and women.[17]

Helen Joyce follows the money in her book, where she points out that when legendary tennis player Martina Navratilova opposed the inclusion of men in women's sports, Athlete Ally dropped her as an ambassador. This organization is funded by Arcus, which partners with President Joe Biden's personal foundation on the Advancing Acceptance initiative that promotes early childhood transition.[18]

Regardless of the true needs of trans people and the desires of the public to protect same-sex spaces, the United States government is being funded by billionaires who funnel "education programs that describe innate gender identity as scientific fact, and sexual orientation as about which genders you are attracted to. And they present trans-identified pupils gaining access to spaces intended for the oppose sex as a civil-rights cause."[19] Dr. Rachel Levine, a transgender "woman" who calls mothers "egg-producers," is the Biden administration's Assistant Secretary of Health.[20] This is a man who doesn't seem healthy in the least. Hiring a man who calls himself a woman was *an intentional decision* on the part of this administration to infiltrate every public school in this nation with this doctrine, from the government down.

By idolizing their ideology, they raise themselves up as the epitome of goodness, superior to *Elohim*. This leads us to another tenet of thought reform, according to Lifton: mystical manipulation.

Mystical Manipulation
(Planned Spontaneity) [21]

- The group has a higher purpose than others outside the group. This may be altruistic, such as saving the world or helping people in need. All things are linked to this higher purpose.
- Seeks to promote specific patterns of behavior and emotion in such a way that it appears to have arisen spontaneously from within the environment, while it actually has been carefully orchestrated.
- Totalist leaders claim to be agents chosen by God, history, or some supernatural force, to carry out the *mystical imperative*.
- The "principles" (God-centered or otherwise) can be put forcibly and claimed exclusively, so that the cult and its beliefs become the only true path to enlightenment.
- The individual then develops the psychology of the pawn, and participates actively in the manipulation of others.
- The leader who becomes the center of the mystical manipulation (or the person in whose name it is done) is more real than God.
- Legitimizes the deception used to recruit new members and/or raise funds.

The Government Is on Our Shoulders

Christians who stay out of politics are fools. When we do, lies become laws. The verse we all repeat at Christmas should wake us up: "For a child will be born to us, a son will be given to us; And *the government* will rest on His shoulders; And His name will be called Wonderful Counselor, Mighty God, Eternal Father, Prince of Peace."[22] Wonderful counselors, arise! What the detransitioner Shape Shifter wanted was a loving, compassionate hug—and for someone to tell him the truth: Male-to-female transitioning is impossible. No matter what Shape Shifter wears, his body parts were still valuable, and keeping them was best for his mental health. His words ring in the air: "I wish someone had protected me from myself." This is a call to arms for the adults in the room. When a teenager's brain is finished developing at age twenty-five or thirty, lifelong decisions can be made with extreme precaution and warnings about risks and side-effects.[23]

Pretending that being a Christian is attending church on Sundays, writing Bible study after Bible study, having conference after conference, and not taking a stand against the cultural crisis targeting effeminate boys and tough girls in our nation is spiritual debauchery. It denies the meaning of Christ's name, who said the Kingdom of Heaven belongs to the children. The government will rest on His shoulders. As the Body of Christ, those shoulders are *our shoulders*. As those who are commanded to speak up for the vulnerable, we have a responsibility in this—not only to define gender for the kids, but also to take a stand about right and wrong.

As brothers and sisters, we are the "hearth that prevents the fire from destroying the house." We must call out in the streets that gender ideology is destructive. Are we going to stand by while trans activists, the persecutors of today's world, threaten us with silence? No. We're not. This is not a time to stand down. This is a time to rise up.

In Washington state, if a child believes he or she is trans and the parents object, the state will go so far as to take the child away from the parents and proceed with medical transition, paid for by the government, all without the parents even knowing where their child is.[24] This happened to a mother who has been raising the alarm ever since. The state accused her of child abuse for not affirming her daughter's "trans identity." As a result, the state took the girl down the road to medicalization, the testosterone wreaked havoc on her mind, and she committed suicide as a ward of the state.[25]

In Canada, a man *went to jail* for not referring to his daughter as a boy with masculine pronouns. His daughter's transition started at school, where teachers exposed her to transgender "educational materials." At eleven years old, she "realized she was male" and school authorities changed her name. When the father did not consent to gender treatment, the courts said that "any attempt to pressure his child to change course would be considered a form of family violence, punishable by law." The judge called the father's failure to approve of testosterone "troublesome" and demanded he use male pronouns when referring to his little girl. The father did not comply. He lost the case, went to jail, and the mother is proceeding with the daughter's transition. He said tearfully:

> "I had a perfectly healthy child a year ago, and that perfectly healthy child has been altered and destroyed for absolutely no good reason. She can never go back to being a girl in the healthy body that she should have had," he said. "She's going to forever have a lower voice. She'll forever have to shave because of facial hair. She won't be able to have children." The father has accused the government of "state-sponsored child abuse."[26]

One of the worst cases is fourteen-year-old Sage in Maryland, whose school counselors met with her *eight times* without her parents' knowledge, encouraging her to proclaim a "male identity." Sage believed her parents were "misgendering her" and took on the name Draco. She ran away from home to meet someone she had met online. That person turned out to be a thirty-two-year-old sex offender who violently raped her, enjoyed "strangling her but not quite to death," and trafficked her in a locked room to so many men she lost count. When authorities rescued her, the Baltimore courts refused to return Sage to her family under the claim that they didn't support her "male identity," yet social services had already cleared the family of such claims.

During the investigation, Sage's seventy-two-year-old grandfather, overcome with emotion, accidently called his granddaughter "she." The judge claimed they were causing emotional abuse by not using "legally required masculine pronouns when referring to Draco." The Baltimore City Department of Juvenile Services placed her in a "secure therapeutic facility" that accommodated her "desire to live as a trans male," which meant placing her with Baltimore's most troubled boys.

Sage cut off her monitoring bracelet and fled. The State Police of Texas Human Trafficking found her beaten, raped, and trafficked *again*. They immediately returned the terrified girl to her parents. Do you know what Sage says now? "I was never a boy. I just wanted friends."[27]

Now we are understanding what it means for the dictionary to change the definition of male and female. Now we are understanding what it means for lies to become laws.

Instead of addressing what is boiling under the surface, these kids are being told to live a lie. The chasm between their brainwashed beliefs and *the reality of sex* only causes more trauma.

Gender ideology checks every box of a thought reform movement. Cisgender, trans man, trans woman, gender "affirming" care, gender fluid, gender queer, gender variant, misgendering, dead-naming, "gen-der-*confirmation* surgery," and "trans-exclusionist hate groups"—these are loaded terms our government demands that we use without question. It is groupthink created by psychologists and philosophers who have no grounding in truth, science, or God. The culture wants us to adopt it, teach it to our children, and speak it—and will punish us if we don't. But when we speak it, we are speaking lies.

This is the key point we must face: Philosophical beliefs are no longer guaranteed protection under the law. That includes religious beliefs. This is where things get serious. When people are silenced, shunned, and canceled for their beliefs, we are experiencing brainwash-ing and mind control. When someone gets fired for believing females are women and males are men—that's communism. Punishing people for their beliefs and eliminating them from public discourse are tactics used by Mao Zedong and Adolf Hitler. They want us to be robots who repeat the party line, even if it's untrue—which is why, I'm sure, so many Christians in leadership have muted their mouths on issues *so biblical it's ridiculous.*

Lifton called this "The Demand for Purity":

The Demand for Purity [28]

- The world becomes sharply divided into the pure and the impure, the absolutely good (the group/ideology) and the absolutely evil (everything outside the group).
- One must continually change or conform to the group "norm."
- Tendencies towards guilt and shame are used as emotional levers for the group's controlling and manipulative influences.
- Once a person has experienced the totalist polarization of good/evil (black/white thinking), he has great difficulty in regaining a more balanced inner sensitivity to the complexities of human morality.
- One must confess when one is not conforming.

I have often considered becoming a university professor in the field of writing and literature, but I have to remind myself that my stance on this would disqualify me, even in Christian universities. Professors who desist have to get "training" in groupthink. Even though I've spent my life engrossed in serving multiethnic, multicultural, at-risk, and underserved people groups, I would have to undergo "inclusion and diversity" training to be sure I repeat the lies propagated by the mob. This is precisely why Jordan Peterson left his tenured position at the University of Toronto, where he originally hoped to be buried.

When Canada made it illegal not to call people by their "preferred pronouns," he knew this would: 1) cause a wave of gender dysphoria—which it did—and 2) limit free speech—which it did. He loved his job; his students loved him. But he didn't believe hiring people based on their race and sexual persuasion was a good formula for a university, so as a philosophy professor, he either had to align himself with his conscience or stay and play. He left. Peterson is a firm voice that the "gender-affirming" doctors are "butchers." He believes the affirmation-only model of therapy is a complete failure and demands for the prosecution of medical personnel for "trans butchery." For this, the College of Psychologists in Ontario threatened to pull his license to practice as a clinical psychologist and ordered he undergo "professional coaching."[29]

This "coaching," which he refused, would "educate him" about supporting an ideology he doesn't believe in. This leads us to another tenet of thought reform used by this movement, which is also used by the Black Lives Matter movement and Critical Race Theory: As a white person, you *must confess* you are racist (though you are not) and make reparations for your evil. People like Peterson must confess their sins and get trained in groupthink to keep their jobs. This is the cult of confession, according to Lifton:

Confession[30]

- "Sin" is defined by the group, not the person.
- Sessions in which one confesses to one's sin are accompanied by patterns of criticism and self-criticism, generally transpiring within small groups with an active and dynamic thrust toward personal change.
- Is an act of symbolic self-surrender.
- Makes it virtually impossible to attain a reasonable balance between worth and humility.
- Often a person will confess to lesser sins while holding on to other secrets (often criticisms/questions/doubts about the group/leaders that may cause them not to advance to a leadership position).

As pressure mounts, people who once felt autonomous in their stance on moral issues are pressed to receive training in this ideology to become better people. If an individual expresses that he or she disagrees with the tenets of the pride movement, woke corporations force an apology. Individual autonomy is a thing of the past; everyone must cooperate with an ideology they do not morally support.

Everyone who stands firm on the basics of biological reality and calls out the gender ideologues lays themselves on the altar. I have experienced this to a *much lesser degree*. If I try to defend myself from false accusations, I am still regarded as a bigot by those who preach "diversity and inclusivity." The worldview of these people is not my own.

And this is essentially the problem. If you believe that God created gender as an immutable fact and profound privilege, you stand in direct opposition to those that don't.

Love and Truth

The last time I had the opportunity to preach in a women's prison, a person undergoing gender transition sat in the front row. I can still see her eyes glued to mine and I can still feel the ache in my heart. We connected. I called her "brother," and we hugged. Those who label me as transphobic do not live inside my soul. I live for an audience of *One*, and I address people as the Holy Spirit directs me.

I grew up in the entertainment industry. As a young model, I was surrounded by gay and lesbian people who were very kind to me. I owe much of my compassion for people in the homosexual lifestyle to my experiences as a model. I spent many hours listening to their stories of rejection by their families—especially their fathers. There's something that happens when someone does your hair; you swap stories, and sometimes there are tears. I felt their emotional turmoil, especially in their most valued relationships.

Recently, my daughter Olivia and I were waited on by a drag-queen-by-night, waiter-by-day in a Mexican restaurant. He showed us pictures of himself with massive fake breasts and loads of makeup. He had just experienced a painful breakup with his boyfriend and cried to us at the table. Because he could see the compassion in our eyes, he opened up about his loneliness and told us he drank alone in his room all night to assuage his pain. We spoke to him in gentle, reassuring tones to tell him he was not alone in the world. We can do great harm to people by not accepting them cart-blanche, the way they are right now, with no agenda but to love them.

When I look at people through a clear lens, I don't see *anyone* as trans or lesbian or gay. I see them as *people*. Cared-for, valued sons and daughters. That's all—and in a perfect world, loving them would be enough. But this is no perfect world, and people get angry when someone questions the road they are taking. Some people walked away from Jesus; some people canceled Him. So be it.

Rowling put it this way:

> The idea that women like me, who've been empathetic to trans people for decades, feeling kinship because they're vulnerable in the same way as women. . . . "hate" trans people because they think sex is real and has lived consequences—is a nonsense. It isn't hate to speak the truth.
>
> Moreover, the "inclusive" language that calls female people "menstruators" and "people with vulvas" strikes many women as dehumanizing and demeaning. . . . for those of us who've had degrading slurs spat at us by violent men, [this language] is not neutral, it's hostile and alienating.[31]

She is right. I feel the same about the "cisgender" label. I am not "cis." I am a woman, a daughter, a wife, a mother, a sister, a friend, and an advocate. If "self-ID" is so important, then that should also be respected.

Chapter Fourteen

I Am the Voice of the Bride

We Will Rise

*God created the only distinction we'll ever need
when he created man and woman.*
—*Riley Gaines*[1]

In 1969, twelve women gathered around a table in New York City. Using consciousness-raising, a technique borrowed from Mao in China, their aim was to stir up discontent among women. No longer did they want women to believe that marriage, home, and family should be the center of their constructive energies. Together, they declared the following manifesto:

"Why are we here today?" the chairwoman asked.
"To make a revolution," they answered.
"What kind of revolution?" she replied.
"The Cultural Revolution," they chanted.
"And how do we make Cultural Revolution?" she demanded.
"By destroying the American family!" they answered.
"How do we destroy the family?" she came back.
"By destroying the American patriarch," they cried exuberantly.
"And how do we destroy the American patriarch?" she probed.
"By taking away his power!"

"How do we do that?"

"By destroying monogamy!" they shouted.

"How can we destroy monogamy?"

"By promoting promiscuity, eroticism, prostitution, abortion, and homosexuality!" they resounded.[2]

These were the fire-breathing dragons who launched the age of raunch. Second-wave feminism was born with a guttural cry. They proceeded to discuss how to advance these initiatives by gathering small groups of women around the nation. In these small groups, women complained about their hard work of homemaking and desire to be free of motherhood. They talked about being oppressed and silenced and bound to the home, while their husbands did exciting work in the corporate marketplace and public sphere. To achieve their dreams of being free from the shackles of home life, children needed to be eliminated. They were a ball and chain. And the real enemy was men.

One of the founders of second-wave feminism was Kate Millet. Her sister Mallory was there on that fateful day in New York City. Today, she says these women desired *nothing less than utter deconstruction of Western society*. Their plan was to invade *every American institution*. Everyone had to be penetrated: The media, education system, K-12, school boards, universities, the judiciary, legislature, executive branches, and even the library system. As Carrie Gress explains in *The End of Woman*, they acquired government funding that ushered Women's Studies into colleges, which acted like feminist brainwashing sessions. The women who graduated from those programs are now running our government. Phyllis Chesler confirms Mallory's story in her book *Politically Incorrect Feminist: Creating a Movement with Bitches, Lunatics, Dykes, Prodigies, Warriors, and Wonder Women*. She calls them "the lost girls."[3]

Today, young women across America can get a master's or even doctorate degree in women's studies with these women as their teachers and scribes. They can even get a doctorate in gender studies and teach the next generation of our great-great-granddaughters these lies. The only problem is, when they graduate, they won't know what a woman is.

This is the power of words to tear a nation down.

The failure of the feminist movement to unite women is glaring at us in neon lights. When women no longer protect developing teen girls, vulnerable boys, and women in prison who have already been subject to abuse, they can no longer pretend to be helping women. Despite the desires of most of them to get it right, it's dead wrong. Driven by child sacrifice, misogynism, and misandry (man-hating, a word they won't teach), this movement is crushingly deceitful. The transgender movement driven into our public-school systems and funneled through media is the final wave to help them accomplish their unrighteous agenda—the annihilation of gender.

The Woman Rides the Beast

The Scarlet Harlot in the Book of Revelations is seated on seven mountains that represent world systems. With the same allegiances as the cult prostitutes, she uses domineering sexuality to gain power and control over men. She steals their role as fathers and husbands and takes dominion over them. Through emasculating them, she gains the illusion of power. This seductress dehumanizes children and revels in the blood of the saints. Her elevated dimorphic sexuality is revealed in her ability to shift genders. Like the goddess of sexuality rampant in Old Testament culture, she turns men into women and women into men. She is the great prostitute of Babylon, the personification of the adulteress. Not only does she lead men to the noose, but she controls the world systems of government. The seven mountains upon which she sits, as Lance Wallnau describes them, are:

1. Arts / Entertainment
2. Government / Law
3. Education
4. Media / News (including social media)
5. Family
6. Religion
7. Business / Science / Medical / Tech / Finance[4]

All of these have been massively infiltrated and governed by the female spirit Revelation talks about.[5] In author Deana Morgan's words, "She deceives all the inhabitants of the earth within her influence, till they become the walking dead due to their stupid and blind submission. But the remnant [of God's elect] do not follow under her control."[6]

The Government Shall Rest upon His Shoulders

As a nation, we have bitten the apple, and its juice is dripping down our chins. *God is a liar! He's trying to limit what we can do!* This agreement with the enemy has flung open the door to children's classrooms, where our government abolished school-led prayer and made posting the Ten Commandments on the wall illegal in 1980. No longer would little boys be taught to *remember God* and little girls be taught to *be guardians of the Word.*

There is a god of the Old Testament named *Baal.* As Jonathan Cahn pulls back the veil in his book *Return of the Gods,* Baal makes people forget.[7] The religious heritage and spiritual foundation of America is being dismantled. The goal is for it to be *forgotten.*

This has happened to people throughout history. God calls His beloved people she / her and they flourish under the banner of His love, and then they prostitute themselves like the adulteress and break His loving heart. Again and again, godly leaders would arise, and the people remember the God who made them and once delivered them from slavery.

After the entrance of *Baal* comes the entrance of *Molech,* the god of child sacrifice. On his heels comes the seductress *Ashtoreth,* who represents the Queen of Heaven, the woman who rides the scarlet beast. She often appeared with the symbols of the moon, the sun, and the stars and is known by her Mesopotamian name Ishtar.[8] She was the original gender bender. With her sexual festivals in June, she was driven by envy and hatred of men. Called the wicked woman in Revelation 2:20, she worshiped like Jezebel and sought to destroy those who questioned her.[9] As the prostitute goddess who removed sexuality from the bonds of marriage, her spirit is the one who is defeated by the Bride of Christ.

When the Gospel of Jesus Christ swept through the Roman empire, goddess worship was driven out, abolished, and became a thing of the past. Yet those gods have returned to American soil. Only one thing will drive them out. The Gospel wiped them out once, and it can do it again.[10]

The Power of the Gospel to Unite Man and Woman

When Adam and Eve sinned, they both tried blaming each other and blaming God, but neither way helped them. If we get defensive and refuse to take an honest look at the ways we've forgotten our name, we will miss the moment that bears the most fruit: The key is in the humbling. When we are in the Refiner's fire, if we bow low in humility, only then can we rise in wisdom—and wisdom will tell us to go back to the beginning and try it God's way. The way of *Elohim* is the way of unity, and that is how we are going to take back our names. The way of humility is the way of surrender.

Now is the prime opportunity to turn, remember, and act. But it takes *surrender*. It takes admitting the Church got it wrong and that forced submission was the least Christlike manner for man to express himself. It takes admitting ungodly men have oppressed and wounded the weaker sex; women *are* more vulnerable, and our voices matter. It takes clarity that God doesn't just hate divorce; more so, He hates violence against women who are called the Daughters of His Eye. He detests pride and arrogance the most (see Proverbs 8:13).

The feminist marchers, right, left, far left—must look in the mirror too. Why are they fighting for men in our bathrooms? What first-world privilege they have! All their energy is expended on infighting and woefully misused—but it can be redirected towards truly helping women. Women in third-world nations are fighting to survive, fighting off their oppressors, fighting to feed their children. Meanwhile American women are fighting one another, banishing men to a subordinate position, castrating them, and calling them women.

After all this shouting and winning rights for women, why are women in America still so unhappy? Why are the largest number of girls in human history turning against femaleness? Why are children addicted to antidepressants like cigarettes? Where is the peace promised by women's "liberation"? Seventy percent of marriages in the United States end in divorce. Women may have positions in the boardroom, but their independence—instead of *interdependence*—is a dagger of separateness in their bedrooms. Did freedom really come from mantras like "Smash the Patriarchy" and "These Boots Were Made for Stomping"? How has feminism hurt men, women, children, God, family, faith, and cracked the foundations of this great nation? How did women speak against the human family and tear it down with their own hands? How did they not realize they could have won men another way?

The first female prime minister of Italy, Georgia Meloni, will not back down on defending the family unit. She stands firm, her face like flint:

We will defend the value of the human being. Every single human being. Because each of us has a unique genetic code that is unrepeatable, and like it or not, that is sacred. We will defend it. We will defend God, country, and family.[11]

The American women who have funneled lies about femininity into the world need to wipe their adulterous mouths and start speaking life with their lips. They need to take care of their homes, husbands, sons, daughters, mothers, fathers, grandmothers, and grandfathers. And they need, like *La Donna and La Nonna* of Italy—the mothers and grandmothers—to lead the way.

The Restoration of the Family

But women *cannot, will not, and should not* attempt to turn the tide of this spirit alone. It will take brothers and sisters, a wall of unity, a hearth around the fire ♂ ♀. The real movement of women who will turn this nation around does not demean men; it upholds them. It appreciates them. It relies on them. We are not goddesses to be worshiped; in God's design, no one dominates. Like *Elohim*, we are to be ordered in perfect unity.

The most powerful antivirus that will disintegrate this ideology is the restoration of the family. At a time like this, we must remember the meaning of our gendered names. We will need the strong shoulders of men and the open eyes of women to teach the next generation the true purpose of biological sex and gender, meaning *masculinity and femininity* and the beauty they behold.

Jesus calls us "the salt of the earth." Salt is a preservative. Without it, food is tasteless and meat rots. By calling us salt He means we will preserve His name, His *shem*, and His lineage. It is up to us to preserve the meaning of God-given gender for this generation. It is up to us to answer the question of the Ethiopian eunuch: *How can I understand this unless someone explains it to me correctly?* It is up to us to know how to answer the question, "What is a Woman?"

It is up to us teach biblical gender identity very, very clearly. It is imperative that we do this. The family is at stake—and the family is the first institution God created that is designed to bring life.

In God's design, we are male and female, man and woman, fathers and mothers, husbands and wives, sons and daughters, brothers and sisters. The male remembers God's ways and passes them on to his children. The female brings life and is the guardian of the home. Man and woman together spell YaH; they are the hand and breath of fire. The father is the benevolent counselor and chief of the tribe. The mother is the strong water-giver and the glue that bonds the family. The son is the arrow warrior, the afflicted one chosen to die on our behalf. The daughter is the apple of his eye, the one he dies to save. Both sons and daughters are builders and repairers in Scripture. They are the hearth around the fire. Sisters are a united force bound by covenant, and brothers are strong barriers of protection. They are *establishers* who will preserve the family line and carry on our legacy.

And our King is coming in glory for His Bride. We are united and forever joined. These are gendered relationships that cannot be forgotten.

The next generation of sons and daughters have everything they need to reestablish truth in our families, schools, and nations—if they do it as *one solid wall*. Not only are young people naturally rising to this, but they are fully equipped to restore the meaning of gender in a way which the older ones are not. Today, young people who follow Jesus can be fearless, vocal influencers who are not easily duped. Because of the internet, they are more able to expose the lies of the enemy and spread the Gospel than any generation before them.

The sons and daughters will prophesy, and they will be given the power and authority to shield the legacy of the family if we teach them to. They are our treasured possession; they have everything they need to be world-changers in their generation. They will be the ones to turn the tide and drive out these demons with the Gospel, but we must prepare them for this calling.

Sister, This Is Your Time to Rise

We must never give up fighting for the family because it is the key to the restoration of our society. We are defenders of freedom in America, defenders of life, liberty, and the pursuit of happiness. We are a nation founded on the tenets of freedom, and we don't back down easily.

When children are given far too many rights to make decisions with long-term consequences, you won't find many American women sitting in their seats. Women are rising. You will see them in school board meetings behind the microphone when a few years ago they wouldn't have dreamt of it. You will find them wearing t-shirts that say "WOMAN: Adult Human Female" in the grocery store. You will find them igniting fury as men in sports steal their daughters' victories. You will find them raising the alarm when men are awarded "Woman of the Year." You will see them taking to social media and combatting the idea that woman is an outfit. You will see them vowing to spend the rest of their lives protecting female prisoners. You will see them as sisters—and suddenly the dividing lines between us disintegrate.

When we return to the original meaning of our name—woman—we will remember who we are. In the oldest definition known to man, woman is an advocate, a stabilizer, and a rescuer. She is the helper-opposite of man, his border-keeper and life-giver. She is the guardian of the home. She is the glue that keeps the nation together. She stands next to man as the hearth around the fire. She is the voice of the Bride.

Jesus said, "I am the Alpha and Omega, the Beginning and the End, the First and the Last." In Hebrew, these letters are the "the *Aleph* and the *Tuv*." The sister's name begins with the *Aleph* 𐤀 and ends with the *Tuv*, † the Cross—the end of the story. Our name is a pictogram of a strong wall united by covenant. When we stand together, we are a force for change. Men and women in unity represent the *Alpha* and the *Omega*, the beginning and the end.

When women see themselves as sisters who stand together as a solid line of defense to *protect* the family, we are better. The children will only benefit from our solidarity and collective wisdom. As Proverbs says:

> Say unto wisdom, "Thou art my sister," and call understanding thy kinswoman.[12]

A circle of sisters is rising as the voice of the bride. We are bound by a promise to protect the children, and we rise fiercest with brothers at our side. We stand in covenant as a dividing wall separating the enemy from the family. And we know the Gospel will demolish the spirits of gender ideology and drive them out. We know this because our King is coming for His Bride.

The Restoration of Gender

Gender is not only a social construct; it is not about pink and blue, ruffles and lace, or trucks and tractors. In the oldest dictionary imaginable, the unchanging Word, being a woman is an *action*. It's the lifeblood in our veins. For centuries people understood this—and if they are honest, they still do.

If we are truly born *for such a time as this*, the time is now to lift our voices in love-laced thunderous, merciful truth. We *must* teach the purpose of biological sex and make gender beautiful again. We must appreciate *masculinity* and *femininity* in their simple, pure, faultless definitions. If we make sure the next generation understands the high calling of their sex and passes these mysteries onto the next generation, we will have done our duty.

Through the continuation of life, the work of our hands, and the nourishment and protection of both sexes, we expand and multiply. The male carries responsibility; the female carries the home. The male carries the name; the female carries the descendants. The male carries protection; the female carries revelation. Together they carry the family, the Church, the nation, and the world. These are gifts not to be disputed. They are the *privilege* of gender.

Male and female: very good. Nobly, perfectly, abundantly good.

An Army of Women

In Psalm 68:11, we read of an army of women.

> The LORD gave the command;
> a great company of women brought the good news. (Psalm 68:11)

They go forth like a host of angels. The picture is of the *Eshet Chayil*, the Woman of Valor. She carries masculine strength, like an army.

- **EXCELLENT: Chayil**[13] **חיל**
  - **Noun Masculine**
  - **Definition:**
    - **Strength, might, efficiency, ability**
    - **Wealth**
    - **Force, whether of men, means, or other resources**

- An army of wealth, virtue, valor, strength
  □ Band of men (soldiers), company, (great) forces, goods, host, might, power, riches, strength, substance, train
  □ Valiant, virtuous, war, worthy

The Woman Wisdom is valiant, and she is worthy. Like the women who followed Jesus from Galilee to the cross and were the first to see the Risen Christ, these women have resources. They provided for the growing kingdom out of their own means.[14] Together with the men, they were a band of soldiers, a company of great forces, and a host of riches with the strength to drive out any demon and break any chain.

Together as women, "the eyes looking out the windows," we have already won the war. As the verse says, "The Lord gives the command; The women who proclaim the *good* tidings are a great host."[15] What is this host? It is *tsâbâ'* in Hebrew:

- **HOST: tsâbâ' צְבָאָה** [16]
  - Noun Masculine
  - That which goes forth, army, war, warfare
    - Organized army
    - Host (of angels)
    - Of Sun, Moon, and Stars
    - Of Whole Creation
  - War, go out to war, service
  - Appointed time
  - Pictograph: ‎צ‎ב‎ם‎ן Strength | House | Man on Side

The ‎ן‎ is a chase or a hunt with a righteous intent. It is the picture of a man on his side and represents the righteousness of the saints. The ‎ם‎ represents the home, family, and nation. The ‎צ‎ represents God. This army is a "mass of persons organized for war." They are a campaign of soldiers prepared for service. They use their strong arms and strong voice to bring good and not harm to the human family. They announce the Good News and proclaim peace. As we see in this definition, the sun, the moon, and the stars do not belong to the harlot. They belong to us. The men are the sun, the women are the moon, and the stars are our children—as Abraham and Sarah once knew.

This is the purpose of women's voices in this hour. This is the appointed time to organize and go to war on behalf of His beloved people, His chosen Bride.

As strong men lay down their lives to bring us life, women will be their front line against the spiritual forces of darkness and their rear guard at home and abroad. It is time for women to uphold men again, to strengthen them for the days to come.

When man and woman stand together, they will rule and subdue. They will take dominion over the spirits of gender confusion by turning the fathers' hearts back to the children, and the children's hearts back to the fathers. They will return woman to her rightful name: the life-giver. A cry for help. More precious than rubies. They will restore the meaning of gender for future generations and lead a host to Christ.

The King of Kings and His Beloved Bride

In the Book of Revelation, we read the end before the beginning. In Revelation 12:1, we see what's called a great sign appear in Heaven. She is a "'Woman clothed with the sun, with the moon under her feet and a crown of twelve stars on her head. She was pregnant and cried out in labor and agony as she was about to give birth . . . She gave birth to a Son, a male child who is going to rule all nations with an iron rod.' He is placed upon a throne with God."[17] A beast tried to devour her and the child, but failed; so he tries coming after her descendants— those who keep the commands of God and hold firmly to the testimony about Jesus.

The fire-breathing dragon of the harlot is burned in an ash heap. Her governmental authority is destroyed, and the woman who rides the beast is no more. "Hallelujah!" we read, "He has judged the notorious prostitute who corrupted the earth with her sexual immorality; and He has avenged the blood of His saints that was on her hands." A second time they cry "Hallelujah!" and then a third time and a fourth time. "For the wedding of the Lamb has come, and his bride has made herself ready."

We see a picture of this glorious Bride in Isaiah 61:10, where she is clothed with garments of salvation and wrapped in a robe of righteousness. She is dressed in fine linen, bright and pure. She is the children of God adorned with valuable jewels, the ultimate picture of femininity at its finest.

And then we see the Ultimate Man coming to rescue her on a white horse in great chivalry:

> His eyes were like a fiery flame, and many crowns were on His head. He had a name written that no one knows except Himself. He wore a robe stained with blood, and His name is the Word of God. The armies that were in heaven followed Him on white horses, wearing pure white linen. A sharp sword came from His mouth, so that He might strike the nations with it. He will shepherd them with an iron scepter. He will also trample the winepress of the fierce anger of God, the Almighty. And He has a name written on His robe and on His thigh:
> KING OF KINGS
> AND LORD OF LORDS.[18]

In the beginning of this book, we first learned of a Son. Now we come full circle. The Son is coming back for His Bride, and we must be ready to receive Him.

The enemy's strategy to steal our name was just the thing we needed to wake up and put on our battle garments. The woman riding the beast awoke the warrior within us. Like a bride preparing for her wedding day, we are awake, ready, and dressing ourselves in the garments of the King. We are adorning ourselves in the gown we were always meant to wear, adjusting our crowns, and raising our swords. We have taken back our name:

I am not a #NastyWoman. I am Woman Wisdom. I am made in God's image. I am a daughter. I am worth remembering. I am a life-giver. I am a guardian of humanity. I am a wife. I am a mother. I am from the land of the free and the home of the brave. I am an advocate. I am a friend. I am a sister. My name means breath of fire. I am the voice of the bride, and I am ready to rise.

Practical Ways to Take Back Our Name

- **Mentor Younger Women:** Every woman should be mentoring a younger woman and teaching her about her identity in Christ. She will pass this on as a generational legacy that will bear much fruit. Pour into her. Encourage her. Meet for coffee or Zoom and invite her into your home. Take the time to be with her.
- **Stay Connected with a Circle of Sisters:** Surround yourself with faithful women who will pray for you and your family. See below for more info on joining our circle.
- **Watch What You Say:** Choose to bring life with your words. When you mess up, make amends quickly. Practice makes perfect.
- **Make Your Home Your Top Priority:** Create a comfortable, organized, warm environment where the problem of alone-ness is solved and hospitality becomes a way of life.
- **Do unto Others:** Treat people in the Pride community as you'd like to be treated. Focus on their gifts and talents. Call out their identity as daughters, sons, and eunuchs. Keep the door open for relationships. Above all, let them know you love them and are here for them 24/7.
- **Do Not Judge:** When the religious right condemns people for their sexual choices, be like Christ, who stood in the path of their stoning. Pray for them and love them for the long road.
- **Pass It On:** Tell others the meaning of woman, man, male, female, sister, brother, father, mother, son, and daughter. For gifts that memorialize the meaning of our names, go to iama-woman.us.

- **Don't Stand Down:** When it comes to males in female spaces, do not take a knee. Stand up for what is right; defend the right of women and girls to have private changing places, restrooms, and living conditions.
- **Resist and Revolt:** Take a stand against men in women's sports and competitions. Males will continue to injure females and steal their victories if we do not oppose this. This is not a time to be silent. This is a time to speak. Use your voice and your vote to make a difference.
- **Watch Over the Children:** If gender ideology has crept into your public schools, you can stop it. No matter your age and your children's age, you can be a dividing wall and a chamber of protection for young minds. If you put your children in Christian schools, remain vigilant regarding the teaching of human sexuality.
- **Wake Up to Government Control:** Share the information about how thought reform works. Do not partner with agendas that promote transgenderism in young people. To subdue the spirits of gender ideology sweeping across our nation, God's people must pray and push back.
- **Refuse to Bow:** Refuse to allow children to be defined by their sexuality or define others that way. While we must be respectful of others' choices, we do not have to use loaded terms to define people. We are defined by God, period. "What He creates, He names."
- **Familiarize Yourself with Bible Verses about Gender.** For further study, go to iamawoman.us.
- **Love for the Long Road:** Live for an audience of One. If your stance on biblical gender draws persecution and harassment, you are in good company with the prophets and Jesus Himself. Remain firm and immovable.
- **Womanhood Is a Verb, so Treat It Like One:** Be the woman you've read about in this book. Comfort. Support. Rescue. Advocate. Speak up for the vulnerable. Honor men and be

the glue. Teach with love on your lips and grace in your heart. You've got this. I believe in you.

Share This Message

- Challenge your pastor to answer the "What is a Woman?" question. He can invite me to speak on this topic to the congregation. Go to urmore.org/booking for more.
- Gift this book to your women's ministry director, youth leaders, or local business leaders. Carry a few copies in your car to pass this on!
- Be a part of a circle of sisters. To create a united force in your community, we invite you to join or start a Circle of Sisters Book Club or Bible study for mothers, daughters, sisters, and friends. Go to iamawoman.us and https://urmore.org /circleofsisters/ to get started.
- Write a review of the book and email it to support@urmore. org to receive a free gift from our ministry.
- Join our mission to reach underprivileged girls, disadvantaged communities, and incarcerated women with this message. Go to urmore.org/donate to join forces with us to reach women and girls around the world and teach them their value, identity, and purpose in Christ.

Acknowledgments

With special honor to the life and times of Devi Titus: We finally did it! We restored the name woman. Thank you for a job well done. I love you, and I can't wait to see you in Paradise.

To our son Samuel: Special thanks goes to you for all the time you gave up so I could write. Thank you for telling me I'm the world's best mother, and Mary's got some competition with me. You make me laugh every day. Keep reading the Word. You are a world-changer.

To Mom and Dad: The way of the warrior is the way of love. Thank you for allowing me to be both at the same time. I love you.

Linda and Larry: Thank you for teaching Shane, me, Olivia, Zach, and Sam the power of generational legacy. May your love live on through us.

Special thanks goes to: L. Grant Luton, who joyfully answered my endless questions about Hebrew. Steve Martin, my counselor at Wellspring who also supported this work. Thank you to Larry Titus for believing in my gifts to restore the meaning of biblical gender. Thank you to Kathryn Riggs, my brave editor who wrestled through this manuscript and brought out the gold. Finally, to my Circle of Sisters: Megan Carter, Rachelle Fletcher, Deana Morgan, Kristen Smith, Connie Hagen, Jennifer Arnold, Patricia Caro, Trina Titus Lozano, and Val Christner.

You have been my hearth around the fire. Thank you for your strong help in molding me into the woman I am today.

To my husband the Cowboy, who has been twice redeemed—or three times, who's counting? Thank you for relentlessly encouraging me to pursue the dreams in my heart and for all the sacrifices you made for this book to be written. Just when we thought we were falling apart, God was bringing us to unity. Together our influence will be as beautiful as the sand on the shore. I couldn't have done it without you. Here's to us! Always and Forever, me ♀ ♂.

Afterword: The Poetry

Seven years ago, I was standing at the kitchen island chopping celery, onions, and carrots when I heard these words as plain and terrifying as an angel whispering in my ear: "I am going to take you through a crucible." In typical nerdy word girl fashion, I hurried to my online dictionary, typed in the word "crucible," and read:

cru·ci·ble
noun
1. a container subject to very high temperatures, in which different elements interact to create something new.
2. a severe test or trial[1]

The synonyms were *fire, ordeal, cross, gauntlet.* Related words were *grief, affliction, hardship, trial by fire, suffering.* "Great," I thought, "I'll just focus on the part that will *create something new.*"

These are the words He gave me to hold onto in the fire. May they hold you too.

I AM A DAUGHTER

Chosen, wanted, dearly loved.
Cherished, watched, by God above.
In the shadow of my wings, you hide—
Like my people, a chosen bride.

You are wanted, you are seen.
You are priceless, you are clean.
You are sister, daughter, mother—
In my bosom, like no other.

I look upon you—you are more.
For you I have the best in store.
No ear has heard, no eye has seen—
What I am building—for your dreams.

Dancing, laughing, joyous prize.
I see my image in your eyes.
When you hurt, I cry and cry—
You are the Apple of My Eye.

I AM A WOMAN

I am beautiful—I am bold.
I am brilliant—I am bright.
I am young—I am old.
I am loved—I am light.

I am gentle—I am kind.
I am compassion—and I care.
I am daring—I am divine.
I am devoted to you—in prayer.

I am fearless—I am faithful.
I am tried—I am true.
I am generous—I am grateful.
I will forever love you.

I am from the home of the brave
and the land of the free.
This is the Woman
I choose to be.

I AM A WIFE

To but one man.
I am fashioned by God's hand—
I am his complement—his companion,
His lover—and his life.

I am the breath in his bones—
I refuse division and strife.
I will stand in the shallows, on the peaks, in the streams.
I will love till the end—this man of my dreams.

He is bone of my bone, flesh of my flesh—
I get behind him till the day of his death.
On our wedding day, I made my vows—
That was then, this is now.

In the valley of the shadows—I will be his better half.
I will hold his hand—and at the future, I will laugh.
I am gentle grace—the softness at his side.
I will lift my face—and serve him like a bride.

I AM A MOTHER

I nurture. I model. I give. I guide.
I prepare the food and the table—
And keep my home open wide.
I am humble—I am stable—I am dignified.

I am blessed—I am released.
I won't blame, whine, complain.
I have purpose—I have peace.
I know what beauty looks like.

You can't see it in a mirror.
I am grace—
I am gratitude.
I am helpful to my hearers.

I am a healer—a servant.
I am the fragrance of the world.
I am not oppressed—not imprisoned.
I'll be an example to the girls.

I AM A FRIEND

I come along when—
You are hurt, scared, grieved, alone—
And may your heart
My home.

I am a friend.
When joy bounds—I come around.
When hearts break—I have no fear.
I know the stakes—I am near.

I will be silent—I will speak.
On days so bright—on nights so bleak.
I am your keeper—
I will keep.

I will share your joy—and your sorrow.
I am here today—here tomorrow.
When you are up, down, weak, worn—
I am with you in this storm.

I AM A SISTER IN CHRIST

If the waters rise for you to drown—
I will tell you—Hold onto your crown!
I call your name from distant shore
To remind—I love you more.

Do not worry, curse, stress, fear—
Rejoice, rejoice—God is near.
Be not afraid—Your debt's been paid.
You are resilient—You are brilliant.

I will pray till knees are weak—
I will take you up my mountain peak.
I will unveil—I will speak truth.
You and me—Naomi, Ruth.
I am Esther—You are Deborah.
I am the Magdalene.
I am Mary—You are Martha.
I am Rahab—Now and then!

I am the truth—the slayer of lies.
It's not over—We will rise!

Endnotes

Introduction

1 Turning Point USA, "College Student Doesn't KNOW What a Woman Is," YouTube, September 25, 2023, https://www.youtube .com/shorts/46O4nb-AMjs.

2 "Man," American Dictionary of the English Language, https ://webstersdictionary1828.com/Dictionary/man, edited for brevity.

3 Next it reads, "Os homini sublime edit." [Latin for "To man he gave an erect countenance, and bade him gaze on the heavens," a reference to Psalm 8:3-8.]

4 "Woman," American Dictionary of the English Language, https://webstersdictionary1828.com/Dictionary/woman, edited for brevity.

5 "Man," Cambridge Dictionary, https://dictionary.cambridge.org /dictionary/english/man, edited for brevity, changes made in 2022.

6 "Woman," Cambridge Dictionary, https://dictionary.cambridge .org/dictionary/english/woman, edited for brevity.

7   David B. Guralnik, "Male," *Webster's New World Dictionary* (New York City, NY: Warner Books Paperback Edition, Simon & Schuster, 1990), 356.

8   David B. Guralnik, "Female," *Webster's New World Dictionary* (New York City, NY: Warner Books Paperback Edition, Simon & Schuster, 1990), 219.

9   "Male," Merriam-Webster Online Dictionary, https://www.merriam-webster.com/dictionary/male, edited for brevity.

10   "Female," Merriam-Webster Online Dictionary, https://www.merriam-webster.com/dictionary/female, edited for brevity.

11   "Gender Dysphoria in Children," American College of Pediatricians, November 2018, https://acpeds.org/position-stat.

12   "Gender," *Webster's New World Dictionary* (New York City, NY: Warner Books Paperback Edition, Simon & Schuster, 1990), 247.

13   "Gender," Merriam-Webster Online Dictionary, https://www.merriam-webster.com/dictionary/gender.

14   "Gender Identity," Merriam-Webster Online Dictionary, https://www.merriam-webster.com/dictionary/gender identity#dictionary-entry-1, quote by the *Chicago Tribune*.

15   Karina Elwood, "The Teens Fighting to Keep Youngkin's Trans Policies Out of Their Schools," *Washington Post*, September 20, 2023, https://www.washingtonpost.com/education/2023/09/20/youngkin-school-transgender-policies-virginia-beach/. This referred to then-Virginia governor Ralph Northam, a Democrat.

16   Armond White, "The Rolling Stones Redefine Political Anger," *National Review*, September 15, 2023, https://www.nationalreview.com/2023/09/the-rolling-stones-redefine-political-anger/.

17   Benjamin Feamow, "42% of Gen Z Diagnosed with a Mental Health Condition, Survey Reveals," StudyFinds, November 7, 2022, https://studyfinds.org/gen-z-mental-health-condition/#:~:text=Twenty%20percent%20of%20the%201%2C000,with%20daily%20emotional%20distress%20issues.

18 Rachel Hosie, "Unisex Changing Rooms Put Women at Danger of Sexual Assault, Data Reveals," *Independent*, September 2, 2018, https://www.independent.co.uk/life-style/women/sexual-assault -unisex-changing-rooms-sunday-times-women-risk-a8519086 .html#.

19 Louise Perry, *The Case against the Sexual Revolution: A New Guide to Sex in the 21st Century* (Cambridge, UK: Polity Press, 2022), 37.

20 Psalm 119:89; Isaiah 40:8; Malachi 3:6; Numbers 23:19.

21 Matthew 24:35 (NIV).

22 Danny Brown, "Where the Bible Speaks, We Speak – Where the Bible Is Silent, We are Silent," The Preceptor, October 2006, https://www.lavistachurchofchrist.org/cms/where-the-bible -speaks-we-speak-where-the-bible-is-silent-we-are-silent/.

23 Goodreads, George Orwell quotes, https://www.goodreads.com /quotes/6871658-what-i-have-most-wanted-to-do-throughout -the-past.

24 Genesis 9:16 (NIV), emphasis added.

25 See the American College of Pediatricians, "Gender Confusion and Transgender Identity," https://acpeds.org/topics/sexuality -issues-of-youth/gender-confusion-and-transgender-identity.

26 See Genesis 1:27; Psalm 139:13; Jeremiah 1:5.

27 Sam Kneller, "Each Biblical Hebrew Word Is a Precious Jewel to Be Discovered," The Explanation, August 9, 2019, https ://medium.com/the-explanation/each-biblical-hebrew-word-is-a -precious-jewel-to-be-discovered-e07f50ba7071.

Chapter One

1 Erica Chenoneth and Jeremy Pressman, "This Is What We Learned by Counting the Women's Marches," *Washington Post*, February 7, 2017, https://www.washingtonpost.com /news/monkey-cage/wp/2017/02/07/this-is-what-we-learned-by -counting-the-womens-marches/.

2   See pictures at https://www.hollywoodreporter.com/gallery/best
-signs-womens-marches-2017-967685/1-washington-d-c/; see
also Forrest Wickman, "The Best, Nastiest Protest Signs from the
Women's March on Washington," Slate, January 21, 2017, https
://slate.com/human-interest/2017/01/the-best-protest-signs-from
-the-womens-march-on
-washington.html.

3   Amanda Prestigiacomo, "Madonna at #WomensMarch: 'I Have
Thought an Awful Lot about Blowing Up the White House,'
DailyWire, January 22, 2017, https://www.dailywire.com
/news/madonna-womensmarch-i-have-thought-awful-lot-about
-amanda-prestigiacomo.

4   Nina Mariah Donovan, "Poets Corner: NastyWoman by Nina
Donovan," Howl, New York, https://www.howlnewyork.com
/post/poets-corner-nasty-woman-by-nina-donovan.

5   Ibid.

6   Although Donald Trump used the word "nasty" when referring to
Hillary Clinton as a "nasty woman" during a presidential debate,
he elevated women in his cabinet and had women running his
presidential campaign.

7   Damon Linker, "Why Is the Women's March Excluding Pro-Life
Women?" The Week, January 18, 2017, https://theweek.com
/articles/673609/why-womens-march-excluding-prolife-women.

8   Devi Titus was the wife of Larry Titus and the author of the 2017
book *Home Experience: Making Your Home a Place of Love
and Peace*, written with her daughter Trina Titus Lozano and
published by Living Smart Resources.

9   America's Media Watchdog, "Marching to Soros' Tune: 100
Women's March Partners Funded by Left-Wing Billionaire,"
https://www.mrc.org/marching-soros-tune-100-womens-march
-partners-funded-left-wing-billionaire.

10 For framed artwork of my "Identity Poetry" for women, go to
https://urmore.org/product-category/identity-poetry/.

11 "Woman," Wikipedia, https://en.wikipedia.org/wiki/Woman, accessed September 21, 2022. This was the definition at the time of the 2022 Supreme Court hearings. As of this writing, Wikipedia has changed its definition of women to read: "Typically, women inherit a pair of X chromosomes from their parents, and are capable of pregnancy and giving birth from puberty until menopause. More generally, sex differentiation of the female fetus is governed by the lack of a present, or functioning, SRY-gene on either one of the respective sex chromosomes."

12 Victoria's Secret, "Undefinable Global Campaign," https ://vspressroom.com/undefinable-2022/.

Chapter Three

1   L. Grant Luton, *In His Own Words: Messianic Insights into the Hebrew Alphabet, revised & expanded* (Akron, OH: Beth Tikkun Publishing, 2018), 7.

2   H. Res. 8 - Adopting the Rules of the House of Representatives for the One Hundred Seventeenth Congress, and for other purposes, 117th Congress (2021–2022): (5) In clause 15(d)(2) of rule XXIII, https://www.congress.gov/bill/117th-congress/house -resolution/8/text#H9A46EAD744284AECBC3CBD88CE A8C952.

3   Exodus 3:14.

4   Luton, 7.

5   Ibid.

6   "Why the Bible Is Important for Literature Study," Dual Credit at Home, https://dualcreditathome.com/2014/01/bible-important -literature-study/.

7   Lisa Wang, "The Holy Spirit in Emily Brontë's 'Wuthering Heights' and Poetry," *Literary Theology*, Vol. 14, No. 2, Oxford University Press, June 2000, https://www.jstor.org /stable/23924880.

8 See Jeff A. Benner, "The Ancient Pictograph Alphabet," Ancient
   Hebrew Research Center, https://www.ancient-hebrew.org
   /ancient-alphabet/ancient-pictographic-alphabet.htm. See also
   "Bible Lexicons: Ancient Hebrew Alphabet," StudyLight, https
   ://www.studylight.org/lexicons/eng/hebrew/ahl_alphabet
   .html#bet.
9 To do my Hebrew Word Study, *The Secret Meaning of Man and
   Woman,* go to iamawoman.us. As a handy tool, you can also
   download the Hebrew alphabet chart from iamawoman.us.
10 John 1:1 (NASB).
11 Study Light, Strong's #1121 – ben and #1129 – banah.
12 Genesis 1:1
13 Study Light, Strong's #8034 - shem. All my Hebrew definitions
   are compiled from Strong's Concordance, Brown-Drivers-Briggs,
   and the Old Testament Hebrew Lexical Dictionary found at
   https://www.studylight.org/lexicons/eng/hebrew.html.
   For some roots, I use Clark, R' Matityahu *The Etymological
   Dictionary of Biblical Hebrew Based on the Commentaries of
   Samson Raphael Hirsch* (Jerusalem: Feldheim Publishers, 1999).
   For Brevity, all definitions are marked "Study Light, Strong's
   #___ [word]." Those which draw upon Hirsch's work are marked
   Clark, p__.
14 Study Light, Strong's #430 - Elohim
15 "Jewish Concepts: The Name of God" Jewish Virtual Library,
   https://www.jewishvirtuallibrary.org/the-name-of-god.
16 For a deeper study of this, go to iamawoman.us for the Bible
   Study *The Secret Meaning of Man and Woman.*
17 Study Light, Strong's #7307 – ruwach.
18 Luton, xix. On three occasions, Jesus anthropomorphizes the
   spirit and refers to it with the masculine "he." (This is like
   naming a boat "Dolly" and referring to it as a "she.") But in the
   remaining 300+ instances in the New Testament, the spirit is
   consistently neuter—an "it."
19 Proverbs 31:14–26 (NIV).

20   Genesis 1:26–27.

21   Genesis 1:26–31a.

22   Study Light, Strong's #2896 - towb, #3966 – meod.

23   Isaiah 5:20, 21, 23.

24   Study Light, Strong's #3068 -Yehovah and #1933 - hava

25   Study Light, Strong's #1933 – hava.

26   Study Light, Strong's #3443, Yeshuwa, #3068, Yehovah, and
     #3467, yasha.

27   Study Light, Strong's #3444, Yeshuwah.

28   Study Light, Strong's #3467, yasha.

29   Philippians 2:9–10.

Chapter Four

1   Carrie Gress, *The End of Woman: How Smashing the Patriarchy
    Has Destroyed Us* (Carol Stream, IL: Oasis Audio, 2023),
    Chapter One.

2   Carrie Gress, *The End of Woman: How Smashing the Patriarchy
    Has Destroyed Us* (Washington, DC: Regnery Publishing), 2024.

3   "Human Trafficking and Violence: Findings from the Largest
    Global Dataset of Trafficking Survivors," National Library of
    Medicine, November 16, 2021, https://www.ncbi.nlm.nih.gov
    /pmc/articles/PMC8637135/.

4   Louise Perry, *The Case against the Sexual Revolution: A New
    Guide to Sex in the 21st Century* (Cambridge, UK: Polity Press,
    2022), 78.

5   Ibid., 35.

6   "Facts and Figures: Ending Violence against Women," UN
    Women, https://www.unwomen.org/en/what-we-do/ending
    -violence-against
    -women/facts-and-figures, 15–19.

7   Andrew Keiper, "Human Trafficking in America among Worst in
    World: Report," Fox News, June 22, 2019, http://www.foxnews
    /us/human-trafficking-in-america-among-worst-in-world-report.

8   "Facts and Figures," UN Women, 15–19.

9   "Traffickinghub: A Timeline of Pornhub's Rapid Decline," Exodus Cry, September 22, 2022, https://exoduscry.com/articles /traffickinghub-timeline/. See also, Perry, *The Case against the Sexual Revolution*, 101.

10   "Pornhub's 2021 Annual Report Reveals This Year's Most-Watched Porn Categories," Fight the New Drug, https ://fightthenewdrug.org/2021-pornhub-annual-report/.

11   "Traffickinghub," Exodus Cry.

12   Jenna, ex porn actor, quoted in "The Dark Side of Porn: What's Really Going on behind the Scenes," Remojo, May 12, 2023, https://www.remojo.com/post/the-dark-side-of-porn-whats-really -going-on-behind-the-scenes.

13   Regan, ex porn actor, quoted in Remojo, ibid.

14   Perry, *The Case against the Sexual Revolution*, 99. Linda Lovelace and Mike McGrady, *Ordeal: An Autobiography* (New York City, NY: Citadel Press, 1980). Name of show hidden purposefully.

15   "'Teen': Why Has This Porn Category Topped the Charts for 6+ Years?" Fight the New Drug, https://fightthenewdrug.org/this -years-most-popular-genre-of-porn-is-pretty-messed-up/.

16   Bedbible Research Center, "Pornhub Statistics—Analysis of +9,000 Hours of Porn [Shocking]," March 21, 2023, https://bedbible.com /pornhub-statistics/. See also Shrier, *Irreversible Damage*.

17   Matt Fradd "10 Shocking Stats about Teens and Pornography (2023)," Covenant Eyes, May 18, 2023. https://www .covenanteyes.com/2015/04/10/10-shocking-stats-about-teens -and-pornography/; and "Abundant Life Partners with Covenant Eyes: What People Do Online Impacts Their Lives Offline," Abundant Life Fellowship, https://www.abundantlifefellowship .com/Covenant-Eyes.

18   Lyndon Azcuna, "The Porn Pandemic," October 28, 2021, https ://www.lifeplan.org/the-porn-pandemic/#:~:text.

19 "47 Terms that Describe Sexual Behavior, Attraction, and Orientation," Healthline, medically reviewed by Jennifer Litner, PhD, LMFT, CST, February 17, 2023, https://www.healthline .com/health/different-types-of-sexuality.

20 Abigail Shrier, *Irreversible Damage: The Transgender Craze Seducing Our Daughters* (Washington, D.C.: Regnery Publishing, 2020). For the sex education programs she refers to, see Positive Prevention PLUS, "Teen Talk; Be Real, Be Ready," https ://positivepreventionplus.com/.

21 Gender symbol icon vector set illustration by pixelliebe, Adobe Stock photo, used with permission. Licensed. https://stock.adobe .com/Library/urn:aaid:sc:VA6C2:a837bfac-8839-4e86-930f -462dfc4ea80f?asset_id=446882017.

22 Daniel de Visé, "New Studies Find Millions of Young Nonbinary and Transgender Americans," The Hill, January 13, 2023, https ://thehill.com/changing-america/3811406-new-studies-find-millions -of-young-nonbinary-and-transgender-americans/; "Nonbinary LGBTQ Adults in the United States," UCLA Williams Institute School of Law, June 2021, https://williamsinstitute.law.ucla.edu /publications/nonbinary-lgbtq-adults-us/.

23 Robin Respaut and Chad Terhune, "Putting Numbers on the Rise in Children Seeking Gender Care," Reuters, October 6, 2022, https://www.reuters.com/investigates/special-report/usa -transyouth-data/.

24 Ciaran McGrath, "Investigation as Number of Girls Seeking Gender Transition Treatment Rises 4,515%," Express, September 16, 2018, https://www.express.co.uk/news/uk/1018407/gender -transition-treatment-investigation-penny-mordaunt.

25 See "Breaking the Silence: The Reality of De-Transitioning," 7NEWS Spotlight, September 11, 2023, https://www.youtube .com/watch?v=JgW_xtIcpew.

26 "Gender Dysphoria in Children," American College of Pediatricians Physicians Statement, November 2018, https ://acpeds.org/position-statements/gender-dysphoria-in-children.

See also Helen Joyce, *Trans: When Ideology Meets Reality* (London, UK: Oneworld Books, 2022), 33; Shrier, *Irreversible Damage*, 119, 134.

27 Shrier, *Irreversible* Damage, 165, quoting Schneider et al., "Brain Maturation, Cognition and Voice Pattern in a Gender Dysphoria Case under Pubertal Suppression." For more detail on the medical research for this section, see the American College of Pediatricians Statement, "Gender Dysphoria in Children," November 2018.

28 Ibid., 165.

29 Ibid., 165, 169–71.

30 Ibid., 170.

31 Ibid., 171.

32 Ibid., xx–xxii, 165.

33 Perri O. Blumberg, Emily Becker, and Sabrina Talbert, "Here's Your Comprehensive Gender Identity List, as Defined by Psychologists and Sex Experts," *Women's Health Magazine*, quoting Jackie Golob, MS, who works at a private practice at the Centre for Sexual Wellness in Minnesota, https://www .womenshealthmag.com/relationships/a36395721/gender-identity -list/, July 21, 2023. Also referenced, "Gender Identity and Sexuality Terms to Know" video by Women's Health US on same page.

34 Ibid., accessed December 8, 2022. Also referenced, "Gender Identity and Sexuality Terms to Know" video by Women's Health US on same page.

35 This article was recently updated to match the GLAAD's reference guide word for word, making sure the same mantras are repeated again and again.

36 The last three sentences were deleted from the article in 2023 to match the GLAAD reference guide, but I included them because they were in the article for two years.

37 Ibid.

38 Ibid.

39 Study Light, Strong's #1 – ab. Hirsch, p. 1.

40 Study Light, Strong's #1, ibid.

41 Oli London, *Gender Madness: One Man's Devastating Struggle with Woke Ideology and His Battle to Protect Children* (New York City, NY: Skyhorse Publishing, 2023).

42 Her story is told in Matthew 9:20–22, Mark 5:24b–34, and Luke 8:42b–48.

43 Mark 5:34.

44 To study the pictographs in more depth, go to iamawoman.us and get the study, *The Secret Meaning of Man and Woman*.

45 Study Light, Strong's #1323 – bath and #1129 – bana.

46 Psalm 17:8–9 (ESV).

47 "Apple of My Eye', Meaning & Context," No Sweat Shakespeare, https://nosweatshakespeare.com/quotes/famous/apple-of-my-eye/; "Apple of The Eye," Bible Study Tools, https://www.biblestudytools.com/dictionary/apple-of-the-eye/.

48 Jeremiah 8:18–21 (NLT).

49 Luke 7:44.

50 Kristi McLelland, "Jesus & Women: In the First Century and Now," video #1, YouTube, February 18, 2020, https://www.youtube.com/watch?v=N-9GnlkQiLw.

Chapter Five

1 Lois Tverberg, "A Good Eye or a Bad Eye? A Cryptic but Critical Idiom," Our Rabbi Jesus: Insights from Lois Tverberg, January 2, 2019, https://ourrabbijesus.com/articles/a-good-eye-or-a-bad-eye-a-cryptic-but-critical-idiom/. Good Eye is *ayin tovah;* Bad Eye if *ayin ra'ah.*

2 Matthew 6:22–23.

3 Ben Shapiro, "What Does It Mean to Be a Man? | Voddie Baucham," YouTube, July 30, 2023, https://www.youtube.com/watch?v=CMiXQ-iODyk&t=1181s.

4 Ibid.

5 Study Light, Strong's #2145, zâkâr and #2142, zâkar. Clark, 67.

6   *Pearls with Kristi McLelland*, "Episode 11 - Zakhar: Remembering as Moving Forward," November 11, 2022, https ://www.accessmore.com/episode/Ep-11— Zakhar-Remembering -as-Moving-Forward.

7   Read Ecclesiastes 12:3–7 for more commands to remember that are associated with our bodies.

8   Shivimpanin, "INTRO - Secrets of the Hebrew Letters," YouTube, June 9, 2010, https://youtu.be/d0jJhroi5sQ.

9   Luton, 97–98.

10 Ibid., 97.

11 Luton, 98–99, Revelation 3:19–20.

12 For more about the numeric value of 7 and how the Zayin points to Christ, watch the video, "Secret of the Hebrew Letter Zayin," the Living Word, https://www.thelivingword.org.au/grand-design /session25.php.

13 See also Hebrew 1:8.

14 "The Letter Zayin," Hebrew for Christians, https://www .hebrew4christians.com/Grammar/Unit_One/Aleph-Bet/Zayin /zayin.html.

15 Photo courtesy of L. Grant Luton, used with permission.

16 John 19:26.

17 Judges 6:12.

18 Kristen M. Smeltzer and Zachary D. Smeltzer, *Who Do You Say I Am?: Overcoming the Spirit of Identity Theft* (Destiny Oak, 2017).

19 Genesis 3:9 (NLT).

20 Romans 5:12.

21 "What Does It Mean to Be a Man? | Voddie Baucham."

22 Study Light, Strong's #7358 – rechem; Root #7355 – racham.

23 Jeremiah 1:5; Psalm 22:10.

24 "What Does It Mean to Be a Man? | Voddie Baucham."

25 Malachi 4:6 (NASB).

26 Thinkers, "Jordan Peterson – Gender taught as social construct
   in schools: What to do?" YouTube, October 26, 2018,
   https://www.youtube.com/watch?v=KGCN7OHe0qk.

Chapter Six

1   J. K. Rowling, "J. K. Rowling Writes about her Reasons for
   Speaking out on Sex and Gender Issues," jkrowling.com, June 10,
   2020, https://www.jkrowling.com/opinions/j-k-rowling-writes
   -about-her-reasons-for-speaking-out-on-sex-and-gender-issues/.
2   "'Teen': Why Has This Porn Category Topped the Charts for 6+
   Years?" Fight the New Drug, https://fightthenewdrug.org/this
   -years-most-popular-genre-of-porn-is-pretty-messed-up/.
3   Perry, *The Case against the Sexual Revolution*, 27, 29.
4   Matthew Arnold, Goodreads Quotes, https://www.goodreads
   .com/author/quotes/53451.Matthew_Arnold.
5   Study Light, Strong's #5347 -neqebah.
6   Study Light, Strong's #5347 – neqebah. #5344 - naqab;
   Hirsch, 161.
7   Skip Moen, D. Phil., *Guardian Angel: What You Must Know
   about God's Design for Women, abridged edition* (Skip Moen,
   2010), 33.
8   Ibid., 34.
9   Jeremiah 31:22 (NASB).
10 Judges 4:9.
11 Luton, 163–65.
12 Exodus 33:11.
13 Genesis 3:15.
14 For an example of sex education curriculum for young people
   that teaches multiple genders, see Teen Talk, https://teentalk.ca
   /learn-about/gender-identity/.
15 "The Long-Term Decline in Fertility—and What It Means for
   State Budgets," Pew Research Center, December 5, 2022, https
   ://www.pewtrusts.org/en/research-and-analysis/issue

-briefs/2022/12/the-long-term-decline-in-fertility-and-what-it
-means-for-state-budgets.

16   Ronald Reagan, "Remarks to Participants in the March for Life
Rally," Ronald Reagan Presidential Foundation & Institute,
January 22, 1988, https://www.reaganfoundation.org/ronald
-reagan/reagan-quotes-speeches/remarks-to-participants-in-the
-march-for-life-rally/.

17   L. Grant Luton, 173–74.

18   Photo courtesy of L. Grant Luton, used with permission.

19   Thinkers, "Jordan Peterson – Gender Taught as Social Construct
in Schools: What to Do?"

20   Study Light, Strong's #990 – beten.

21   Devi Titus and Trina Titus Lozano, *Home Experience: Making
Your Home a Place of Love and Peace,* ibid.

22   Genesis 12:8.

23   R. Hirsch, *The Hirsch Chumash* (New York, Feldheim Publishers,
2002), 303.

24   Blue Letter Bible, Strong's G3616 – oikodespotéō.

25   Blue Letter Bible, Strong's G3626 – oikourós.

26   Titus and Lozano, *Home Experience: Making Your Home a Place
of Love and Peace.*

27   Proverbs 31:13–31.

28   Isaiah 38:1b.

29   Luton, 78.

Chapter Seven

1   Matt Walsh, *What Is a Woman?: One Man's Journey to Answer
the Question of a Generation* (Nashville, TN: Daily Wire Books,
2022).

2   (Now called Middle Eastern). Some include Assyrian, Acadian,
Babylonian, and Egyptian.

3   Kristi McLelland, "Ezer Kenegdo," New Lens Biblical Studies, https://newlensbiblicalstudies.teachable.com/courses/1401822/lectures/32198938.

4   Study Light, Strong's #5397 – neshemah.

5   McLelland, "Ezer Kenegdo."

6   "Stereotypes and Biased Language," Purdue University Online Writing Lab (OWL), https://owl.purdue.edu/owl/general_writing/academic_writing/using_appropriate_language/stereotypes_and_biased_language.html. See also "Statement on Gender and Language," NCTE Position Statements, October 25, 2018, https://ncte.org/statement/genderfairuseoflang/.

7   Adam Sabes, "Purdue writing guide: Words with 'MAN' should be avoided'" Campus Reform, February 20, 2018, https://www.campusreform.org/article/purdue-writing-guide-words-with-man-should-be-avoided/10539

8   Study Light, Strong's #120 - adam

9   Study Light, Strong's #H5647 – abad.

10 Study Light, Strong's #H8014 – shamar.

11 Moen, 37.

12 Genesis 2:16–17. Moen 37, 39.

13 Ibid., 38–39.

14 Genesis 2:18 (NLT).

15 Study Light, Strong's #905 – bad.

16 Study Light, Strong's #8378 – taavah.

17 McLelland, "Ezer Kenegdo."

18 Study Light, Strong's #7451 – ra.

19 Ecclesiastes 4:9–10.

20 Moen, 42.

21 Tiphani Montgomery, "THE WIFE IS A WARNING SYSTEM!!!" YouTube, September 26, 2023, https://www.youtube.com/watch?v=_wZQ6x5Xgzs.

22 Moen, 42.

23 Study Light, Strong's #5828 – ezer, #5826 – azar. Clark, 183. Moen, 55–57.

24   Kristi McLelland, "God's First Words about Woman," https
     ://newlensbiblicalstudies.teachable.com/courses/1401822
     /lectures/32198938.

25   Deuteronomy 33:26, 29 (NIV), emphasis added

26   Ps. 33:20 (ESV), emphasis added

27   Ps. 70:5 (ESV), emphasis added

28   Psalm 121, (HCSB and ESV combined), emphasis added.

29   Moen, 54.

30   Clark, 183.

31   Moen, 54.

32   See Devi Titus's message "I AM WOMAN" on the *I AM A
     WOMAN Podcast*, Season 1 Episode 8: Jennifer Strickland,
     "I AM A WOMAN with DEVI TITUS," YouTube, March 8,
     2023, https://youtu.be/crraKS_pskY?si=fFhLwNAdt-N-vVm2.

33   Genesis 4:1; Study Light, Strong's #3045 – yada.

34   Moen, 55.

35   McLelland, "Ezer Kenegdo."

36   Genesis 2:18, 20; Study Light, Strong's #5048 – neged.

37   Blue Letter Bible, Strong's #H5046 – nagad.

38   Kisha Gallagher, "The Biblical Role of Women Part II", GRACE
     IN TORAH, https://graceintorah.net/2013/05/19/the
     -biblical-role-of-women-part-ii/. See also Moen, 108. See also
     "God's Word to Women," Word Study, Ezer Kenegdo, https
     ://godswordtowomen.org/ezerkenegdo.htm.

39   Rabbi Sholmo Riskin, "Prashat Bereishit: A Help Opposite?
     The Florida Jewish News, October 2003. Quoted by Moen, 60.

40   Gallagher, "The Biblical Role of Women Part II."

41   Moen, 61.

42   "God's Word to Women."

43   Septuagint, abbreviated LXX.

44   John 20:15; Mark 16:1; Luke 23:55–11.

45   John 4:25–26.

46   Proverbs 31:26 (NIV).

47 Genesis 2:24.
48 Jeremiah 31:22.

Chapter Eight

1 "I am a Wife" by Jennifer Strickland, https://urmore.org/product /i-am-a-wife.
2 Moen, 11.
3 Genesis 2:21–23 (NASB).
4 Study Light, Strong's #6763 – tsela.
5 Moen, 44 See also Gallagher, "The Biblical Role of Women Part II."
6 Malachi 2:1–15; 1 Peter 3:7.
7 Study Light, Strong's #802 -ishshah; Clark 17.
8 Proverbs 25:15; 25:11, paraphrase.
9 Genesis 2:7; Isaiah 40:7.
10 Proverbs 12:4.
11 Proverbs 21:9.
12 Gallagher, "The Biblical Role of Women Part XI," GRACE in TORAH, https://graceintorah.net/2015/11/03/the-biblical-role-of -women-part-xi/.
13 Proverbs 12:18.
14 Study Light - Strong's #376 – iysh; Clark, 9.
15 Study Light, Strong's #784 – esh.
16 Gallagher, "The Biblical Role of Women Part XI."
17 Exodus 24:17 (ESV).
18 Gallagher, "Man, Woman, and Fire."
19 Ibid.
20 Proverbs 3:15-18, 26; 31:10–12 (NLT).
21 Genesis 2:21–24 (NASB).
22 Study Light, Strong's #1692 – dabaq.
23 Proverbs 5:15–23 NLT.
24 See Louise Perry, *The Case against the Sexual Revolution: A New Guide to Sex in the 21st Century.*

25 Wikipedia, "Lists of Universities with BDSM Clubs," https
    ://en.wikipedia.org/wiki/List_of_universities_with_BDSM_clubs.
26 Wikipedia, "Sex Week at Yale," https://en.wikipedia.org/wiki
    /Sex_Week_at_Yale.
27 Perry, 15.
28 Perry, 15, 20.
29 Perry, 67.
30 Song of Solomon 7:10.
31 Honore de Blazac, AZ Quotes, https://www.azquotes.com
    /author/858-Honore_de_Balzac.
32 Moen, 70.
33 See Moen, Chapter 7.
34 Genesis 3:14–19 (NASB).
35 Study Light, Strong's #7451 – ra.
36 Study Light, Strong's #6087; Moen, 76.
37 Moen, 78.
38 Genesis 3:21.
39 Moen,113. Leviticus 8:7, 13; Numbers 20:28.
40 Song of Solomon 8:6 (NLT).

Chapter Nine

1 Revelation 17:1–6 (HSCB). The NASB uses the word "harlot" for
   "prostitute."
2 Revelation 17:15.
3 Revelation 17:9.
4 Revelation 17:14.
5 Ephesians 6:12.
6 Study Light, Strong's #517 – em.
7 Study Light, ibid.
8 Hirsch, p.11.
9 Isaiah 49:15–16 (NASB).
10 Isaiah 66:13.
11 Isaiah 42:14 (NASB).

12 Kisha Gallagher, GRACE in TORAH, "The Biblical Role of Women Part IX," https://graceintorah.net/2014/12/22/the -biblical-role-of-women-part-ix/.

13 Genesis 17:1–6, 15–16 (NASB).

14 Ibid.

15 Study Light, Strong's #8283 - Sarah; Abram means "exalted father" and Sarai means "princess." Abram became Abraham, which means *father of a multitude*. Sarai became Sarah meaning "noblewoman."

16 Erick S. Gray, Goodreads Quotes, https://www.goodreads.com /author/quotes/149580.Erick_S_Gray.

17 Study Light, Strong's #2332 – Chavvah, #2331 – chavah, #2324, chava.

18 Luton, 105.

19 John 20:15–18.

20 Study Light, Strong's #5046 – neged, #5046 - nagad.

21 For a deeper understanding of the commonly debated verses about women speaking in the congregations, see Skip Moen, *Guardian Angel*, Chapters 12 and 13. See also Lysa TerKeurst, Jim Cress, and Joel Muddamalle, "Therapy & Theology: Commonly Debated and Misunderstood Bible Verses About Women," Official Proverbs 31 Ministries, YouTube, November 3, 2022, https://www.youtube.com/watch?v=1I7s3EwyUNY.

22 1 Timothy 1:5; Galatians 3:28.

23 Ephesians 4:11–13 (NIV).

24 Romans 12:6–7 (NIV).

25 A listing of spiritual gifts is found in 1 Corinthians 12:8–10, Ephesians 4:7–13, Isaiah 11:2–3, and Romans 12:3–8.

26 1 Timothy 2:8–10.

27 Ezekiel 16:4–14; Isaiah 4:2–6.

28 TerKeurst, Cress, and Muddamalle, "Therapy & Theology."

29 Moen, 137.

30 Mark 16:11–14.

31 1 Corinthians 14:34–35 (NASB).

32   Moen, 144–46.

33   Ibid.

34   Gilbert Bilezikian, *Beyond Sex Roles: What the Bible Says about a Woman's Roles in Church and Family* (Ada, MI: Baker Academic, 2002), 174–78; Moen 144.

35   Moen, 149. Scripturally, the only role that is specifically designated for certain males was the Levitical priesthood. For a Greek understanding of the gendered pronouns referring to overseers, see Moen, 148–49.

36   The Greek makes it clear that Junia is a female apostle. See Moen, 146–48.

37   Acts 21:9; 1 Corinthians 14:1.

38   Margo Mowczko, 5Q, "Women Leaders in the New Testament," quoted from margmowczko.com, August 22, 2015. "The following list is of first-century women ministers and church leaders mentioned in the New Testament: Philip's daughters (Acts 21:9), Priscilla (Acts 18:26; Rom. 16:3-5, etc.), Phoebe (Rom. 16:1-2), Junia (Rom. 16:7), possibly Chloe (1 Cor. 1:11), Euodia and Syntyche (Phil. 4:2-3), Nympha (Col. 4:15), Apphia (Phlm. 2), 'the chosen lady' (2 John 1), 'the chosen sister' (2 John 13), and probably Lydia (Acts 16:40), etc," https://5qcentral.com/women-leaders-nt/.

39   NASB.

40   Psalm 144:11–13 (NASB).

41   Genesis 1:27b–28.

42   Judges 4:9.

Chapter Ten

1   Jennifer Strickland, "Protecting Children from Trafficking & Exploitation with Landon Starbuck: Part 1 & 2," YouTube, April 6, 2023, https://www.youtube.com/watch?v=LI-DXS-N9Vg.

2   Teen Vogue, "5 Misconceptions about Sex and Gender," YouTube, March 19, 2019, https://www.youtube.com/watch?v=2S0e-i117vY.

3   Ibid.

4   Dr. Robert J. Lifton, *Thought Reform and The Future of Immortality* (First Edition, New York: Basic Books, 1987), Chapter 15.

5   George Orwell, *1984* (Boston, MA: Harcourt, Inc., 1949), 77.

6   The International Churches of Christ was the fastest-growing Christian cult in the United States, also called the ICC or the Boston Movement, and was led by Kip McKean. It has since been dismantled. Later on, I became instrumental in helping others understand their false teaching.

7   Stephen Martin, *The Heresy of Mind Control: Recognizing Con artists, Tyrants, and Spiritual Abusers in Leadership* (Nashville, TN: ACW Press, 2009).

8   The letter I wrote to the ICC can be found here: Jennifer Porter, "The Truth Has Set Me Free," www.reveal.org/library/stories /jporter.html.

9   See Lifton, *Thought Reform and the Psychology of Totalism*, Chapter 22, and *The Future of Immortality*, Chapter 15.

10   Goodreads, Thomas Campbell Quotes, from *My Big TOE: Awakening*, https://www.goodreads.com/search?utf8 =√&q=thomas+campbell&search_type=quotes&search %5Bfield%5D=on.

11   Lifton.

12   Ibid. These words are Lifton's own, but I edited them here for brevity.

13   Bill C-16, House of Commons of Canada, First Session, Forty-second Parliament, first reading, May 17, 2016, https://www .parl/ca/DocumentViewer/en/42-1/bill/C-16/first-reading. See also, TVO Today, "Genders, Rights and Freedom of Speech," YouTube, October 26, 2016, https://www.youtube.com /watch?v=kasiov0ytEc.

14   "George Orwell's 1984 Should Be Required Reading in Schools," Reddit, opinion, midshipmans_hat, https://www.reddit.com/r

/IntellectualDarkWeb/comments/12id0l8/george_orwells_1984
_should_be_required_reading_in/.

15 Jared Gould, "Students Caught Using Wrong Pronouns at Harvard
    May Violate Harassment Policies," Campus Reform, October 4,
    2022, https://www.campusreform.org/article?id=20328.

16 Lifton. These words are Lifton's own, but I edited them here for
    brevity.

17 Perri O. Blumberg, Emily Becker, and Sabrina Talbert, *Women's
    Health Magazine*, "Here's Your Comprehensive Gender Identity
    List, as Defined by Psychologists and Sex Experts," quoting Jackie
    Golob, MS, who works at a private practice at the Centre for
    Sexual Wellness in Minnesota, https://www.womenshealthmag
    .com/relationships/a36395721/gender-identity-list/, July 21, 2023.

18 "U.S. Teen Girls Experiencing Increased Sadness and Violence,"
    CDC, last reviewed February 13, 2023, https://www.cdc.gov
    /media/releases/2023/p0213-yrbs.html.

19 GLSEN is formerly the "Gay and Lesbian Independent School
    Teachers Network," which supplies curriculum materials to
    lecture students on sexual orientation and gender. "The A-Z of
    Awesome—Because Self Expression and Identity Matter," LEGO,
    June 1, 2022, https://www.lego.com/en-us/aboutus/news/2022
    /may/the-a-z-of-awesome-because-self-expression-and-identity
    -matter.

20 Abigail Shrier, *Irreversible Damage: The Transgender Craze
    Seducing our Daughters* (Washington, DC: Regnery Publishing,
    2020), 69.

21 Ibid., 64–66.

22 See Positive Prevention PLUS, *Teen Talk; Be Real, Be Ready*.

23 Shrier, 68.

24 I highly recommend the Just Say Yes Relationships & Sexual
    Health Programs, https://justsayyes.org/relationships-sexual
    -health/.

25 LEGO, "The A-Z of Awesome | An Alphabet of LGBTQIA+ LEGO Builds," YouTube, June 1, 2022, https://www.youtube.com /watch?v=837WdHmZw3E.

26 Lifton. These words are Lifton's own, but I edited them here for brevity.

27 Lifton, *Thought Reform and the Psychology of Totalism*, 421.

28 US Flag Code §7. (e) reads: "The flag of the United States of America should be at the center and at the highest point of the group when a number of flags of States or localities or pennants of societies are grouped and displayed from staffs." See also Anders Hagstrom, "Biden Says Transgender People 'Shape Our Nation's Soul' in Official Proclamation," Fox News, March 20, 2023, https://www.foxnews.com/politics/biden-transgender -people-shape-nations-soul-official-proclamation.

29 Andrea Cavalier, "Biden Is Slammed on Social Media for US Flag Code Violation by Putting Pride Design Front and Center at White House Event," *Daily Mail*, June 11, 2023, https://www.dailymail. co.uk/news/article-12183631/Biden-slammed-social-media-Flag -Code-violation.html.

30 Samuel Lovett, "Tavistock Gender Clinic Facing Legal Action over 'Failure of Care' Claims," *Independent*, August 11, 2022, https://www.independent.co.uk/news/health/tavistock-gender -clinic-lawyers-latest-b2143006.html; and Sue Evans, "I Worked at the Tavistock Gender Clinic. This Is Why Closing It Was the Right Move.," *Dallas News*, April 22, 2023, https://www .dallasnews.com/opinion/commentary/2023/04/22/i-worked-at -the-tavistock-gender-clinic-this-is-why-closing-it-was-the-right -move/.

31 "LGBTQ+ Pride Flags and What They Stand For," Volvo, December 12, 2022, https://www.volvogroup.com/en/news-and -media/news/2021/jun/lgbtq-pride-flags-and-what-they -stand-for.html#:~:text=Gender Queer Pride Flag,-The Gender Queer&text=The lavender, a mix of,binary and the third gender.

32   To name a few: Montana State University "Glossary of Helpful
      Terms," https://www.montana.edu/lgbtq/glossary.html; LGBTQIA
      Resource Center, UC Davis, https://lgbtqia.ucdavis.edu/educated
      /glossary; and Brown University LGBTQ Center, https://www
      .brown.edu/campus-life/support/lgbtq/http:/brown.edu/campus
      -life/support/lgbtq/campus
      -resources/key-terms.
33   Brown University LGBTQ Center.
34   Megan Lasher, https://www.seventeen.com/author/208796
      /megan-lasher/.
35   CatholicVote, "Boys Are Boys, Girls Are Girls," YouTube,
      December 3, 2022, https://www.youtube.com/watch?v
      =GL510E5Najc.
36   "The A-Z of Awesome | An Alphabet of LGBTQIA+ LEGO
      Builds."

Chapter Eleven

1   Jordan Peterson, https://www.jordanbpeterson.com/about/.
2   Hannah Grossman and Ashley Carnahan, "Detransitioned
      Boy Castrated by Doctors Warns Kids about Perils of Gender
      Ideology: 'Patient for Life'," Fox News, July 21, 2023, https
      ://www.foxnews.com/media/detransitioned-boy-castrated-by
      -doctors-warns-kids-about-perils-of-gender-affirming-care.
      His real name is withheld for privacy reasons.
3   Helen Joyce, *Trans: When Ideology Meets Reality* (London, UK:
      Oneworld Publications, 2021), 32.
4   Ibid., 32.
5   Grossman and Carnahan, "Detransitioned Boy Castrated by
      Doctors Warns Kids about Perils of Gender Ideology."
6   See "Expert Submission of Dr. Stephen B. Levine, M.D.," March
      12, 2020, https://www.legis.state.pa.us/WU01/LI/TR
      /Transcripts/2020_0046_0001_TSTMNY.pdf. See also "Gender
      Confusion and Transgender Identity," the American College of

Pediatricians, https://acpeds.org/topics/sexuality-issues-of-youth/gender-confusion-and-transgender-identity.

7 Levine, ibid.

8 See American College of Pediatricians, "Gender Dysphoria in Children."

9 Alan Rutherford, LPC, "Nine Functions of the Prefrontal Cortex," https://www.alanrutherfordlpc.com/resources/nine-functions-of-the-prefrontal-cortex.

10 N. Dafny, G. C. Rosenfeld, "Neurobiology of Drugs of Abuse," Conn's Translational Neuroscience, 2017,https://www.sciencedirect.com/topics/medicine-and-dentistry/prefrontal-cortex#:~:text=The%20PFC%20is%20involved%20in,and%20modulation%20of%20social%20behavior.

11 "The Teen Brain: 7 Things to Know," National Institute of Mental Health, https://www.sciencedirect.com/topics/medicine-and-dentistry/prefrontal-cortex#:~:text=The%20PFC%20is%20involved%20in,and%20mohttps://www.nimh.nih.gov/health/publications/the-teen-brain-7-things-to-know#:~:text=The%20brain%20finishes%20developing%20and,%20prioritizing,%20and%20making%20good%20decisionsdulation%20of%20social%20behavior.

12 Samuel Lovett, "Tavistock Gender Clinic Facing Legal Action over 'Failure of Care Claims," Independent, August 11, 2022, https://www.independent.co.uk/news/health/tavistock-gender-clinic-lawyers-latest-b2143006.html.

13 Sue Evans, "I Worked at the Tavistock Gender Clinic. This Is Why Closing It Was the Right Move," April 22, Dallas News, April 22, 2023, https://www.dallasnews.com/opinion/commentary/2023/04/22/i-worked-at-the-tavistock-gender-clinic-this-is-why-closing-it-was-the-right-move/.

14 Ibid.

15 National Library of Medicine, "Orchiectomy," last updated August 28, 2023, https://www.ncbi.nlm.nih.gov/books/NBK562336/#:~:text=Orchidectomy%20involves%20the%20

surgical%20removal,with%20locally%20advanced%20
prostate%20cancer.

16   Blue Letter Bible, Strong's #3875 – parakletos.

17   Proverbs 31:8–9.

18   For more information see "Gender Confusion and Transgender
Identity," American College of Pediatricians, https://acpeds.org
/topics/sexuality-issues-of-youth/gender-confusion-and
-transgender-identity.

19   "The Myth about Suicide and Gender Dysphoric Children," the
American College of Pediatricians, https://acpeds.org/assets/for
-GID-page-1-The-Myth-About-Suicide-and-Gender-Dysphoric
-Children-handout.pdf.

20   "Ibid.

21   The Daily Signal, "'My Childhood Was RUINED:' Detransitioner
Chloe Cole Talks about Trans Procedures," YouTube, July 27,
2023, https://www.youtube.com/watch?v=DSGgR3W_jjg. See
also, The Daily Signal, "Former Trans Kid Chloe Cole on Why
She Left Transgenderism," YouTube, January 11, 2023, https
://www.youtube.com/watch?v=3am6G-D-VtQ.

22   Sadie is a pseudonym. Her identity is hidden to protect her
identity.

23   The Blaire White Project, YouTube, https://www.youtube.com
/@TheBlaireWhiteProject.

24   Soft White Underbelly, "Ex (Detransitioning) Trans Woman
Interview—Shape Shifter," YouTube, March 23, 2023, https
://www.youtube.com/watch?v=xsbtaXqfg1o&t=5s.

25   Blair White, "Jazz Jennings: The Trans Kid Tragedy America
Claps For," YouTube, September 26, 2023, https://www.youtube
.com/watch?v=VN5T1_eI00Q.

26   Ibid.

27   Lifton, p. 430–32, edited for brevity.

28   Abigail Shrier, *Irreversible Damage: The Transgender Craze
Seducing Our Daughters* (Washington, DC: Regnery Publishing,
2020), xxi.

29   Ibid.

30   See Gays Against Groomers, https://www.gaysagainstgroomers
     .com/about; Kathleen Stock, https://kathleenstock.substack
     .com/; Blaire White Project, https://www.youtube.com
     /@TheBlaireWhiteProject.

31   Lifton, 433–35, edited for brevity.

32   According to mind control expert Stephen Martin, "A significant
     word in these verses is 'cause to stumble' or 'cause to sin' in Matt.
     18:6, 8, 9; Mark 9:42, 43, 45, 47; Luke 17:2 (NASB95). The
     original Greek word is scandalizo from which we get our English
     word scandalize. According to *W. E. Vine's Expository Dictionary
     of New Testament Words*, it signifies 'to put a snare or stumbling
     block in the way.'"

33   Cat Cattinson, 'My Body Was Never the Problem' - Cat Cattinson
     Speaks Out against the Medicalization of Minors," YouTube,
     October 20, 2022, https://youtu.be/2HS7Gxc4tSg?si
     =s5EM9NViGwvkDx47.

Chapter Twelve

1   Christian Response Forum, "Jordan Peterson—If you love
    someone you'll help them avoid hell - Christian Response Forum
    #shorts," YouTube, January 2, 2022, https://www.youtube.com
    /watch?v+a21BjqmqU8M.

2   Becket Cook, "A Mother's Prayer for Her Gay Son – the Becket
    Cook Show Ep. 106," YouTube, January 19, 2023, https://www
    .youtube.com/watch?v=uFWl9eWkmWg.

3   Caleb Kaltenbach, *Messy Grace: How a Pastor with Gay
    Parents Learned to Love Others without Sacrificing Conviction*
    (Colorado Springs, CO: WaterBrook, 2015).

4   Acts 6:5, 8–15; 7:1–60.

5   Isaiah 53:7–8 (NLT).

6   Acts 8:26–40 (NLT).

7   "Reaching the Youth of America" with Christian Boudreau on
    the *I AM A WOMAN Podcast*, https://urmore.org/episode
    /reaching-the-youth-of-america/.

8   The Whosoevers, https://thewhosoevers.com.

9   Deuteronomy 23:1.

10 Isaiah 41:9 (NLT).

11 Study Light, Strong's 3047 – yad.

12 Study Light, Strong's 5463 - cegar

13 Study Light, Strong's #7453 – rea and #7462, raah. Clark, p. 246

14 John 15:15.

15 Mark 1:41 (KJ21).

16 Matthew 14:14 (KJ21).

17 Mark 6:34, (KJ21).

18 Matthew 9:36 (KJ21).

19 Luke 19:5 (NASB).

20 Bereshith בְּרֵאשִׁית, the first seven letters of the Bible, tell the story
    of the Gospel. See also L. Grant Luton, *God Prepares a World:
    Messianic Insights into the Book of Genesis* (Beth Tikkun
    Publishing, 2019), 13.

21 Luke 18:9–14, (NLT).

22 Read Luke 14:7–24 (NLT).

23 Luke 6:32–35.

24 Luke 6:41–42.

25 Psalm 139:4; Proverbs 3:34; Proverbs 29:23; Matthew 23:12;
    Luke 1:52; James 4:6; 1 Peter 5:5. To take the "Pride Test" to help
    you clean out the pride in your heart, go to urmore.org/pridetest.

26 Charla Janecka, "Looking Between the Surface: Loving People
    with Sexual and Gender Identity Concerns, Part 1 and 2," UR
    More, August 10, 2023, https://urmore.org/episode/looking
    -beneath-the-surface-loving-people-with-sexual-and-gender
    -identity-concerns-part-1/.

27 Luke 19:1–10.

28 Paul David Tripp, *New Morning Mercies: A Daily Gospel Devotional* (Wheaton, IL: Crossway, 2014), August 6.

29 Luton, 7.

Chapter Thirteen

1   "J. K. Rowling Reflects on Twitter Backlash and Her Stance on Gender Issues," (Excerpts from "The Witch Trials of J. K. Rowling: Episode 5,) the Rowling Library, March 14, 2023, https://www.therowlinglibrary.com/2023/03/14/j-k-rowling -reflects-on-twitter-backlash-and-her-stance-on-gender-issues -excerpts-from-the-witch-trials-of-j-k-rowling-episode-5/.

2   Hirsch, 7.

3   Study Light, Strong's #269 – achowth.

4   Study Light, Strong's #251 – ach.

5   *Trans* back cover copy, the *Telegraph*.

6   J. K. Rowling, "J. K. Rowling Writes about her Reasons for Speaking out on Sex and Gender Issues," June 10, 2020, https ://www.jkrowling.com/opinions/j-k-rowling-writes-about-her -reasons-for-speaking-out-on-sex-and-gender-issues/.

7   Ibid.

8   Megan Phelps-Roper podcast, *The Witch Trials of J. K. Rowling*—for anyone who wants to understand the full story of Rowling's stance and the backlash she has received, this is worth listening to.

9   Rowling, "J. K. Rowling Writes about her Reasons for Speaking out on Sex and Gender Issues."

10 Ibid.

11 Ibid.

12 Kathleen Stock, *Material Girls: Why Reality Matters for Feminism* (London, UK: Fleet, 2022).

13 Julie Bindel, "Kathleen Stock: 'I Won't Be Silenced'," UnHerd, November 4, 2021, https://unherd.com/2021/11/kathleen-stock -i-wont-be-silenced/.

14   Ibid.

15   Rowling, "J. K. Rowling Writes about Her Reasons for Speaking out on Sex and Gender Issues."

16   Haroon Siddique, "Maya Forstater Was Discriminated against Gender-Critical Beliefs, Tribunal Rules," *Guardian*, July 6, 2022, https://www.theguardian.com/society/2022/jul/06/maya-forstater -was-discriminated-against-over-gender-critical-beliefs-tribunal-rules.

17   See the stories of Oberlin College coach Kim Russell, California P.E. teacher Jessica Tapia, and Google engineer James Damoore.

18   Joyce, 227.

19   Ibid., 230.

20   Hannah Grossman, "Rachel Levine Praises Gender Clinic Pushing Biological Sex Revisionism, Referring to Moms as 'Egg Producer,'"
Fox News, August 16, 2023, https://www.foxnews.com/media /rachel-levine-praises-gender-clinic-pushing-biological-sex -revisionism-referring-moms-egg-producer.

21   Lifton, 422–23, edited for brevity.

22   Isaiah 9:6, emphasis added.

23   See Expert Submission of Dr. Stephen B. Levine, M.D., March 12, 2020, " https://www.legis.state.pa.us/WU01/LI/TR /Transcripts/2020_0046_0001_TSTMNY.pdf; see also American College of Pediatrics, "Gender Confusion and Transgender Identity," https://acpeds.org/topics/sexuality-issues-of-youth /gender-confusion-and-transgender-identity.

24   "Bill Offering Protections to Transgender Youth in Washington Signed into Law," KIRO 7, May 10, 2023, https://www.kiro7 .com/news/local/bill-offering-protections-transgender-youth -washington-signed-into-law/SQ2ZCEBPPNGUPDELFAIWN7BDRU /; see also "Washington Bill Would Allow Transgender Medical Procedures for Minors without Parental Consent," FOX 12, April 17, 2023, https://www.kptv.com/2023/04/17/washington -bill-would-allow-transgender-medical-procedures-minors -without-parental-consent/.

25 Her story is told in the documentary, "Gender Transformation: The Untold Realities," Epoch TV, https://gendertransformation .com/.

26 Tre Goins-Phillips, "Canadian Father Jailed for Speaking Out against Biological Daughter's Gender Transition," CBN, March 20, 2021, https://www2.cbn.com/news/world/canadian-father -jailed-speaking-out-against-biological-daughters-gender -transition.

27 Luke Rosa, "Mother of Sex Trafficked Teen Files Lawsuit after Girl Was Held in Boys Group Home to 'Affirm' Her Trans Identity," *Daily Wire*, August 25, 2023, https://www.dailywire .com/news/maryland-refused-to-give-back-a-virginia-runaway -because-her-parents-misgendered-her-then-she-was-sex -trafficked-mother-says. See also: Luke Rosa, "Maryland Refused to Give Back a Virginia Runaway Because Her Parents 'Misgendered Her.' Then She Was Sex Trafficked, Mother Says," Daily Wire, January 19, 2023, https://www.dailywire.com/news /maryland-refused-to-give-back-a-virginia-runaway-because-her -parents-misgendered-her-then-she-was-sex-trafficked-mother-says.

28 Lifton, 423–25, edited for brevity.

29 Jordan Peterson, "I'm Being Professionally Canceled for My Moral Stance on Trans Butchery," *New York Post*, September 5, 2023, https://nypost.com/2023/09/05/im-being-professionally -canceled-for-my-moral-stance-on-trans-butchery/.

30 Lifton, 425–27, edited for brevity.

31 Rowling, "J. K. Rowling Writes about her Reasons for Speaking out on Sex and Gender Issues."

Chapter Fourteen

1   Kristen Altus, "Riley Gaines out to End the Use of 'Biological' Gender Terminology," Fox Business, September 22, 2023, https ://www.foxbusiness.com/sports/riley-gaines-end-use-biological -gender-terminology.

2   Carrie Gress, "Second-Wave Feminists Pushed the Sexual
    Revolution to End America, and It's Working," *Federalist*,
    April 19, 2022, https://thefederalist.com/2022/04/19/second-wave
    -feminists-pushed-the-sexual-revolution-to-end-america-and-its
    -working/.
3   Ibid.
4   Parent Compass, "7 Mountains of Influence – Family Is 1 – Lance
    Wallnau," YouTube, November 4, 2022, https://www.youtube.
    com/watch?v=6KcVGq5ZCXI.
5   See Revelation 17–18 and 20–22.
6   Deana Morgan, personal interview.
7   Jonathan Cahn, *The Return of the Gods* (Chicago, IL: Frontline,
    2022).
8   Cahn, 73–75.
9   Cahn, Chapters 17–21.
10 Cahn, 236.
11 Cassius, "Giorgia Meloni's Electrifying Speech at the World
    Congress of Families, English subtitles," YouTube, April 17, 2019,
    https://www.youtube.com/watch?v=y_Z1LClnhsk.
12 Proverbs 7:4 (KJ21).
13 Study Light, Strong's #2428 – Chayil.
14 Luke 8:1–3.
15 Psalm 68:11 (NASB).
16 Study Light, Strong's #6635 – tsaba.
17 Revelation 12:1, 5–6.
18 Revelations 19:11-16.

Afterword: The Poetry

1   This is my paraphrase.